Deleuze and the Gynesis of Horror

Deleuze and the Gynesis of Horror

From Monstrous Births to the Birth of the Monster

Sunny Romack

BLOOMSBURY ACADEMIC
NEW YORK • LONDON • OXFORD • NEW DELHI • SYDNEY

BLOOMSBURY ACADEMIC
Bloomsbury Publishing Inc
1385 Broadway, New York, NY 10018, USA
50 Bedford Square, London, WC1B 3DP, UK
29 Earlsfort Terrace, Dublin 2, Ireland

BLOOMSBURY, BLOOMSBURY ACADEMIC and the Diana logo are trademarks of
Bloomsbury Publishing Plc

First published in the United States of America 2020
This paperback edition published in 2022

Copyright © Sunny Romack, 2020

For legal purposes the Acknowledgments on p. vii constitute an extension
of this copyright page.

Cover design by Louise Dugdale
Cover image: Still from Ex Machina (2014) © Mary Evans/AF Archive/Film4

All rights reserved. No part of this publication may be reproduced or transmitted in any form or by any means, electronic or mechanical, including photocopying, recording, or any information storage or retrieval system, without prior permission in writing from the publishers.

Bloomsbury Publishing Inc does not have any control over, or responsibility for, any third-party websites referred to or in this book. All internet addresses given in this book were correct at the time of going to press. The author and publisher regret any inconvenience caused if addresses have changed or sites have ceased to exist, but can accept no responsibility for any such changes.

Library of Congress Cataloging-in-Publication Data
Names: Romack, Sunny, 1979- author.
Title: Deleuze and the gynesis of horror: from monstrous births to the
birth of the monster / Sunny Romack.
Description: New York: Bloomsbury Academic, 2020. | Includes
bibliographical references, filmography, and index.
Identifiers: LCCN 2020013012 | ISBN 9781501358456 (hardback) |
ISBN 9781501358432 (pdf) | ISBN 9781501358449 (ebook)
Subjects: LCSH: Deleuze, Gilles, 1925-1995. | Horror films–History and criticism. | Motherhood in motion pictures. | Mothers in motion pictures. | Monsters in motion pictures. | Feminism and motion pictures.
Classification: LCC PN1995.9.H6 H39 2020 | DDC 791.43/6164–dc23
LC record available at https://lccn.loc.gov/2020013012

ISBN: HB: 978-1-5013-5845-6
PB: 978-1-5013-6932-2
ePDF: 978-1-5013-5843-2
eBook: 978-1-5013-5844-9

Typeset by Deanta Global Publishing Services, Chennai, India

To find out more about our authors and books visit
www.bloomsbury.com and sign up for our newsletters.

Contents

Acknowledgments — vii

Introduction — 1
    Essential Motherhood and Egalitarian Feminism: The Conundrum of Sexual Difference — 3
    Beyond the Binary: Opening up the Body without Organs — 11
    Schizosophy of the Monstrous — 19

1 Mother, (m)Other — 27
    Transcendental Empiricism: Deleuze's Cinematic Philosophy — 29
    The "Volatile Body" in Schizoanalysis — 35
    Pure Difference and the Post-human Family — 45

2 Mother (of) Monsters — 55
    Becoming the Monstrous-Feminine — 60
    Last (wo)Man Standing, or The Final Girl in Schizoanalysis — 69
    Molar Beings, Molecular Becomings, and the Putting into Discourse of "Woman" — 72

3 Meet Your Makers — 79
    Becoming-Woman: The "Universal Girl" and the Ever-Shrinking Man — 79
    Escaping (or Not) the Binary Machine — 85
    Law of the Father versus the Law of the Jungle — 91
    The Psychomechanics of Becoming-Monster — 97

4 It's a Monster (Baby) — 111
    The Blood ~~Is~~ Gives Life: Evolution in *Underworld* — 113
    Prey Becomes Predator: Molecular Ruptures in *Twilight*'s Hegemonic Narrative — 122
    The Post-human Resistance — 135

5 The Post-human Family — 141
    Queering Creation — 144
    The Spiral of Time — 150

    Family as Survivor Assemblage   157
    Molecular Motherhood, or the Monstrous Body (Re)imagined   169

Notes   183
References   187
Films   190
Index   191

Acknowledgments

The enthusiasm of my students for exploring gender in the horror film was what inspired me to undertake this project. I would like to thank Rocky Colavito and the faculty members of our Horror Living and Learning Community at Butler University for encouraging me to pursue this idea. An early version of Chapter 2 was presented at the Popular Culture Association Conference in 2018, and the excitement with which it was received persuaded me that a book applying Deleuzian theories to analysis of gender in film might well be called for.

Special thanks to the instructors and colleagues who have supported and encouraged me over the years, most of all my dear friend Amy Montz, who has spent the last decade fearlessly climbing writing mountains alongside me; David Blakesley, who inspired me to return to the horror films I had long feared with an amazing undergraduate course in the rhetoric of film; Elizabeth Klaver, who introduced me to gender theory way back when; and finally to Ann Hall, who generously provided feedback on a draft of this manuscript. To Katie Gallof, who championed this project from the first, and the entire team at Bloomsbury Academic, thank you for helping make this a much better book.

Without the love, support, and encouragement of my partner Brandon, this project would never have been completed. I have him and my grandparents R. L. and Carol Parrott to thank for teaching me what family is for.

Introduction

Motherhood.

For each of us, that word conjures different images: our own mothers, perhaps, or the women or men who "mothered" us when we were children. Perhaps we picture our best friend with her three children, or our wives holding our newborn infants. Perhaps we picture our mothers with their mothers, in the kitchen, cooking a holiday meal.

A Google Image search for *mother* returns endless images of (mostly white, able-bodied, middle-class, presumably heterosexual) women cuddling perfectly coiffed infants in immaculate nurseries or reading books to sleepy little angels under trees in flowering meadows. My twenty-, thirty-, and forty-something friends' Instagrams depict moms and toddlers proudly displaying finger-paint-stained hands, moms beaming beside daughters and sons dressed for school dances, moms eating ice cream with Girl Scouts and Little Leaguers. Whether authentic, staged, or curated, what these images reveal is that, as Nancy Chodorow has said, we have a cultural idea of *motherhood*, and whether that idea(l) matches up with the reality of our lived experiences, the ideal is still powerful. It shapes public opinion and public policy. It defines the standard "good" mothers must strive for. And it stands uncomfortably alongside our idea(l)s of what it means to be a woman. For a mother, after all, is not just an idea. She is also a body.

A woman's body.

This is a book about horror film. Specifically, it is a book about the maternal in horror film, one which engages a radically alternative perspective to the commonly practiced psychoanalytic lens of feminist film analysis. In so doing—in demonstrating within horror film feminist concepts such as Moira Gatens's imaginary body, Elizabeth Grosz's volatile body, and Rosi Braidotti's monstrous body, all ideas drawn from the "schizoid" philosophy of Gilles Deleuze and Felix Guattari—this book aims to radicalize how *difference* is conceived in both feminism and film analysis. If this book has any value, it lies foremost in its argument for reshaping our cultural perspective on sexual difference, at a time when difference—of sex, gender, race, ethnicity, ability, national origin, religion, class, language, or sexual orientation—remains personally and politically dangerous. In sum, my argument is that, as Kimberly Jackson has said, we find ourselves in an interstitial moment in which changing gender roles have nullified the patriarchal order without an alternative to that order having yet emerged; hence, the films in this collection reveal the contested place of the maternal in a society that, clinging to egalitarian feminism and other notions of equal rather than equitable treatment of minorities and marginalized communities, still denies sexual difference. Even more problematically, in an echo of what Alice Jardine observed when writing about "gynesis," what Jackson has called "the postfeminist mindset" encourages us to believe feminist goals have been achieved, while all the while the masculinist mindset of the patriarchal order has not been overturned: Whiteness, heterosexuality, and binary gender are still taken as the natural order of things, while social, political, economic, and cultural capital remain largely in the hands of corporate and government institutions designed to benefit most the wealthy, white, heterosexual male majority.

The other, equally important aim of this project, to be more fully elucidated in the next chapter, is to demonstrate within the horror genre how Deleuzian schizoanalysis allows us to distinguish "molar" films—those films which reify patriarchal ideology, in some cases by erasing, othering, or demonizing the maternal, in others by using motherhood to "redomesticate" the mother-monster—from more "molecular" films. Molecular films, as future chapters will explain, may subvert any and all notions of "order" by incorporating viewers into a cinematic assemblage that, in expression, like the maternal allows for no boundaries or borders between "inside" and "outside," between Self and Other, and in content, celebrates the metamorphic potential of the monster, whose "becoming" cannot be fixed or frozen into binary identities such as masculine or feminine, dualities the patriarchal order needs it subjects ordered into. I intend this book to suggest a way out of the postpatriarchal/postfeminist limbo in which we find ourselves, by encouraging us to embrace what Deleuze and Guattari called *pure difference*, or difference-in-itself.

Essential Motherhood and Egalitarian Feminism: The Conundrum of Sexual Difference

Sexual difference is perhaps nowhere more inescapable than in reproduction, in which the equality of men and women cannot be rendered in the familiar, comfortable discourse of sameness—*treat everyone the same*—because the roles male and female bodies play in reproduction are, simply, different. The power of the female body to nurture and deliver life, a power the male body cannot (as of yet) replicate, has been constrained throughout Western history by prohibitions against female sexual and reproductive freedom. Lacking the womb, men have sought to control the womb by dictating when (after marriage) and by whom (the husband) a woman could be impregnated. Yet in the twentieth and twenty-first centuries, medical and social advances increasingly placed women in control of their own sexual and reproductive destinies, so that today, it is entirely possible and indeed not uncommon for women to conceive via artificial insemination, in which the only part of a man still required for reproduction is sperm. With the phallus thus relegated to a passive, ejaculatory rather than an active, penetrative role in conception, it seems *the womb* has achieved even greater centrality in Western culture. It is therefore likely no accident that in recent years debates over women's reproductive rights have once again risen to a fever pitch.

What has perhaps received less attention than debates over the legality of abortion, access to birth control, or abstinence-only education is the hegemonic idea(l) of motherhood itself. My first brush with this ideal and its importance to the patriarchy came in 1992, when then vice president Dan Quayle launched his now-infamous attack on the sitcom character Murphy Brown for becoming a (fictional) single mom. In its front-page story, *The New York Times* reported that Quayle accused the character of "mocking the importance of fathers, by bearing a child alone, and calling it just another 'lifestyle choice'" (Fortin 2018). At the time, the feminist response, encapsulated in comments made by the show's creator Diane English, was to highlight the hypocrisy of an administration opposed to a woman's choice (that is, to abortion) condemning a single woman for choosing to have and raise her child. While true, as I look back on this early battle in the so-called culture wars, I cannot help thinking that the feminist response missed the point—a point Quayle himself seemed aware of. "They said that I believe single mothers and their children are not families. That is a lie," *The New York Times* reported Quayle saying in response to English's remark that "'if the Vice President thinks it's disgraceful for an unmarried woman to bear a child, . . . and if he believes that a woman cannot adequately raise a child without a father, then he'd better make sure abortion remains safe and legal'" (Fortin 2018).

Are single mothers and their children *families*? If they are, why do we feel the need to distinguish single mothers from, simply, mothers? The question of what *legitimizes* motherhood was barely addressed by the Murphy Brown debate, with feminists like English swiftly pointing the dial toward a woman's "right to choose." Yet that reaction glossed over the crux of Quayle's objection to Murphy Brown: that by mothering without fathering, she was not denying her child the advantages of a second wage-earner or caregiver (roles anyone, even someone not biologically related to the child, could fulfill), but was, rather, denying Man's role as The Father. A *real* mother would not do that, Quayle's argument seemed to say. A real mother would recognize the importance of The Father, not for any role he would play in rearing the child, but, as feminist scholar Patrice Diquinzio explains, because in phallocentric culture, it is The Father who stands at the center of what it means to be a family, although women continue to provide the brunt of childcare within the home (Diquinzio 1999: ii). The Father's central authority within this family structure, and The Mother's subservience to The Father's will despite his absence from the home, provides the masculinist basis for much of Western society's socio-industrial complex (Diquinzio 1999: ii), a point both Tony Williams and Kimberly Jackson have noted when (psycho)analyzing the political functions of the nuclear family within our wider industrial-capitalist, patriarchal society. Harkening back to Freud, Williams notes that "civilization relies on repression, often molding individuals in ways detrimental to their individual potentials" (2014: 13)—in this instance, by naturalizing binary, phallocentric gender norms vis-à-vis the nuclear family.

Nor has The Mother in the twenty-first century lost her cultural weight. Decades after the Murphy Brown episode, early into my tenure as an academic, I was asked to articulate the feminist perspective on abortion at a panel invited by a student organization. Although intended as neither a pro-life nor a pro-choice event, the panel created a stir in the local community, and in addition to a hearty student turnout, members of a local evangelical Christian congregation showed up. I took the podium first, and in relating the "feminist perspective" (I was careful to note in my remarks that there is not one, monolithic "feminist perspective" on anything, let alone a topic as fraught as abortion), I attempted to change the conversation, to help those listening understand abortion less as an abstraction, more as a concrete, nuanced circumstance faced by women who in reality look quite different from the unwed, middle-class, white suburban teenagers so often depicted in movies and television: women who report feeling they have no choice but to terminate their pregnancies because of financial insecurity (the need to work or stay in school, or a lack of health insurance to pay for prenatal care, labor, and delivery) and, moreover, women who may be not only married but also *already* mothers who feel they cannot provide for another child.[1] I hoped my audience could move beyond simplistic moral arguments and consider how socioeconomic realities constrict a woman's ability to "choose"—that is, how a woman's material circumstances may override her option to choose or not to choose abortion on purely moral grounds, either her own or someone else's. Yet at the end of the evening, as the panel was wrapping up, a female congregant stood and shouted to the students: "They're lying to you! A real mother would not have an abortion!"

What exactly this woman thought we panelists were lying about is, to me, superfluous to her underlying thesis: that a *real* mother would not, *could not*, terminate a pregnancy. This *real* mother, as an idea/ideal, inhabits a virtual realm divorced from the actual, embodied experiences of mothering—from maternal bodies that hunger, tire, labor, love, desire, exult, fear, and hope in endless variations, not just one maternal body from another but each maternal body from itself during any given month, week, day, or hour. And yet, for all of that, this "real mother" seemed to many people in that room to be no less real.

On the one hand, such a hegemonic ideal of motherhood provides a convenient out via which the privileged white middle class can ignore inequalities like those highlighted in my presentation, upholding a supposedly moral argument about the sanctity of life while turning a blind eye to the significant percentage of women who report seeking abortions because they could not afford (another) child. On the other hand, as with Vice President Quayle's condemnation of single motherhood, something deeper resonated within this woman's comments, namely the codification of an inviolable maternal instinct onto the body of a *real* mother, who, by extension, is a *real woman*, so that the logic falls out like so: For a real woman, every pregnancy is a joyful experience, regardless of her circumstance, for every real woman has both the instinct and desire for motherhood.

Disembodying motherhood from actual maternal bodies creates the conditions under which such ideals of "essential motherhood" (more on this in a moment) can exist. It also creates the conditions under which motherhood has become a proverbial Gordian knot for feminism. To be clear, despite popular (often conservative) depictions of it as so, feminism is not anti-motherhood. Feminism does oppose in principle the patriarchal notion that a woman's value to society can be equated with her reproductive capabilities—that women exist to become mothers, in other words. Consequently, feminism argues that the choice of when, or whether, to become a mother should rest with each woman as an individual; therefore, each woman must be granted unequivocal control over her reproductive decisions (which, of course, means unequivocal control over her body). Unfortunately, this fantasy, comforting as it may be, remains only that, a fantasy, in our current binary system. For once we acknowledge the myth that is "equality" in our postpatriarchal, postfeminist society, we find ourselves facing a complicated answer to a seemingly simple question: *Is motherhood a choice?*

Not according to feminist scholar Kelly Oliver, who argues that women often still feel motherhood is their only vehicle for personal fulfillment and/or that once they become mothers, all other avenues for fulfillment—career, education, art, politics—must be, if not abandoned, at least curtailed (2010: 768). Meanwhile, let us not forget that, as Oliver points out, worldwide as well as in the US women and children are far more likely than men to live in poverty. Such women face more than the sacrifice of a career—they face the challenge of finding work that will allow them to adequately feed, clothe, and house their children (Oliver 2010: 769). The "choice" to become a mother, then, carries real consequences for real bodies, the bodies of mothers and the children they must provide for in a society that continues to deny women the same economic opportunities as men. Feminism's argument that women should be able to choose whether or when to become mothers assumes that all women really can *have it all*—fulfilling careers, political power, financial stability, and, if they so desire, children. It is a pleasant fiction, but one that denies the embodied experience of mothering in a society fundamentally inequitable on many levels, not only in terms of gender but also in terms of race, sexual orientation, disability, and so on.

There is another aspect to the hegemonic ideal of motherhood as well, one with implications for the conflation of motherhood with womanhood upon which the film analysis in this book will dwell. All the images I described at the beginning of this introduction, all those happy mothers with happy children, reinforce what Diquinzio calls the "ideological formation" of essential motherhood, which makes mothering into "a function of women's essentially female nature, women's biological reproductive capacities, and/or human evolutionary development," and thus not only assumes that all women will and should want to become mothers but also "requires women's exclusive and selfless attention to and care of children based on women's psychological and emotional capacities for empathy, awareness of the needs of others, and self-sacrifice" (1999: xiii). The "psychological and emotional capacities" Diquinzio describes as being culturally ascribed/inscribed on/to women is what we often call the *maternal instinct*. Thus, the ideological function of essential motherhood is to naturalize a cultural demand placed on women for social, political, and economic purposes, making childcare the responsibility of the mother as a pseudo-biological extension of her female body's role in pregnancy and childbirth and correlating the mental health and happiness of women with the bearing and rearing of children (Diquinzio 1999).

None of this is to say that some women do not find emotional satisfaction in mothering. Undoubtedly many do. Yet the equation of the female body with an alleged maternal instinct denies the reality that, for many women, mothering is the opposite of satisfying. There are even women who, as the BBC reports, regret having children:

> "If I could turn the clock back I would not have had children," says Rachel who is now in her 50s. She has three children—her youngest is 17—and for most of this time she has been a single mother, which is when the reality hit her. "There were times where I didn't feel mature enough to be responsible for . . . this little person that needed me for existence. . . . I just felt like screaming that actually it's not all it's cracked up to be. If you're really maternal then . . . you've got everything you've wanted, but when you're not maternal all you've done is trap yourself. . . . But I feel guilty for saying that, because I love my children dearly." (Mackenzie 2018)

If you're really maternal, this mother says. In that, I hear echoes of the woman who objected to the content of our faculty panel on abortion, convinced as she was that an essential aspect of womanliness, written into our very female DNA, is the desire to become a mother, and furthermore the belief that mothering will adhere to a particular cultural stereotype of total self-sacrifice *for the good of the children*. As Diquinzio explains, essential motherhood extends the biological role the female body plays in reproduction outward into cultural expectations that women should "have a certain bond with or connection to the children to whom they give birth, . . . love their children unconditionally, empathize completely with their children, [and] meet their children's needs selflessly" (1999: 89), either because women's bodies are designed to create spiritual, psychological, and social bonds with a fetus during pregnancy or because women, naturally and universally, possess an instinct for mothering in ways that most benefit the patriarchy.

While feminism continues to lobby for access to birth control, including abortion services, that in theory allow women to choose when and if to become mothers, stories such as the one reported in the BBC drive home the hegemonic forces surrounding that "if." *If* I do not want to be a mother, am I really a *woman*? Obviously, feminists would say yes. Some, like Diquinzio, have even argued for a "paradoxical politics of mothering" to validate that "some persons, including some women, will have little or nothing to offer in caring for children, and some persons, including some women, will want little or nothing to do with it" (1999: 249). Although Diquinzio's position moves us in the right direction, such a politics can only ever be paradoxical, and therefore unable to unseat the hegemonic power of essential motherhood, so long as feminism remains disembodied, allowing for the perpetuation of cultural ideals of motherhood that rely upon the *sameness* of women's bodies: bodies defined by the category Woman (with slight variations in race, age, sexual orientation, and so on), onto which can be written the biological, evolutionary, or instinctive desire for motherhood.

Perhaps this argument for embodied feminism sounds contradictory, since it is the reproductive capacity of the female body that lies at the heart of essential motherhood. Indeed, feminists like Oliver, drawing on Iris Marion Young, have highlighted the dangers of seeking political or professional equality for women by "finding positive value in pregnancy, childbirth, and motherhood [which] could be used to justify women's exile to the domestic sphere" (2010: 763). Oliver in fact traces exactly how "restor[ation] of desire and subjectivity to the maternal body" (764) results in a return to domestic exile in romantic comedies like *Knocked Up*, *Juno*, and *Labor Pains*, which, like the *Twilight* films to be discussed later in this book, promote a regressive, heteronormative narrative of the allegedly desiring, subjective maternal body. Such films reveal the tension between the patriarchy's elevation of cultural ideals of motherhood and the patriarchal abjectification of the (pregnant) female body, now coupled with "the eroticization of the pregnant body ... in very traditional ways that make women's bodies the object of the gaze in Hollywood films. That is to say, [women's] bodies and their desires are imagined for others, for men, for the viewing audience, and not for themselves or as women themselves experience their own sexuality or desires" (Oliver 2010: 765).

Oliver's argument makes clear that merely reembodying feminism within a patriarchal society will not untie the Gordian knot of motherhood for feminism, for the maternal/female bodies Oliver describes are still constructed as the generic Woman's body, a body imagined by, and for, men. To speak of Mothers, then, is no less totalizing than to speak of Women, reducing as it does individuals to categories, flattening the different, embodied experiences that make *this* woman a mother, *that* mother a woman, *this* woman still *a* woman whether or not she is also a mother. Moreover, to return to my earlier observation about the centrality of the womb in an era of de-phallicized artificial insemination, the romantic comedies Oliver analyzes, again much like the *Twilight* series, "idealize heterosexual sex as the origins of life" as they "reassure us that babies are not products of technology but rather of passion, and that sexual desire is necessary to fulfill the desire for babies" (Oliver 2010: 771). In other words, Mothers still need Fathers, whether or not their children do.

Why motherhood? That is a question I asked myself when I began to conceive this project. Has not enough been written about the maternal in horror? What new territory, even when applying an alternative, schizosophic lens to traditionally psychoanalyzed films, could really be left to cover? The territory, I discovered, is exactly where Oliver finds feminism's attempted revaluation of feminine-maternal subjectivity becoming instead the chains that bind women once more to domestic exile in romantic comedies. It is the territory that cannot be traversed so long as we seek to create space for women in a binary, phallocentric society, in which women will always be defined first and foremost by our difference *from men*.

In this sense, it is easy to understand why so many egalitarian feminists have argued against embodied approaches to feminism. For the female-feminine *body*, binarily constructed as the antithesis of male-masculine logic and rationality, has often been used to reify phallocentrism, misogyny, and the patriarchy, or in short to justify women's oppression. Egalitarian or "equality" feminism sought instead to argue for women's rights by positing that men and women are essentially *the same*, and therefore should be treated as equals. However, in terms of menstruation, pregnancy, and lactation, the female body again takes precedence as the site of difference, as everything that makes a woman not-male, *female*. Thus it is no wonder that, quite apart from the romantic comedies Oliver analyzes, horror films, which focus so emphatically on bodies—both the bodies onscreen that are tortured, mutilated, and destroyed and the bodies in the audience, the *viewer's* body, which respond to scenes of horror, violence, and death—should focus also on the maternal body. Freudian psychoanalysis has certainly found fertile ground for theorizing the various ways in which horror films "horrify" by reifying terror of sexual difference vis-à-vis the maternal body.

For the social, cultural, and political implications of women's embodied "otherness" to be fully understood in horror film, it is necessary to understand first that, for egalitarian feminism, motherhood and maternity have presented a seemingly unsolvable conundrum, since once the female body assumes its role in procreation, our differences from the male body cannot be denied. Diquinzio describes this as a "dilemma of difference" in which "feminism and feminist theory deny or disavow women's difference, and differences among women, in order to argue for women's equality and to mobilize women as a group" (1999: xv), only to have these denials and disavowals ultimately reinforce the phallocentric assumption that masculinity is naturally superior to femininity and therefore women, in order to be equal, should aspire to be more like men (preferably white, middle-class, able-bodied, heterosexual men). The masculinist worldview is hereby left unquestioned, as is the underlying dualistic male/female thinking, as egalitarian feminism inadvertently tends toward precisely the same cultural delusion as phallocentrism, albeit from a gynocentric perspective, as it imaginatively constructs a generic, disembodied female subject which "presupposes that there is some set of situations and experiences that are shared by all women, and/or that there is a women's perspective—a view of the world, a mode of acquiring knowledge—shared by all women," a flattening of female difference that "may lead to the political misrepresentations of women's interests or the representations of some women's interests at the expense of others" (Diquinzio 1999: 69). Egalitarian feminism has certainly been accused of this with regard to its championing of the concerns of white, heterosexual, middle-class, cisgender women, seemingly in ignorance of the circumstances or experiences of women of color, queer women, trans women, and women with disabilities, as though white, heterosexual, able-bodied, middle-class experience represents the universal nature of womanliness, absorbing all other female identities within it.

Embodying theories of difference is frightening for feminists because of the traditional use of *the body* to other and oppress women. I understand this. As a woman, I empathize with it. Nevertheless, my argument in this book is that what needs to change is not the way we understand Women (as a generic, and artificial, category of representation) but rather, as Deleuze and Guattari say, the way we understand *difference*. If we continue to operate from dualistic thinking that defines woman as man's Other, feminism will never be able to theorize motherhood in ways that do not reduce women to our biological, reproductive functions, or in ways that address the inequalities experienced by women of different races, ages, ethnicities, religions, classes, national origins, dis/abilities, and sexual orientations, or in ways that result in real choices for women and in more stable, more secure, *happier* families for us all. Reconceiving difference beyond otherness, I contend, is the only real path to freedom from the postpatriarchal moment in which we find ourselves—the only true line of flight from the patriarchal model feminism destabilized but, as Kimberly Jackson has said, did not provide an alternative to. As Deleuze would say, egalitarian feminism left intact our *social delirium*, our belief in the received wisdom, established truth, and higher values that led to the inscription of gender norms onto biological bodies in the first place as well as the master/slave molar opposition of male to female, masculine to feminine that ultimately resulted in universal enslavement even for those seeking to become "masters."[2] "We live in a society undergirded by racism and sexism and propelled by capitalism; in such a culture, we are all shaped by invisible systems of power and privilege," Jackson writes, "for if 'woman' is not a unified category, then neither is 'man'" (2016: 13).

Beyond the Binary: Opening up the Body without Organs

Horror is likely not the first genre to spring to mind when we think of family-friendly entertainment, in no small part because horror films enjoy tearing families apart, by means both literal and figurative. In *Hearths of Darkness: The Family in American Horror Film*, Tony Williams relates how "the Reagan era attempted to restore family values by attacking feminism and restoring male hegemony," yet these efforts were undermined by socioeconomic upheaval as traditionally male industries such as mining and manufacturing disappeared, leading to "the creation of low-income 'feminine' service jobs and the destabilization of patriarchal family foundations" (2014: 18), that is, Nancy Chodorow's nuclear family idea/ideal of the absent-dominant breadwinner Father and domesticated-subservient homemaker Mother. Williams goes on to relate how, from the 1960s onward, rising rates of divorce and reports of domestic violence, child abuse, and family dysfunction led to the conclusion that "the traditional family was finished. The very virulent nature of [1980s] slasher films reveals an unconscious patriarchal hysteria trying to hold back contradictory tensions, especially those involving changing gender roles" (2014: 19).

Jackson picks up Williams's argument in examining films from our current postpatriarchal, postfeminist moment. She, like other theorists, contends that the changes to patriarchal society wrought by second-wave feminism resulted in a sort of masculine identity crisis that only worsened in the face of economic pressures brought about in large part by globalization, as Williams describes. Hence, both Williams and Jackson trace a similar trajectory for "the family" in American horror films. In the 1950s and early 1960s, the horror film family was still a source of protection for protagonists, though it also stood in need of protection from outside forces. By the late 1960s/early 1970s, however, the family had become, according to Williams, "morally bankrupt," a condition for which women and children were to blame (see, for instance, *Rosemary's Baby* and *The Exorcist*)—no doubt a cultural scapegoating of women's demands for equality, which a conservative, patriarchal agenda pointed to as responsible for the public and domestic upheaval of this era. Eventually, however, by the late 1970s/early 1980s, blame for the family's demise shifted from mothers and children onto fathers, as we see, for instance, in *The Amityville Horror*, *Poltergeist*, and *The Shining* (Williams 2014; Jackson 2016). And now? According to Jackson, the twenty-first-century horror film maintains the father's "guilt" for being too "weak" to fulfill the traditionally masculine role of protecting his offspring, but with the added wrinkle that "[i]t then falls to the women and children to attempt to save the family" (2016: 3).

Take, for instance, the 2018 film *A Quiet Place*, which follows the Abbott family (father, mother, three children) through a postapocalyptic landscape overrun by monsters that hunt by sound. A year after the family loses one son to the monsters, we discover the mother, Evelyn, almost nine months pregnant, placing her within that tradition of postapocalyptic female protagonists (Sarah Connor of the *Terminator* franchise, Laurie Grimes of *The Walking Dead*) whose wombs represent the hope of (hu)mankind. For whether the human population is threatened by robots, zombies, pandemics, vampires, or aliens, after society collapses the most essential function of a woman once again becomes reproduction.

Let me pause here to note that one reason I have ranged so widely in choosing films for this project, including any film with both fantastic (including science fiction) *and* horror elements, although not every such film would be considered part of the horror genre, is to trace what I call the "politics of reproduction" at play in these films, all of which exhibit strong horror elements.³ On the one hand, we find films like *Twilight* and *A Quiet Place* which, amid their horror, celebrate hegemonic, heteronormative ideals of essential motherhood, much as Oliver's romantic comedies do. For despite Steve Jones's recent argument that survival-horror films (his term) are not explicitly pro-life or pro-choice, since they emphasize "how difficult choice-making is for [their] lead protagonists" and as such offer "a valuable contribution to the abortion debate, acknowledging that individuals matter . . . and imbuing personal choices about one's life-path with political significance" (2015: 428), choice is rarely figured as such in the postapocalyptic world. Sarah Connor's son (obviously, it could not be a daughter) is to be humanity's only hope against the machines; therefore, Sarah must survive attempts to retroactively abort her son by killing her, his *vessel*, before he is born. Once he is born, she must devote her life to preparing him to become humanity's savior—a future Sarah will not live to see. Likewise, Laurie Grimes's pregnancy may be seen as punishment for an extramarital affair, the consequence of her sexual liberation a brutal death in childbirth, resurrection as a zombie, and a second brutal death at the hands of her son, yet up until her daughter is born, Laurie's maternal body—the body that can bring life into a world devastatingly depopulated—is of utmost concern to the characters, not for Laurie's sake, but for the sake of the child in her womb.

In terms of its essentializing function, then, Evelyn Abbott's pregnancy has much in common with both Sarah Connor's and Laurie Grimes's. Yet *A Quiet Place* goes a step further in making Evelyn's maternal body the locus of the film's horror. In the climactic scene, Evelyn, surrounded by monsters, must give birth alone, in a bathtub, *in total silence*. Thus, while some survival-horror films depict parenting itself as "an overwhelming burden . . . not to be taken lightly" (Jones 2015: 432), the Abbotts, to the consternation of some viewers, have chosen to bring another child into their postapocalyptic world, even going so far as to construct a soundproof room in which to raise the baby. In the much-hyped bathtub birth scene, Evelyn's survival, like Sarah's, like Laurie's, comes to matter not only for her sake—or her other children's—but for the sake of the baby she carries inside her.

A Quiet Place thus again evacuates the woman's (as distinct from the mother's) body from the maternal equation, ascribing value to women based primarily on their reproductive functions—for if mom dies, so does baby. And like Sarah, like Laurie, who, although she briefly considers abortion, ultimately "chooses life," Evelyn proves willing to endure any amount of pain for her child, as a *real* mother should.[4] Still, not all horror films glorify essential motherhood. Many—and herein an embodied philosophy of affirmative sexual difference begins to emerge, albeit obliquely—treat pregnancy itself as monstrous, as, in Julia Kristeva's terms, more like a *possession*. Although Kristeva was speaking of pregnancy in real life, there is no denying that horror film has exploited the idea that pregnancy "opens the body to otherness in ways that make the experience porous physically and mentally" (Oliver 2010: 772).

Certainly, the openness of the pregnant body has been used to horrific effect in pregnancy-possession films like *Rosemary's Baby*, *The Rite*, *Devil's Due*, and the horror comedy *Prevenge*. Nonetheless, pregnancy's very porosity also creates space for "a more porous notion of subjectivity than philosophers typically provide" (Oliver 2010: 773). For the pregnant body *is a body*, and moreover a body open to change in ways more insistently obvious than the non-pregnant body—which is to say, the pregnant body is visibly in the process of *becoming different from itself* as the internal changes of pregnancy are externalized in the body that is pregnant. In that sense, the pregnant body, so often treated as grotesque, shameful, and abject through a phallocentric lens, might be *the* embodiment of how we experience life at the beginning of the twenty-first century. I refer here not only to the rapid pace of social, political, economic, and environmental change in a global, technological society, although that pace has certainly undermined the notion of a stable, static subjectivity upon which patriarchal Western capitalism depends, but also to changes in our understanding of what it means to be human.

At the time of this writing, advances in artificial intelligence have prompted scientists, philosophers, and science fiction writers to question how we define consciousness and sentience—and what happens if those qualities are taken on by machines. Zoological research has challenged the anthropocentric binary between humans and animals, demonstrating that humans do not hold a monopoly on intelligence, empathy, and morality and may not be as different from, or superior to, other animals as we would like to think. In the field of forestry, botanists have discovered that trees are able to communicate with one another via vibrations in the root system, challenging both humankind's claim to primacy through language and the plant/animal binary. Even the very definition of *human* appears to be changing, as scientists have discovered that less than half—just 43 percent—of our cells are actually human, the rest belonging to the microscopic organisms of our life-essential microbiome (which we now know are introduced to infants as they exit the mother's birth canal).⁵ In *Metamorphoses: Towards a Materialist Theory of Becoming*, Deleuzoguattarian philosopher Rosi Braidotti maintains that the "social mutations" (2002: 264) spurred by these and other wide-ranging discoveries, from military-industrial technology to the World Wide Web, have made contemporary politics largely a matter of "the management of the insecurity and fears induced by the perennial state of change. From a Deleuzian perspective I would say that a constant state of crisis is what our system is all about. Be it a crisis of human 'Life,' humans rights, or human reproduction, post-industrial societies are confronted by the threat to the generic category of human" (Braidotti 2002: 264).

We can state, then, that the patriarchal structures that relied on constancy for their flourishment have lost the battle for re-production, in the sense of reproduction as repetition of categories and identities most beneficial to patriarchal power across generations. The delusion of identification and representation—that there is a *this* (fixed, stable, and static) to be compared to or judged against *that*—falls apart when confronted with fluctuations of our most established values, such as what we mean by human life, or indeed, by life. Thus, we should expect to see, and we do, the pregnant body occupying a contested space within postpatriarchal, postfeminist twenty-first-century imaginations that have broken with, but have yet to break free from, the (so-called) Truths of the old order.

Before I go further, however, I want to make clear that I am not endorsing a disembodied, albeit gynocentric, philosophy in which the pregnant body *symbolizes* change. As a schizosophist, as I will explore throughout this book, I am not interested in symbology or representation of any kind; I am interested in ethology and embodiment. Moreover, I am interested in exploring why the maternal remains a subject of fascination for horror film and whether, or how, contemplating the body (actual, individual bodies) vis-à-vis the embodied experiences of motherhood and/or pregnancy might facilitate an escape from the gender binary. I am *not* interested in reconstructing that binary as gynocentric, which, as I argue in the next chapter, would in fact be no escape at all. My goal is foregoing binarism's otherness for an embodied, nonrepresentational, radically affirmative theory of difference as difference-in-itself. My aim, therefore, is not to argue for what the pregnant or maternal body *represents*. Representation is antithetical to the philosophies of Deleuze and Guattari. In Deleuzoguattarian philosophy, or "schizosophy," all representation is false, for representation depends upon stability and solidity when in fact each of us is constantly engaged in a fluid process of becoming different-from-ourselves. Thus, schizosophic difference is difference over time, temporal and also qualitative, not difference from any "ideal form" but only from ourselves-over-time (Deleuze 1995). The person who embraces the qualitative, temporal nature of difference may become the Body without Organs, or BwO, freed from representations and from the molar plane that tries to categorize, hierarchize, and freeze individuals into stable, static subjects. The BwO undergoes a ceaseless process of molecular becomings, and from its schizosophical vantage point, recognizes and accepts that it can never be identified as a whole or unified Subject. (Much more will be said on this in the next chapter.)

Simply put, getting from our binary state to the BwO requires more than replacing phallocentrism with gynocentrism, although recuperating the value of the feminine must be understood as indispensable to this project. To become the BwO requires a radical rethinking (or *unthinking*) of our current dualistic system of identification and representation, particularly where sexual difference is concerned. My argument here is that the maternal body, much like Deleuze and Guattari's not-uncontroversial concept of becoming-woman (to be taken up in Chapter 3), may move us closer to thinking the actual, embodied experience of becoming and thereby closer to becoming the BwO because the mother's body challenges the binary construction closed/open, as well as the phallocentric privileging of that (the masculine) which is contained, solid, and "pure" over that (the feminine) which is porous, fluid, and "contaminated." The BwO is by necessity a body which is open. As I will argue at the end of this introduction, one reason vampires, aliens, cyborgs, werewolves, mutants, and even zombies have become heroic, sympathetic figures in recent horror film has to do with the crisis of the generic category *human* which Braidotti points to in *Metamorphoses*—with our recognition that sameness, solidity, and stability are not only delusions but are also, and more importantly, undesirable ways of being, or attempting *to be*, in a world which, now more than ever, for our very survival in the face of rapid, ceaseless change demands fluid becomings.

If we were to replace phallocentrism with gynocentrism, such a system would remain binary and demand molar subjectivity of the women (and men) it "represents." Undoing phallocentrism is therefore not enough, although again, it is a necessary component of a larger process of unraveling binary thinking. Outside of horror film, as feminist theorist Rosemary Betterton describes, artists have in part begun this work by challenging hegemonic, patriarchal understandings of the alternatively eroticized-and-abjectified pregnant body.

In one such instance that speaks directly to my argument, Betterton analyzes artist Cindy Sherman's use of "the grotesque and comedic potential of horror to interrogate what it means to be—or what is meant to be—maternal" (2006: 93). Betterton argues that Sherman's photography "reworks, deforms, and conflates signifiers of sexual identity" as "the pregnant body is figured as both sexual and monstrous through prosthetic devices" (2006: 93), including the "faked" pregnancy of an elderly woman. As "a means of denaturalizing the maternal body, or as Donna Haraway puts it, 'queering what counts as nature,'" Betterton explains how the "seduction and repulsion of the 'pregnant senile hag' not only disturbs the categories of sexual and maternal identity, but . . . our very understanding of what bodies can be" (2006: 96).[6]

Betterton writes of the "discomfort" Sherman's viewers experience when confronted with images like the "pregnant senile hag" that distort belief in a *natural* body. One word for these images might be "monstrous." As both Betterton and Braidotti have argued, defining what is monstrous reinforces "a same/other binary between what is sacred and mutant, normal and abnormal, whether it be between sexual, racial, or human/nonhuman categories" (Betterton 2006: 82). Yet I will argue throughout this book that encounters with the monstrous (especially those encounters which, in their affective power, destabilize, distort, or discomfit viewers' experiences of *their* bodies) can be made to demolish rather than reify the same/other binary. That is, as Betterton notes, Braidotti's project in *Metamorphoses* is "finding new figurations of hybrids and monsters as possible models for a 'materialist theory of becoming,'" for the "challenge that the hybrid, the anomalous, the monstrous others throw in our direction is nothing less than a disassociation from [the Victorian sensibility] which pathologized and criminalized difference" (Betterton 2006: 87). The challenge the monstrous-maternal body throws in the direction of feminism is no less a challenge to disassociate ourselves first from the mindset that attitudes toward masculinity and femininity can be changed without simultaneously questioning the binary construction of same/other, male/female, and secondly from the belief that our bodies are natural, beyond coding or representation—a given that never changes.

To conceive of the body as a *given* requires distancing ourselves from embodied, nonrepresentational experiences. For instance, like other philosophers Elizabeth Grosz points out that the term *phallus* is not synonymous with penis; the phallus is the penis given cultural status in a phallocentric society, a status then coded onto the (so-called) natural male body, even as the *lack* of a penis is coded onto the female body to justify the oppression of women (Grosz 1994). In *Gynesis: Configurations of Woman and Modernity*—the oft-overlooked feminist philosophical treatise from whence my project takes its name—Alice Jardine argued that feminism had not gone far enough in questioning the received truth and established wisdom of patriarchal society. Jardine's work highlights the postpatriarchal/postfeminist moment Jackson more recently identified, as women find ourselves caught between, on the one hand, misogynist mindsets in which women are excluded from phallocentric society based on female-feminine difference (as is the case with essential motherhood) and, on the other, feminist mindsets in which women may operate within phallocentric spheres so long as we value masculinity over femininity, operating within the patriarchy without challenging its structures too deeply. Hence the "strong woman" of the twentieth- and twenty-first-century horror film, whom Kathryn Cady and Thomas Oates describe as "embody[ing] physical strength and emotional toughness" in moments of peril "while happily coupling in domestic tranquility after the threat has passed. This performance of both power and traditional femininity represents an ethos quite acceptable to contemporary ways of viewing women as capable and strong although still always essentially embodying feminine difference" (2016: 322–3). Despite its victories, this is what egalitarian feminism ultimately earned women: the right to *be more like men* in a world still designed by, and for, men. Under either mindset, woman remains man's Other, demarcated as not-male, whereas we could, on the other hand, "start with the simple recognition that if man and woman exist, they do so only within the symbolic" (Jardine 1985: 48).

The starting point of schizosophic sexual difference is accepting that, although we may experience our male and female bodies as masculine or feminine, these experiences are not natural extensions of physical, biological, or evolutionary processes but, quite to the contrary, are "determined by language, and by the political . . . in the form of artistic, theoretical, economic and power, class and sexual systems at any given moment" (Jardine 1985: 48). Obviously, other feminists have made this argument—that gender is a social construction and not a biological given is hardly a new idea. Yet even corporeal theories of gender such as that forwarded by Judith Butler have not succeeded in fundamentally unraveling binary gender's received wisdom or established values, nor our dualistic thinking about masculinity and femininity. This leaves us, at the start of a new millennium, at the same impasse Jardine pointed to at the end of the last: unable to theorize sexual difference in ways that do not treat difference as *negative*.

In the chapters to come, I argue that Freudian psychoanalysis, despite its many and significant contributions to horror film studies, has not led us beyond this impasse because psychoanalysis, like the Aristotelian system of classification upon which it rests, is inherently dualistic. Under the psychoanalytic system, itself based on Platonic notions of an Ideal Form, the "ideal" human subject is white, heterosexual, middle-class, able-bodied, and male—yet this does not make every white, straight, able-bodied middle-class man "ideal." At best, as Teresa Rizzo argues, it makes him a facsimile, worthy only insofar as he measures up to the "original," that is, the Ideal (Rizzo 2012: 42). Furthermore, Rizzo goes on to explain that for women, as for people of color, queer individuals, those of the working classes, or those with disabilities, such a system of classification denies the validity of an existence unrelated to whiteness, heterosexuality, middle-classness, dis/ability, or maleness. In other words, in this representational system, difference is always difference *from* the Ideal, a measure of the ways in which one is or is not hegemonically *human*, where humanity is defined by/as whiteness, maleness, middle-classness, able-bodiedness, and heterosexuality. To merely reimagine the Ideal Form differently—as, for instance, black, or queer, or female—would only change the nature of oppression, when our feminist goal should be to eradicate oppressive systems. I argue, then, that we must begin to think differently about difference. In the final section of this introduction, I posit that if monsters have traditionally been conceived of as the ultimate embodiment of difference, as the (generic) human's Other, perhaps the time has come for us all to become monsters.

Schizosophy of the Monstrous

When Jardine, writing from the postmodernist perspective, questioned whether any revolutionary movement (such as feminism) could ever escape its oppressive binary history, she asked whether a far more radical rethinking of all Western "ways of knowing" might be necessary to create an actually equitable society (1985: 23–4), as Deleuze also pointed out (2005). Similarly, Rosi Braidotti, drawing from both Deleuze and Luce Irigaray, advocates a "nomadic subjectivity," a radical unthinking of binarism that allows for affirmative conceptions of difference as difference-in-itself in which "the point is not to know who we are, but rather what, at last, we want to become, how to represent the mutations, changes, and transformations, rather than Being in its classical modes" (2002: 2).

To apply Braidotti to my own work, I believe what we need is a way to reach what Henri Bergson called our *inner states* and learn to see ourselves as his *living things constantly becoming*. Only then will we be able to reconstruct what the next chapter will call our "imaginary bodies" in ways that make freer, that make safer, that make more equitable *every* person's lived experiences. Although horror, as theorists from Noël Carroll to Tony Williams have pointed out, has by and large been a conservative genre, concerned with wholeness (if only via incompleteness), horror film may have transgressive/progressive potential because, in primarily molecular horror films, viewers may be *affected* into becoming monsters-who-are-not-monstrous. In this instance, monstrousness has not been normalized or naturalized. Rather, as I will explain when turning to schizoanalysis in the next chapter, viewers of molecular films may learn to discard a dualistic model of difference that demands our identities stand as sharply delineated, closed-off categories in favor of conceptions of difference that embrace fluid, possible becomings lived somewhere within the slash between self/Other.

Obviously, the implications of a nomadic subjectivity go beyond film theory. Braidotti argues that, in the twenty-first century, "we live in permanent processes of transition, hybridization, and nomadization" (2002: 2). If we are not careful, in this postpatriarchal, postfeminist moment our society may fall back into oppressive and repressive modes of thinking out of sociocultural panic about how such betwixtness overturns the powerful and powerfully entrenched ideological structures that have underpinned Western society for centuries—structures that rely on fixed, static, molar subjects. The Victorian era gave us monsters who were monsters because they differed from the Freudian subject's Platonic ideal: not-male; not-heterosexual; not-white; not-able-bodied; not-European; not-middle-class. While the social and political revolutions of the twentieth century may have challenged the belief that women, persons of color, different socioeconomic groups, queer people, and individuals with disabilities should be excluded from the rights enjoyed by able-bodied, middle-class, white European heterosexual males, these movements, including feminism, have not gone far enough in denying the primacy of that ideal. As Deleuze would say, like Kant we have allowed the established order to remain intact. Now, in the twenty-first century, as diversity is slowly giving way to inclusivity, in which the margins have not only moved closer to the center but, through liberatory ideologies, have begun to demand that the center reshape itself in the image of those who were not only excluded from but frankly never even considered when white, European, patriarchal institutions were established, I believe the monster is taking on the role of challenging the "naturalness" of the (white, middle-class, cisgender, heterosexual, able-bodied) body, as well as negate-ive theories of difference. As I hope to show in the following chapters, monsters in the new millennium have acquired a new cache as the post-human, a "techno-terratological phenomenon that privileges the deviant or the mutant" and thereby "gives a new twist to the centuries-old connection between the feminine and the monstrous" (Braidotti 2002: 179).

In the chapters to come, my first argument is that this "new twist" to the monstrous-feminine, in which female heroes like *Alien's* Ripley or *Underworld's* Selene are as much monster-as-hero (Selene being a vampire and Ripley, by *Alien: Resurrection*, being an alien-human hybrid clone), speaks to our new millennium's desire for affirmative difference. Braidotti certainly hails this development in horror, science fiction, and fantasy, claiming that it "actively contributes to . . . an emphasis on hybrid and mutant identities and transgender bodies" (2002: 183), with the result that what Barbara Creed called "the monstrous-feminine" now more than ever reflects the panic of the patriarchy as patriarchal structures have at last begun to bend under the combined pressure of minoritarian viewpoints pushing at the white, male, European center.

However, as hopeful as Braidotti's "post-human, bio-centered egalitarianism" sounds, we must recognize that the patriarchy has not yet died a quiet death. Since Braidotti was writing in 2002, hegemonic culture has responded to the disruptive power of the mother-monster by returning to the hegemonic ideal of the nuclear family—which, as Chodorow claims, stands at the heart of patriarchal power structures—and, as this book will argue, has used motherhood itself to redomesticate the monster. In presenting a four-point "cartography of the women-monsters nexus" (Braidotti 2002: 193) in horror film dependent on what I call the films' politics of reproduction—films like *The Matrix* which shift the capacity for reproduction from mothers to technology or machines; films like *Rosemary's Baby* which equate female insemination with possession by demonic or alien forces; films like *Alien* which transfer birth from females to males; and films like *Psycho* in which men "transform" into women, as the result of unresolved Oedipal crises—Braidotti maintains that "[t]his fantasmagoric of unnatural births and unrepresentable sexualities of the most hybrid kind plays with alternative body-forms, . . . the counterpoint to the emphasis that dominant post-industrial culture has placed on the construction of clean, healthy, fit, white, decent, law-abiding, heterosexual and forever young bodies" (2002: 199–200). Braidotti's argument is that liberative, revolutionary ideologies will only ever succeed in truly destabilizing the established order, creating space for new possibilities of becoming, when we embrace an affirmative philosophy of difference in which "the metamorphic company of monsters—those existential aristocrats who have already undergone the mutation—can provide not only a solace, but an ethical model" (2002: 211).

Like Braidotti, I find it intriguing that reproduction, so long the purview of the patriarchy which, as Ann Hall maintains, has sought to re-produce "sameness and the status quo," might also be a vehicle for embodying a liberating schizosophy of monstrousness—which is to say that the Othered and monstrous-ized female body might now be an "ethical model" for affirmative, qualitative theories of difference. Nevertheless, like Jardine and Jackson, I fear declaring this victory too soon. Hence, in large part this book concerns itself with distinguishing those films that continue to treat motherhood as essential to female difference in the most negative sense from those films that embody an ethical model of difference as difference-in-itself. It is to this monstrous philosophy of motherhood the rest of this book will turn.

Although Deleuze was the first philosopher to write seriously of cinema as philosophical, Deleuzian film theory—what Anna Powell calls "schizoanalysis"—has been late in finding a seat at the theoretical table. The majority of film scholarship in the twentieth and twenty-first centuries, particularly that concerned with gender, has drawn from Freudian psychoanalysis, a system I, like Powell, call "cinepsychoanalysis." Because, as theorists from Barbara Creed to Tony Williams have pointed out, horror's conflation of the monstrous Other with the feminine has proven fertile ground for feminist film critics, cinepsychoanalysis has therefore dominated the field of horror film studies—which has been fortunate, since cinepsychoanalysis has done much to help us understand the oftentimes misogynist, typically hegemonic ends of horror. Yet, in the twenty-first century, as horror and its monsters, including mother-monsters, take on a new dimension and Otherness, which is to say *difference,* has become an inescapable concern of our diverse, hyperconnected, rapidly changing global world, it is time schizoanalysis is allowed to contribute to feminist film studies what cinepsychoanalysis has not: namely, an affirmative theory of sexual difference.

For those readers unfamiliar with the schizoid philosophy or "schizosophy" of Gilles Deleuze and his partner, Felix Guattari, and/or with horror film analysis, I want to offer reassurance that this book seeks to make the application of schizosophy to horror film analysis clear and accessible, both describing and demonstrating the techniques of schizoanalysis. In addition to positing an argument about the contested place of the monstrous-maternal in contemporary horror film and what this contestation reveals about/points toward for feminism, I also intend this book to enable those who want to *do* schizoanalysis to find concrete examples of how to apply schizosophy to film. Therefore, much more will be said about schizosophy and schizoanalysis as this book progresses, and readers unfamiliar with either schizoanalysis or cinepsychoanalysis (or both) will find definition and application of terms particular to both approaches in the ensuing chapters.

I would also here note that this book employs (or attempts to employ) the rhizomatic structure of Deleuze and Guattari's own philosophic writings, bringing readers to "plateaus" of understanding about the politics of reproduction in horror film before deliberately dropping readers off from that theoretical and/or analytical plateau. In Chapter 1, "Mother, (m)Other," I continue to discuss the problem of "mothering" for feminism under an allegedly egalitarian, yet still binary, framework of gender that posits equality for women and men based on the sameness of the sexes. I will therefore argue that feminist film theory's inability to theorize difference as difference-in-itself stems from the phallocentric gender binary reflected in (and perhaps reinforced by) cinepsychoanalysis—the most common approach to analyzing gender in the horror film. Moreover, I will argue that failing to theorize difference has allowed hegemonic ideals of motherhood to dominate a disembodied cultural construction of women-as-mothers, essentializing motherhood into a natural extension of the female body's reproductive capacity.

Having in this introduction outlined both the oppressive uses to which essential motherhood has been employed against women and the failure of egalitarian feminism to redress the very real problems of "mothering" in a postpatriarchal society, in this first chapter I argue for schizosophic theories of embodied, qualitative, and radically affirmative difference as difference-in-itself, and I explain how schizoanalysis's embodied approach to film viewing suggests that the cinematic assemblage has the power to realize those theories by *changing* the viewer. I will explain how, through the techniques of horror film, viewers may be destabilized from unified subjectivity—affected into becoming-camera, becoming-alien, becoming-fire, and so on—and, like Freudian conceptions of the (monstrous) female body, may be opened to becomings: to our bodies' fluidity, seepage, and flow. This chapter concludes by articulating the distinction between molar and molecular films and suggests that it is through the monster's molecular potential for "queering" nature that feminism may at last find freedom from the gender binary.

Chapter 2, "Mother (of) Monsters," tackles one of the most analyzed "mother-monster" horror film franchises: *Alien*. This chapter addresses the abjection of the maternal body famously highlighted by cinepsychoanalyst Barbara Creed, but argues from a schizoanalytic perspective that, because the abject breaks down borders, abjection also creates opportunities for molecular becomings—for awareness of our non-natural, culturally over-coded bodies as "living things constantly becoming." I then turn from the liberative potential of Braidotti's "monstrous philosophy" experienced through Ripley's becoming-alien to the franchise's far more molar twenty-first-century prequels, *Prometheus* and *Alien: Covenant*, arguing that these films shift focus from mothers to monsters and in so doing reify the hegemonic gender binary in which reproduction becomes about (re)producing sameness. Because *Prometheus* and *Alien: Covenant* have been hailed by some as feminist films, after contrasting the prequels' molar elements with the originals' molecular expressions, I explore how Jardine's theory of gynesis—the "putting into discourse of woman" (1985: 25)—has, rather than advancing the feminist project, served to reify Woman's position as Man's other.

Chapter 3, "Meet Your Makers," picks up the thread of the monster man creates, exploring Ann Hall's contention that, for the patriarchy, reproduction is about reproducing sameness—a whole, ideal, perfected form of life. I also propose that Deleuze and Guattari's "becoming-woman" remains such a problematic concept for feminism in part because it leaves the male body unexplored, a universal given—the generic *hu*man—and explore this argument through three films centered around male creators: *The Island of Dr. Moreau*; *Ex Machina*; and *Mary Shelley's Frankenstein*.

Chapter 4, "It's a Monster (Baby)," returns to the concept of essential motherhood and examines how this patriarchal notion is invoked to redomesticate the mother-monster in the *Twilight* films and, with less hegemonic success, the *Underworld* films. I analyze the coincidence of molar expression and hegemonic content in the abstinence-only, pro-life *Twilight* franchise, while also highlighting the franchise's many molecular moments that threaten to disrupt the overarching, ultimately successful patriarchal narrative. By contrast, I argue that the original *Underworld* films allow for the becomings of their monstrous heroes Selene and Michael, yet despite the films' fluid contents and expressions, when Selene becomes a mother-monster in the most recent sequels, the franchise does not manage to overcome feminism's dilemma of difference, as the vanishing of

Selene's daughter from the narrative indicates that feminism still has not found a way for "motherhood" to exist alongside "womanhood."

Finally, Chapter 5, "The Post-human Family," explores the rise of the heroic/sympathetic monster in twenty-first-century horror films. In this chapter, I schizoanalyze how what Braidotti calls the "post-human" also impacts the construction of the nuclear family in the molecular films *Bram Stoker's Dracula*, *Interview with the Vampire*, *Only Lovers Left Alive*, and *28 Days Later*. And yet, I argue, none of these molecular films shows us a pregnancy, which is why in this final chapter I look at the pregnant body as we find it in *Mad Max: Fury Road*, schizoanalyzing the film's molecular elements, as well as its capacity to break down borders and boundaries without either abjectifying or eroticizing its mothers. Ultimately, I argue that the film's blending of science fiction, fantasy, and horror is necessary for destabilizing the generic category of "the human," enabling us all to become-monster.

1

Mother, (m)Other

Gilles Deleuze (1925–95) was among the first philosophers of the twentieth century to take seriously what was at the time a relatively untheorized art: cinema. In fact, Deleuze insisted that *film itself* can be a philosophic medium, embodying the "transcendental empiricism" he argued for as a means of escape from the cultural, political, personal, and philosophical trap of an egoistic self.

This is not to say, however, that Deleuze saw film as *representing* philosophic thought. Rather, Deleuze viewed film as a mechanism via which viewers might *experience* the "self" not as a separate, divided, stable, subjective entity but as *a* self, uncategorizable by culturally determined norms and expectations inscribed onto human bodies by a culture that has deluded its members into believing our "selves" could ever be organized into identities or frozen into subjects. To Deleuze, the only reality was "virtuality," the ceaseless becoming of a self-in-flux across time: *a* self always engaged in becoming different from *itself*. Such a virtual or potential self cannot be thought into being, for in the act of thinking-of-self we fix and freeze the self we are thinking of, thereby arresting the potentiality of becoming. Hence, our habituated ways of thinking—our (mis)perceptions or delusions of *a* self as The Self—in fact serve only to confine us into dualistic modes of being. According to Deleuze and his philosophic partner, the psychologist Felix Guattari, the "schizo"—the disordered mind able to exist without either boundaries between "self" and "other" or the fiction of reality and subjectivity to stabilize it—was the only "free" mind: free because the schizo had accepted reality as delusion and refused to participate in the great social delirium of granting to imagined, cultural fictions the status of generalizable, universal Truth.

For those readers unfamiliar with Deleuze and Guattari, a brief (and necessarily truncated) introduction to their philosophical partnership may clarify how Deleuze later applied their collaboratively devised "schizosophy" to his individual work on cinema. Deleuze and Guattari began their collaboration during the economic and political upheaval of late-1960s France, when French philosophy became overtly political in its attempts to demonstrate how *identity*, far from being the purview of an individual, is socially constructed and constrained, with the goal that such an understanding would ultimately free individuals from hegemonic restraints. Their first collaborative work *Anti-Oedipus* set out to dismantle Freudianism, in which neuroses and psychoses were produced by improper gender identification within the patriarchal nuclear family, as well as Marxism, in which neuroses and psychoses were created by inequitable, unjust socioeconomic conditions. In the first place, Deleuze and Guattari objected to Freud's and Marx's attempts to segregate the psychological/individual from the cultural/social realm; they argued instead for a synthetic theory capable of interrogating the interplay between the individual/social, wherein identity is constantly *becoming*—constantly *produced* as individuals assemble with social, cultural, political, educational, religious, economic, and other institutions. Moreover, Deleuze and Guattari proposed, in direct contravention of Freudian psychoanalysis, that there is no stable, static ego (or subject), for the self is, again, constantly becoming different from *its*-self. Even more importantly, they proposed that the "economy of desire" that produces these becomings is not motivated by *lack*, as it is in Freudianism, but is instead affirmative and creative: a desiring-production. The "social machine," as Deleuze and Guattari call it, seeks to repress desiring-production, forming/forcing individuals into stable, static subjects submissive to the status quo—"good" citizens who go to work, spend money, obey laws, pay taxes, have children, and so on.

In the figure of "the schizo," Deleuze and Guattari pointed to an individual unrestrained by social and cultural institutions (including the family), motivated not by conformity to sociocultural expectations but by the self-constituting desire to create an ever-evolving, autonomous self. Their second collaboration *A Thousand Plateaus: Capitalism and Schizophrenia* sought to present an affirmative philosophy of difference indebted to dynamic systems theory, in which material systems reach thresholds (or "plateaus") that reduce or restrict their movements, constricting the "flow" of desiring-production—such as what happens to the individual when it confronts social, political, economic, or even linguistic structures that tend toward actuality, or systems meant to fix, freeze, and order individuals into (hegemonic) subjects. The schizo resists and ultimately rejects this fixing, freezing, and ordering, remaining an "open" system of desiring-production, or what Deleuze and Guattari called the Body without Organs (BwO); but, Deleuze and Guattari note, there are also *systems* that tend in the opposite direction from actuality, in which desiring-production is always progressing toward a virtual state that will never be realized or attained, never finished or frozen, leaving the individual open to those ceaseless assemblages and constant becomings.[1]

To say that Deleuze and Guattari turned philosophy on its head would be an understatement. Furthermore, their ideas, radical in themselves, were further radicalized by Deleuze's later insistence that cinema was the modern era's most excellent medium, or mechanism, for embodying the schizosophic principles he and Guattari identified. Yet, for all its radicality, Deleuze's cinematic schizosophy was not the theoretical approach adopted once film came to be theorized in the mid- to late-twentieth century. Instead, film theorists, particularly those interested in gender, gravitated toward a theory Deleuze and Guattari vehemently and systematically rejected: Freudian psychoanalysis.

Before delving deeper into the maternal—the concept that animates the project of this book—let us step back, taking this time to examine in more detail both Deleuze's cinematic philosophy as it has been applied by contemporary film theorists (especially those concerned with horror) and Deleuze and Guattari's schizoid philosophy, which gives rise to schizoanalysis as a film theory in many ways counterposed to psychoanalytic film theory. Yet we must tread carefully, being sure not to draw another, and false, binary between psychoanalysis and schizoanalysis. Much about these theories can inform and enhance the other, even as schizoanalysis brings a more nuanced, inclusive, and embodied approach to film analysis that might point us toward a society no longer threatened by "the Other"—a society open to embracing difference as difference-in-itself.

Transcendental Empiricism: Deleuze's Cinematic Philosophy

Schizoanalysis relies on dissolution of the ego, the film viewer's loss of the sense of "self" as one loses track of whether one is "inside" or "outside" the film event. In *Pure Immanence: Essays on A Life*, Deleuze writes that our consciousness solidifies into dualisms (me/not me, inside/outside) "only when a subject is produced at the same time as its object, both being outside the field and appearing as 'transcendents'. . . . [A]s long as consciousness traverses the transcendental field at an infinite speed everywhere diffused, nothing is able to reveal it" (2005: 26). In film, the viewer's consciousness operates at this "infinite speed" as our brains work to process a deluge of stimulation delivered to and through our optic and auditory nerves. Film may therefore be one of those open or virtual systems that destabilizes the production of a fixed-and-frozen Self that could consciously perceive or conceive the images, sounds, movements, special effects, and edits of the film event as a stable, unified object capable of producing a cinematic or spectatorial *subject*.

Deleuze composed two works on the philosophy of cinema, *Cinema 1* and *Cinema 2*, popularly known as his Cinema Books. Nevertheless, *applying* Deleuze's theories is often easier said than done—which, as other schizophilosophers have noted, is one reason why Deleuze's work has so long remained obscure outside his native France.[2] Perhaps the most striking feature of schizoanalysis is that it foregoes the "model of the eye, which traditionally has been the most important model for perceiving, conceiving, imagining, and judging representation and difference ('I see,' 'I think,' 'I imagine' . . . all through the noble sense of sight, which presupposes an 'I' that transcends experience) for a model of the brain" wherein "the brain itself functions like the screen. It is here that we make assemblages and rhizomatic connections" (Pisters 2003: 7). In defining schizoanalysis, Anna Powell distinguishes its methods and aims from those of what will hereafter be referred to as cinepsychoanalysis. Her explanation also helps explain why *the body* is central to Deleuzian film philosophy, a point that will resonate throughout discussions of both horror and maternity in this book. In contrast to Freud's ordered, three-part psyche (id, ego, and superego), and in explanation of how the schizoanalytic viewer differs from the psychoanalytic spectator in ways that challenge the idea of cinema as a monolithic cultural apparatus for producing cinematic subjects, Deleuze and Guattari, following Henri Bergson, propose that

> there are two different selves, one of which is the external projection and social representation of the other. The internal operations of the self are reached by deep introspection, a process that leads us to grasp our inner states as living things constantly *becoming*. . . .[wherein] identity is in constant flux and process. Perception [of cinema] takes place on a direct, visceral level rather than at a subjective level. Cinema is an intensive sensory event of colour, light, and movement. If our subjectivity is not fixed, then our identity in the viewing experience is not a rigid template, but a fluid becoming. (Powell 2005: 19–20, 207)

Deleuze's point, captured eloquently by Powell, was that the cinematic viewing experience has the power to *change* the viewer because film viewing is an embodied encounter experienced in and through the brain, not through the (allegedly transcendent) eye/I. Schizoanalysis maintains that, when highly affected by a film, as viewers we approach this transcendental (not "transcendent") introspective experience in which sensation overtakes or replaces thought. Whereas cinepsychoanalysis has focused on detached, symbolic readings of film and analysis of spectatorial identification with characters, schizoanalysis focuses on "excessive forms of cinematography, *mise-en-scéne,* editing and sound . . . the pivotal tools of horror, used to arouse visual sensations and 'horrify' the viewer. Theories of representation and narrative structure neglect the primacy of corporeal affect" (Powell 2005: 2), that is, how a horror film *affects* the viewer's body, as our hearts race, our stomachs clench, and our palms sweat. Yet it is this *affectively corporeal* experience of film viewing that may serve to dissolve our egos, even for a moment, creating space for viewers to *become*—an experience that cannot be undone even after the film ends and viewers begin to think as "I/eye" again.

In other words, the aim of schizoanalysis as both Anna Powell and Teresa Rizzo have applied it to film has been to theorize how films go about affecting our viewing bodies in ways that allow us to reach those "internal operations of the self," freeing us to see ourselves not as fixed, stable identities—our external, social projections—but, as Bergson said, "as living things constantly becoming." However, like Powell, I do not mean to discount the contributions made to film and gender studies by those cinepsychoanalysts who have "map[ped] social and political meaning onto the representations of fantasy," nor can it be denied that "[f]ear and desire have subjective specificity and operate within a socially learned framework" (2005: 204). Nevertheless, like Powell, I argue that because the people, places, and things we see on film are rendered *virtually*, their "representational capacity" does not overtake the embodied effect of cinema as viewers "are moved by, and move with, lighting, montage, and the camera's motion in space and time" (2005: 201).

Again, without drawing a binary between schizoanalysis and cinepsychoanalysis, it nonetheless seems that cinepsychoanalysis, by focusing exclusively on film-as-representation, lacks the ability of schizoanalysis to illuminate cinema's transformative potential, since it is through a film's affective force, a force even stronger in horror than in other types of film,[3] that film *produces* thought in a complex interaction between optic and auditory nerves and neurologic pathways, or as Deleuze put it, *the brain is the screen.* If we consider how our brains, interpreting information gained through our optic nerves, convince us that the images on film exist in spatial and temporal relation to one another, we may recall Deleuze writing of our "indefinite life" that has no "moments, close as they may be one to another, but only between-times, between-moments; . . . the immensity of an empty time where one sees the event yet to come and already happened" (2005: 29). Cinema for Deleuze, as a collection of images filmed at different times, in different spaces, then assembled to appear continuous, even seamless, was at its most philosophic when it revealed this time-image, the image of time as immanent; for it could be said that film *is* editing, since it is in editing, the literal between-times and between-moments, that cinematic time and space as we have come to know it becomes possible. In this instance, as in others, film provides the opportunity for viewers to reflect on "perception itself" (Powell 2005: 202). Such reflection may, and often does, continue after the film has ended, since "perception and reflection vibrate in us at different speeds. Ideally, Deleuze wants us to approach each film as a direct event, letting it work on us without preconceptions" (Powell 2005: 202)—the very "preconceptions" the eye/I of cinepsychoanalysis, steeped as it is in representation and identification, would weld us to. Yet approaching film as a "direct event," rather than as a text onto which preconceived concepts can be mapped, requires a framework for analyzing the affective potential of film's aesthetic and technological components, such as camera movement, light and color, editing techniques, and sound and visual effects. This is what schizoanalysis provides: a theory of film viewing that does not treat film as solely a representation of reality (as cinepsychoanalysis does) but instead as an embodied event with the expressive capacity to affect a viewer, whose "internal operations" can then be changed by and through the film event.

Schizoanalysis requires more than adopting a new set of tools for film analysis, however, for schizoanalysis operates from a paradigm radically different than the paradigm of psychoanalysis. In schizoanalysis, Freudian "[p]sychic interiority is replaced by an immanence in which desire is process and energy. Here, ideas are dynamic events or 'lines of flight' that can take us into 'a fibrous web of directions'. . . . The term 'rhizome' (or lateral, multi-forked root system) suggests the nomadic movement of thought by the intensities of a self in process" (Powell 2005: 21–2). Rhizomatic thinking could not diverge more sharply from representational thinking, for rhizomatic thinking is non-hierarchic, non-dualistic, and non-chronologic (Pisters 2003: 6). Rhizomatic thinking instead remains *open* and *multiplicitous* and therefore, as this chapter will argue, able to think *difference* differently than is possible in representational schemas, which depend upon oppositions and dualisms such as self/other, beginning/end, masculine/feminine, and normal/abnormal.

Schizoanalysis argues essentially that the affected film viewer may become the schizo, no longer seeking stability via Identity but, rather, open(ed) to becoming what Deleuze and Guattari call the BwO. Becoming has no beginning or end; it inevitably occurs *in the middle*, somewhere between and/or within the connections we make with people, places, ideas, and so on. Deleuze and Guattari called these endlessly combining and recombining (or reterritorializing and deterritorializing) connections *assemblages*. Deleuze in particular was greatly influenced by David Hume's theory of relations, an exteriorized (rather than internalized) "harlequin world of multicolored patterns and non-totalizable fragments where communication takes place through external relations" (Deleuze 2005: 38). This exteriorized theory of relations is reflected in the schizosophic assemblage, as Deleuze and Guattari posit that we assemble with events, ideas, people, technologies, and so on throughout our lives. In those moments of assemblage, we *become*.

To put it another way, we could say that we do not discover or even create ideas or knowledge but, through communication with those "external relations," we *become with* ideas and knowledge. Hence, as we are constantly assembling with events, ideas, people, and technologies—including the technology of cinema—we are never beings, fixed, frozen, stable, or static. We are instead becomings, for "what is universal or constant in the human mind is never one idea or another ... but only the ways of passing from one particular idea to another" (Deleuze 2005: 39). The passing-between *is* becoming, and as later chapters will argue, becoming is always *becoming something else*.

Becoming is a wholly different way of experiencing the world than the one imagined by the ordered psyche of the Freudian subject. Yet Powell is careful to note that Deleuze and Guattari do not conflate schizophrenia, as a mental health condition, with the philosophical concept of the schizo (2005: 21). Schizoanalysis neither valorizes nor glamourizes mental illness, for "the schizo," as Deleuze and Guattari use the term, describes not a person with a clinical condition but the "free man, irresponsible, solitary, and joyous, finally able to say and do something simple in his own name, without asking permission, a desire lacking nothing, a flux that overcomes barriers and codes, a name that no longer designate[s] any ego whatever" (Deleuze and Guattari 2009: 131). The schizo stands as antithesis to the ordered, unified, egoistic Freudian subject, in search always of identity and wholeness. Moreover, schizoanalysis is an *ethological* approach, one "interested not in what a body *is*, but rather in the body's capacity to affect and be affected" (Rizzo 2012: 58).

Hence, while cinepsychoanalysis treats film as an *apparatus* for producing egoistic, hegemonic subjects, à la Plato's allegory of the cave, Deleuze focused on cinema as an assemblage (*agencement* in the original French): the arrangement, layout, or joining together of heterogenous elements. Assemblages do not form a unified whole, for an assemblage is never a finished product; the assemblage, as Thomas Nail explains, is more than "a mixture of heterogenous elements" (2017: 24). Assemblages are always in flux, always assembling, dissembling, and reassembling, each time with different conditions, different elements, and different agents, all of which affect and are affected by one another, as well as being coexistent.

In the cinematic assemblage, the element of the viewer's *body* is as integral as the viewer's psyche. Discarding the model of the eye/I, which melds those "preconceived notions" onto a filmic text to decipher symbols and representations, in favor of Deleuze's model of the brain that experiences film *directly*, unmediated by psychic representation, means elevating a film's style and technique to a level of importance equal to narrative and content. When Deleuze describes the brain *as* the screen, he is referring to "the brain as a 'relatively undifferentiated matter' into which thinking and art might introduce new connections that didn't preexist them—as it were, the brain as materiality of 'a life' yet to be invented, prior and irreducible to consciousness as well as machines" (Rajchman 2005: 20). Deleuze thus rejected purely representational film theories, because representation assumes a preexistent reality which the conscious Self, or subject, interprets, fits into existing schema, and chooses either to accept or reject. For Deleuze, because there is no preexistent reality, there can be no representation; therefore, the film viewer is not decoding symbols but is rather *connecting*, on a neural level, *through the brain*, with the cinematic experience. The optic and auditory nerves are forming an assemblage with the technology of cinema (light, sound, color, editing, camera movement, special effects) in ways that *affect* the viewer's body, as anyone who has ever felt the urge to faint or gag during a gruesome scene will know.

Although cinepsychoanalysis is correct in identifying the ways in which, through identification and representation, film may be productive of what Powell calls "ideational thought," what schizoanalysis brings to the theoretical table is the recognition that film also involves "perceptual and neurological processes" as viewers "connect our corporeal machine and the film's technological and aesthetic machine. If our engagement is intense, we think in and through the body in a powerful experiential response" (Powell 2005: 116). In other words, in the embodied encounter between brain and screen, ideas are introduced that have the literal potential to *change the viewer's mind*. But of course, if it is the body we are thinking through, then before returning to the maternal in horror film, the feminist implications for schizosophic understandings of "the body" need to be elucidated.

The "Volatile Body" in Schizoanalysis

First and foremost, schizosophy does not treat bodies as stable, statics beings but as temporal becomings, as "affective and processual" (Rizzo 2012: 66) or what Elizabeth Grosz calls *volatile*. Secondly, following Bergson, schizosophy views difference as *qualitative*, as internal and non-dialectical, not as difference from any external Other (Rizzo 2012: 68). If, as Rizzo explains, our bodies are constantly becoming, our identities and subjectivities are also constantly in flux, never fixed or stable, making "the individual itself . . . a kind of assemblage that operates on both the molar and the molecular levels" (2012: 66).

The importance of molarity and molecularity to schizoanalysis cannot be overstated. In *A Thousand Plateaus*, Deleuze and Guattari conceived of the molar plane as hierarchically organized; it is within the molar plane that we find individuals fixed or frozen into subjects as a means of categorizing and conceptualizing them. Consequently, molarity creates divisions, and therefore dualisms, between subjects and objects. By contrast, the molecular plane remains in flux, for here the virtuality of things is not fixed or frozen. The molecular plane is made up of things becoming, things in their in-betweenness; and because becomings, in their state of flux, cannot be differentiated one from the other, molecularity is closer than molarity to the plane of immanence where *all* is virtual, (co)existing at once as endless possibility and multiplicity.

As I schizoanalyze the films in this collection, the main thrust of my project will be to distinguish between those films which, by virtue of their molecularity, might open viewers to such immanent experience because these films are concerned with *experience*, with the viewer's embodied responses to light, sound, camera movement, editing, and so on, more so than with the *representation* of what characters or symbols "mean." *Meaning* is the dominant concern of molar films. Although no film is entirely molar or entirely molecular, but rather will contain elements of both, one of my aims is to demonstrate both the subversive potential of primarily molecular films and the hegemonic reinforcement of primarily molar films, for again, representation requires preexistent reality and becomes the basis for dualisms—in fact, representation requires subjectivity and objectivity, the fixing and freezing of the virtual into the actual for the purposes of separation, division, and categorization. Consequently, a molar film is primarily concerned with representation and the actual, not with the immanent or the virtual, and therefore the molar film is more likely to reinforce rather than subvert the hegemonic status quo, particularly where gender, sexual orientation, race, class, and other, intersecting markers of culturally inscribed identity are concerned.

However, it would be a mistake to conceive of the molar and molecular as dualistically opposed. Rather, as Rizzo maintains, the molar is always attempting to operate upon the molecular, fixing and freezing becomings into beings, yet becomings have no sooner been fixed or frozen than attempts at molar organization dissolve into further molecular becomings. The coexistence of molarity and molecularity not only in film (every molar film will demonstrate some molecular elements, and vice versa) but also in the experience of living in continually transforming human bodies leads to Grosz's depiction of the body's *volatility*. Such an affective, temporal conception of the body is particularly important for an ethological film theory like schizoanalysis, since "film can, and often does, imagine bodies and identities outside boundaries, hierarchies, and fixed categories. [Schizoanalysis] has the ability to go beyond the discussion of bodies on the screen to that of the relationship between the body and the screen" (Rizzo 2012: 68). Thinking the body in terms of its *possibilities*, rather than in terms of a fixed, hierarchized identity, furthermore requires thinking the body *in specificity*—as a body that, in terms of race, age, class, dis/ability, sexual orientation, or gender (not to mention size, language, education, or religion), will experience different contexts differently from other bodies.[4] Hence different bodies will affect and be affected by assemblages, including cinematic assemblages, differently.

This is not a question of determining what bodies onscreen *represent* for the viewer. It is a question of how each viewer experiences the cinematic assemblage of which they form a part. According to schizosophy, representation is a fallacy made up of "four great 'illusions,'" namely identity, opposition, analogy, and resemblance (Grosz 1994: 164), which, Deleuze said, we are taught to understand restrictively—what is me, what is not me; what is like me, what is not like me—when it is also entirely possible to see difference not in relation to Self but simply as *difference-in-itself*. So opposed to the dominant, representational way of thinking was Deleuze that in *Difference and Repetition* he called its four operations the "branches of the Caught. On precisely these branches, difference is crucified" (1995: 138). By formulating a theory of *pure difference*, on the other hand, Deleuze and Guattari present a radically alternative conception of "the body and its connections with other bodies, both human and nonhuman, animate and inanimate, linking [bodies] to material objects and social practices" without "subordinat[ing] the body to a unity or homogeneity of the kind provided by the body's subordination to consciousness or to biological organization" (Grosz 1994: 164–5), wherein biology itself becomes a molar plane that fixes, freezes, and orders molecular bodies, in much the same way psychoanalysis organizes the body according to a psychic interiority of desire and identification (the son's identification with the phallic father, the daughter's identification with the castrated mother). Elizabeth Grosz therefore maintains that although Deleuze and Guattari did not explicitly endorse liberatory ideologies such as feminism, their way of understanding difference as difference-in-itself may remove "metaphysical oppositions and concepts" (1994: 164) that permit women to construct our own stories, and selves, free from the representational fetters of the phallocentric imagination, just as Alice Jardine envisioned. It is these sorts of accounts the molecular films in this book attempt to create.

Still, it must be acknowledged that Deleuze and Guattari's work is late in coming to the feminist table. Perhaps following from their adamantly nonbinary thinking, Deleuze and Guattari's schizosophy does not at first blush seem to argue for women's equality. Nonetheless, in recent years feminist scholars have begun to recognize what a theory of pure difference could do for feminism, by enabling us to think the body *as a body*. While (sound) feminist objections to theorizing women's bodies were already discussed in this volume's introduction, schizosophic redefinition of the body as "neither biological nor physical, static nor ahistorical, but lived and situated, changing and culturally constructed" (Rizzo 2012: 49) might provide a line of flight from phallocentrism without setting up an equally oppressive binary of gynocentrism. Returning to Deleuze and Guattari's theory of systems that tend toward the *actual*, schizosophy leads us to acknowledge what Moira Gatens calls an *imaginary body* in which the culturally devised and historically devised meanings inscribed on our bodies generate "emotional investment" in molar categories of identity (race, gender, sexual orientation, and so on) that are then "lived and experienced" as though those meanings are *actual*; hence, "[t]he body . . . is always shadowed and informed by an imaginary body" (Rizzo 2012: 49). True to its schizosophic roots, Gatens's imaginary body is nonbinary—that is, Gatens does not argue for a real (physical)/imaginary (representative) body division, but instead maintains that the imaginary body and the physical body exist in what she calls an "intersection" in which one continuously informs the other (Gatens 1996). Importantly for schizoanalysis, then, Gatens's imaginary body enables us to understand *a body* temporally "as a series of connections that . . . determine what that body can do. . . . Film viewing could be understood as one of these encounters" or connections (Rizzo 2012: 51, 52).

Let us not fail to appreciate how revolutionary the imaginary body could be for our understanding of identity. Gatens's imaginary body is a complete departure from the boundary-obsessed, subject/object process of ego formation concretized in Freudian psychoanalysis and long accepted as truth in philosophy and feminism. The concept of "self" in psychoanalysis has always been dependent upon the existence of an "other" (in Freudianism, typically the mother) against which, through either rejection or identification, we define our *self*. Although they accept that the existence of an/other is necessary for us to operate as distinct entities with individual agency, both Gatens and Grosz argue that self-differentiation begins not with separation but with *connection*. Hence, Lacan's mirror stage can best be described as *a* self "not understood in opposition to the other, but by means of an affective connection with the other . . . , always becoming different from itself as a result of encounters with others . . . mean[ing] that the positive potential of difference can be mobilized" (Rizzo 2012: 51–2).

Without reconceiving of our bodies as temporal and processual—as never finished or whole and, therefore, always open to change—and furthermore without reconceiving the relationship of self to "other" as affectual rather than oppositional, how can we hope to dissolve the gender binary? Feminist theorist Alice Jardine reminds us that psychoanalysis was "born from women's 'hystericality'" (1985: 89), which was understood in opposition to men's rationality and which, when applied through film theory, "finds its most insistent denotations in psychoanalytic fictions" (1985: 90) that posit the woman (or homosexual, or person of color) as Other—*other than* the white, able-bodied, heterosexual, cisgender, middle-class male. Thus, cinepsychoanalysis, despite its many contributions to film and gender theory, may in fact reify the gender binary because, whether viewed from a phallocentric or gynocentric vantage point, psychoanalysis tends toward seeing difference as negative, as *difference from* something (or someone) else.

Representational in its thinking and therefore dependent upon identity, opposition, analogy, and resemblance—Deleuze's "four branches of the Caught"—cinepsychoanalysis has no frame of reference for describing difference as difference-in-itself. Take, for instance, Barbara Creed's famous analysis of the womb in horror film. "In many [horror] films the monster commits her or his dreadful acts in a location which resembles the womb" in its "dark, narrow, winding passages leading to a central room, cellar, or other symbolic place of birth," or perhaps "the monstrous womb belongs to a woman or a female creature who is about to give birth to an alien being or brood of terrifying creatures... thus giving concrete expression to [the womb's] monstrous nature" (Creed 1993: 53). Representing either phallocentric panic at maternity's disturbance of egoistic boundaries (a body contained within another body) and/or repressed male desire to rejoin the oneness of the Mother by going back to the womb—this is how Creed insists the monstrous-maternal must be read in horror film, whether characters are trapped in an uncharted cave system fighting mutant cannibals (as in *The Descent*) or impregnated with an alien spawn that eviscerates its host as it is born (as in *Alien*). In the terms via which cinepsychoanalysis understands difference, one horror film is much like another; its symbols always represent what amounts to the same thing: negation of the (feminine) Other to preserve the (masculine) self.

But is this really all horror film does, or all it can do? Jardine tells us that "where the tools of representation—narrative, characters—are recognized as existing only at the level of fantasies that have entrapped us," to "analyze those fantasies is to ask for repetition" (1985: 59). Powell agrees. She argues that, as horror "obsessively returns to the trope of wholeness, its consequent graphic disintegration and its possible renewal" (2005: 88), continuing to *do* cinepsychoanalysis may inadvertently serve to more firmly entrench binary, phallocentric emphasis on wholeness, even via incompleteness. On the other hand, schizoanalysis, by shifting focus from unity to fluidity—from neither wholeness nor incompleteness but to the processes of becoming which occur between the two—may help us discover films that affect viewers in ways that might free us from binary thinking and dualistic opposition, as well as from the obsessive, subjective need to find unity and identity.

Just as importantly, for all that it has given us in terms of understanding the representational work of gender in horror film, cinepsychoanalysis has also proven insufficient for theorizing how different film viewers might experience films differently. Even feminist film critics like Barbara Creed and Carol Clover tend to operate within the paradigm of cinema as a cultural apparatus, theorizing what films represent to viewers by assuming that women, because they are women, will experience representational and symbolic fictions in the same way (Rizzo 2012: 45). Cinepsychoanalytic theories of spectatorship such as that originally posited by Laura Mulvey, for instance, have argued that horror film provides masochistic pleasure for women, sadistic pleasure for men, as though all men will naturally and inevitably identify with male characters, all women with female characters. But how might a lesbian viewer respond to the representation of woman-as-other in horror film? What about a transgender woman? A black woman? Cinepsychoanalysis offers no satisfying answers to these questions. Obviously, there are no answers, for just as there is no woman-in-general, there is no *viewer in general*, no subsuming of the specificity of individual, embodied experience within monolithic categories such as lesbian, trans, and person of color. My point, and the point of schizoanalysis, is, as Rizzo has argued, that sexual orientation, gender identity, race, and ability are not categories that define individuals, nor do these categories determine their viewing responses. Perhaps one of the most important issues left unaddressed by cinepsychoanalysis, then, is the capacity to theorize *viewers'* bodies in their specificity, to better articulate the cultural work accomplished through the cinematic viewing experience. Here, as Rizzo points out, schizoanalysis can provide much-needed insight. Schizoanalysis may more effectively ask the question of how different viewers might respond differently to horror film, since unlike cinepsychoanalysis, schizoanalysis has not already decided how the eye/I will read a horror film, nor what those readings might mean for disembodied spectators who can be lumped into totalizing categories such as Women, Women of Color, Queer Women—and Mothers.

As this book progresses, it will become clear that schizoanalysis incorporates many of the tools and theories of cinepsychoanalysis in understanding the cultural representations produced in film. But whereas cinepsychoanalysis assumes that those representations are a fixed point—a point of reference all Women or all Men will similarly respond to—schizoanalysis offers far more specificity in understanding how horror film creates affective responses in viewers. Likewise, schizoanalysis does not hierarchize those responses by assuming an "ideal" (white, middle-class, able-bodied, heterosexual, cisgender) male or female viewer. Thus, schizoanalysis is unlikely to produce the supposedly *universal* readings of the symbols and tropes of horror film so familiar from the work of cinepsychoanalysts. Schizoanalysis is, frankly, uninterested in producing readings of that sort. Instead of interpretations of what a horror film *means*, what schizoanalysis seeks is a clearer understanding of how a horror film *works*, on viewers. Such an understanding is important for gender and film theory because, as I aim to show in this book, by combining analysis of content and style into a conception of cinema not as an apparatus but as an assemblage that includes the viewer's body, in all its specificity, schizoanalysis can help us understand the affective impact of film—its potential to *change* us—and moreover to distinguish those films which reify hegemonic ways of being (molar films) from those which open viewers up to possible becomings (molecular films).

As we consider an embodied or ethological approach to film viewing, it will be important to keep in mind that schizosophy has no more room for binarism or dualistic opposition than it does for representation. Drawing from Nietzsche, Deleuze saw the origins of dualisms and binary thinking as stemming from the impetus to make *thinking* about *judging*, for we can only judge one "thing" against another when both objects are fixed and stable, not while they are in flux. To Deleuze, as to Nietzsche, this turn from thought to judgment, this impetus to fix and freeze subjects and objects in service of categorizing and (de)valuing them, presents us with "*the triumph of 'reaction' over active life and of negation over affirmative thought*" (Deleuze 2005: 68).

Like Nietzsche, Deleuze and Guattari proposed a radical escape from the trap of dualistic thinking. Like Nietzsche, they wanted to reveal the falsity of those "so-called higher values," our established ideals—to question knowing, morality, and all the domains of science, religion, family, government, biology, culture, history, and so on which Kant, for all of his denunciation of "false knowledge," did not do: "Kant denounces false claims to knowledge, but he doesn't question the ideal of knowing. . . . [T]he domains remain intact, and the interests of reason, sacred" (Deleuze 2005: 70). Egalitarian feminism questioned the established wisdom that men were superior to women, yet it left the domains of binary gender and masculine privilege unassailed, asserting women's sameness to men as a reason for women to enjoy male privileges (of power, money, and access). Egalitarian feminism did not question the (so-called) true knowledge of the patriarchy: that masculinity is to be valued over femininity, that these gendered categories are somehow true or natural in and of themselves, and that women must become more *like* men in order to enjoy the privileges *of* men. Hence, the egalitarian feminism of the 1960s and 1970s represents a social tipping point during which, as Deleuze observed, our "values can change" but "what is essential hasn't changed: the perspectives or the evaluations on which these values, whether old or new, depend.... [W]e are still asked to accept 'the real as it is'—but *this 'real as it is' is precisely what the higher values have made of reality*" (2005: 71). It is this delusion of "the real as it is" that Deleuze considered the great social delirium, and it is this delirium he wished to see us wake up to—and escape from.

In place of binary thinking or dualisms, we find schizosophy's radical affirmation of difference as qualitative (as difference-in-itself) and radical dismissal of any notion of a preexistent Ideal Form against which the Self could be measured. Deleuze and Guattari likewise conceived of desire in starkly different terms than Freud. In psychoanalysis, desire is most often (psycho)sexual and typically motivated by lack (the desire to *become more* or to *be something else*). In schizosophy, desire is rendered as "productive" and this, Grosz says, "seems to offer women ... the promise of at last a position other than the passive objects of desire, castrated in themselves, requiring the fulfillment provided by men and the phallus" (1994: 182). When Deleuze and Guattari speak of *desiring machines*, it is Nietzsche's *will to power* to which they refer, not as a drive to dominate but as the drive to create. Creation involves what Deleuze describes as the "lightening" of burdens, freedom from the fiction of reality our thinking/judging minds and dualistic cultures have convinced us of: "To create is to lighten, to unburden life, to invent new possibilities of life. The creator is legislator—dancer" (Deleuze 2005: 69). In fact, these two sentences neatly capture the essence of what schizosophists mean when we refer to schizosophy as *radically affirmative*—as always and completely on the side of *life*. Deleuze writes of what he calls "active forces" as "affirm[ing], and affirm[ing] their difference," whereas "reactive forces" focus on "opposition to what they are not ... [T]hrough negation, they arrive at a semblance of affirmation. Affirmation and negation are thus the qualia of the will to power" (2005: 74).[5]

Let us consider how the will to power plays out in applying schizosophy to film theory. One major project of this book is to demonstrate the ways schizoanalysis helps us distinguish those films with primarily molar elements from films with primarily molecular elements, and to understand the different cultural work that may be achieved via molarity and molecularity. Molarity *reacts* to established "truths" and places forces in binary opposition, affirming self by negating Other (that which differs, like the monster). Consequent to this affirmation-by-negation, molarity also reinforces hegemonic ideals, received wisdom, and established values. Molecularity, on the other hand, is *active*, creative, in flux, and therefore does not rely on dualisms. Molecularity instead reveals temporal becomings, dissolves boundaries, and destabilizes the primacy of subjectivity, the eye/I who perceives and thinks.

In terms of egalitarian feminism's attempts to re-order gender relations, we could say, as Deleuze does, that "[e]ven when they win, reactive forces are still reactive.... Our masters are slaves that have triumphed in a universal becoming-slave" (2005: 76), for we have not managed to free ourselves from binary thinking. As a step toward outlining the logic of this book, which concerns itself with the maternal in horror film, it is worth quoting Deleuze here at length:

> When nihilism triumphs, then and only then does the will to power stop meaning "to create" and start to signify instead "to want power," "to want to dominate" (thus to attribute to oneself or have others attribute to one established values: money, honors, power, and so on). Yet that kind of will to power is precisely that of the slave; it is the way in which the slave or the impotent conceives of power, the idea he has of it and that *he applies when he triumphs*. (2005: 77)

Insofar as women "triumphed" under egalitarian feminism, it was by gaining access to patriarchal power, in no small part by devaluing femininity—persisting in the belief that receiving "money, honors, power, and so on" should be predicated upon displaying those characteristics, namely masculine characteristics, that patriarchal society valued. It did not seem to enter into egalitarian feminism's mindset that those values might be values only because we have agreed to hold them as such, only because we have collectively, as men *and* women, bought into the fictional reality that not only is masculinity superior to femininity but, just as importantly, that masculinity and femininity also exist independently of cultural norms inscribed onto biological bodies, that there is in fact *a gender binary*. Nor, as was discussed in the introduction, did sexual difference find a place within this conversation. Rather, egalitarian feminism continued essentially to operate from a definition of difference-as-lack, of woman as castrated (lacking the phallus), a negate-ive and reactive force that succeeded only in helping slaves (women) become masters within a master/slave system in which the masters (men), as Deleuze says, were always-already slaves themselves.

Hence, the triumphs of egalitarian feminism, although I do not mean to dismiss the material and social impacts this movement had on the lives of (some) women, can only be viewed as triumphs in the most nihilistic sense. For in the master/slave dichotomy, to win—to become a master—means nothing more than embracing a new form of slavery. What Deleuze and Guattari's radically affirmative schizosophy argues for instead is the schizo, the freeing of ourselves from dualistic thinking in order to embrace and affirm *difference,* for "as long as we replace old values with new ones that only amount to new combinations between reactive forces and the will to nothingness, nothing has changed" (Deleuze 2005: 81). This, too, Grosz realizes, cautioning, like Jardine, that in a phallocentric world, women can only attain so much power—the power afforded to us by the patriarchy, most often in exchange for our tacit agreement that our difference from men is negative, as we continue to valorize the masculine over the feminine and deny ourselves any perspective on our own female or feminine becomings (Grosz 1994: 182). If we are to truly escape the gender binary, we, as this project proposes, need to begin theorizing women's embodied experiences *in specificity,* within a model of radically affirmative, qualitative difference as difference-in-itself.

Such escape from dualistic thinking is described by Deleuze and Guattari in numerous writings as tracing a line of flight, an image that evokes birds dancing across the sky and, not coincidentally, recalls Deleuze's comparison of the lightened, unburdened creator to a dancer. Tracing a line of flight from dualistic thinking involves becoming a BwO. While some of this discussion must be reserved for later chapters, because the BwO, particularly in discussions of horror, can invoke decidedly gruesome images, it is necessary here to comment on what others have critiqued as the violence at the core of Deleuze and Guattari's radically affirmative philosophy.

For as much as Deleuze admired Nietzsche, Deleuze was not a nihilist. Deleuze saw in Nietzsche a process for doing what Kant did not: escaping our delusions of reality by questioning the established values culture has handed to us. But where Nietzsche remained at the lowest possible point of this degeneration, the individual toppling into an abyss of meaninglessness, Deleuze envisioned the point from which the creator, or dancer, might begin to soar. At just the moment that the individual embraces the impossibility of remaining within the binary machine that has trapped it, "thanks to this rupture, the will to nothingness . . . becomes the will to deny reactive life itself, and inspires in man the wish to actively destroy himself. Beyond the last man, then, there is still *the man who wants to die.* And at this moment of the completion of nihilism (midnight), everything is ready—ready for a transmutation" (Deleuze 2005: 82).

At just the moment when self-destruction appears the only option, Deleuze finds possibility and potential for becoming. Evacuated of concepts, freed from dualisms, attuned to the delirium of reality, the BwO, although we might be tempted to say it is the endpoint of becoming, is in fact the entryway that makes all other becomings possible. The BwO, in other words, is not the destruction of life, but an escape from the reactive forces that constrict and imprison life's potential. Yet becoming-schizo *does* bring an individual to the precipice of madness, of suicide. Thus, there is a certain amount of, if not outright violence, at the very least dissolution of self that walks right up to the edge of the abyss. Herein perhaps lies the answer to why horror film may have such molecular potential. For although we could certainly reach the emptiness-which-activates-transmutation through contemplation or meditation, it makes sense that horror film can also so affect us, not by emptying us (as contemplation and meditation would) but by using saturation of image, sound, and feeling to disorient us, overwhelming and thereby destabilizing our thinking subjectivities so that, as viewers, we find ourselves opening up to becoming the BwO. From there, freed from binary thinking and its negation of difference, we have the potential for endless other becomings.

It is here that joy returns to schizosophy. Deleuze says of transmutation that it "elevates multiplicity and becoming to their highest power and makes of them objects of an affirmation" (2005: 84). In the radically affirmative embracing of difference as difference-in-itself, we find the "practical joy of the diverse" (2005: 84).

Pure Difference and the Post-human Family

Let us not pretend tracing a line of flight from the gender binary will be easy, especially given schizosophy's reliance on embodiment and the ways the body has been used to "other" and oppress women. Nevertheless, I persist in advocating for schizosophy and schizoanalysis, quite simply because I see no other road forward for feminist film theory that does not fall prey to the binary trap. As Rosi Braidotti has said,

> it would be a defeat to have the dialectics of the sexes merely reversed for the benefit of women—mostly white, highly-educated women—while leaving the power structures practically unchanged. I think it would be most beneficial

to all concerned if the tensions that are built into the [contemporary] crisis of ["human"] values were allowed to explode within feminism, bringing its paradoxes to the fore. (2002: 210)

I propose in this book that motherhood and the maternal stand as two of feminism's most enduring and important paradoxes. Yet to theorize only motherhood would be to ignore the equally conflicted concept of fatherhood. For as much of the conflation of the feminine with the *natural* (and therefore the uncontained and uncontrollable) body has served to oppress women, Grosz argues that failure to theorize with any specificity the male body has also contributed to phallocentric fear of the female (m)Other, since "the specificities of the masculine have always been hidden under the generality of the universal, the human,... the generic 'person.' Thus what remains unanalyzed, what men can have no distance on, is the mystery... of the unspoken male body" (1994: 198).

Consider how phallocentrism has resisted theorizing seminal fluid as fluid (Grosz 1994: 199). Instead, phallocentrism renders what is actually a fluid a solid with the "capacity to fertilize, to father, to produce an object," thereby "extend[ing] bodily interests beyond the male body's skin... in the mother whom he has impregnated and the child thereby produced, making them *his* products, possessions, and responsibilities" (Grosz 1994: 199). Within binary gender, Grosz explains, it has been necessary to solidify seminal fluid because "phallicizing the male body, ... subordinating the rest of the body to the valorized functioning of the penis, ... involves the constitution of the sealed-up, impermeable body" (1994: 201) that can be opposed to the openness of the female body. The female body's openness, as Creed (following Julia Kristeva) has argued, leads to the abjectification of the female body in horror film: that which oozes, bleeds, putrefies, excretes, expectorates, and so on. Grosz goes so far as to suggest that beyond mere openness, what the phallocentric imagination detests is the idea of *flow,* or that the male body, too, might become a "passive receptacle" like the female body, "conceived as... the nesting place of [the man's] product—the fetus" (1994: 201).[6]

What many of the films analyzed in this book reveal is undoubtedly what cinepsychoanalysis proposes: phallocentric fear of the open, leaky female body from which feminine contagion might flow—the castrated or castrating mother the male child must separate himself from. Nonetheless, viewed from a schizosophic perspective, we might see certain of these films as a tentative, if not wholly positive or successful, critique of this phallocentric denial of male fluidity. What the male scientist Victor Frankenstein, like many of his filmic (and literary) successors, creates may be "monstrous," yet time and time again, horror punishes these parthenogenetic pioneers perhaps not for taking on the female role so much as for attempting to negate the female's role in (pro)creation. Certainly we could read these films as a reification of essential motherhood, assigning women's role as that of mothers (and nothing else), but the chapters to follow will demonstrate that at least some of these films, the more molecular films, could also be understood as recognizing a "two-way" or reciprocal flow between male and female bodies as reproductive *partners*, in which, as Grosz says, the female body is co-productive of, not merely a "nesting place" for, life. In this sort of nonbinary reproductive model, sexual difference is essential *and* affirmative, as sexual difference in schizosophy must be. Affirmative, qualitative models of sexual difference, therefore, may be the first step toward defining motherhood and fatherhood—or, simply, parenthood—outside of a binary model of gender that hegemonically constructs those experiences as artificially naturalized extensions of male and female reproductive capacities—an argument I will return to in this book's final chapter.

For now, it is enough to stress that what egalitarian feminism has not gained by insisting on equality-via-sameness of/within the sexes (that women are *the same* as men, and therefore all women are the same as all other women, all men the same as all other men) schizosophic models of embodied difference might enable us to finally achieve. For although "there will always remain a kind of outsideness or alienness of the experiences and lived reality of each sex for the other . . . [w]hen respected, this difference . . . involves each relating to the other without being engulfed or overwhelmed" (Grosz 1994: 207). Within our current binary conception of gender, unfortunately, this "gulf" of sexual difference has proven so disgusting to the masculinist need to reproduce sameness and solidify identity that such difference can only be negative—Woman must be castrated, related to only as Man's Other, viewed as fluid, filthy, alien, *monstrous*. Cinepsychoanalysis of horror film has driven this point home quite fruitfully in recent decades. However, if we want to move beyond pointing out how women in horror film are othered, we need both new, affirmative, qualitative models of sexual difference and *an erasure of the desire to code characteristics as masculine or feminine*, as though those characteristics are natural extensions of male or female bodies. We must therefore trace a line of flight from binary thinking about gender, which means stepping back for a moment to consider how this binary thinking arises, particularly within the context of the family.

Deleuze, drawing from Hume, notes that most of what we consider to be real or true is based primarily on predictive schemas developed through observation and habituation. That is, when we observe what seem to be "similar cases," as Deleuze puts it, we imaginatively combine those cases to create an expectation for what is happening/will be happening, while ignoring any differences between these cases (Deleuze 2005: 40–1). Thus, the "principle of habit as fusion of similar cases in the imagination and the principle of experience as observation of distinct cases in the understanding . . . combine to produce both the relation and the inference that follows from the relation (belief), through which causality functions" (Deleuze 2005: 41). Applying the functionality of causal relations to gender roles, we can see that binary gender has been constructed in this way: We believe men and women think, feel and act in certain ways—ways we have come to code masculine and feminine—because that is what we observe, and it becomes what we expect (habit) without our realizing that what we are observing is not a naturally occurring state; rather, we are observing socially conditioned beings acting in ways that are not biologically or even evolutionarily innate, but which are culturally programmed: what those beings were habituated to think, feel, or do as a man or wo-man. Deleuze thereby points to our absurd (although wholly understandable) tendency to construct our world out of observations that form and were formed by expectations, which then form habits, which we then believe are Truth, the Way of Things. Hence delirium becomes reality, though in truth, it is only still delirium.

What would be required to free us from this delirium? Deleuze posits the dissolution of self—the schizo who sees delirium *as delirium*. Thus, the role of imagination or phantasy in normalizing this delirium, in effect the psychological and ideological trick of convincing ourselves that the fictive is the actual, becomes paramount. Deleuze, like Hume, ascribed to human imagination the influence of passions, which "have the effect of restricting the range of the mind, fixating it on privileged ideas and objects, for the basis of passion is not egotism but *partiality*, which is much worse" (Deleuze 2005: 46). In a theoretical turn that bears directly upon the project of this book, Deleuze writes: "We are passionate in the first place about our parents, about those who are close to us and are like us. . . . The problem is . . . how to go beyond partialities . . . to an 'extended generosity,' how to stretch passions and give them an extension they don't have on their own" (2005: 46–7).

Let us think of *the family* as one institution that creates partialities. Tony Williams explains that "the family is the ideal launching pad for producing gendered beings. It has a specific social and psychic function, policing desire, social relationships, and artistic expression. According to Freud's scenario, the male child must relinquish identification with the pre-Oedipal feminine maternal realm to gain access to the Law of the Father" (2014: 13). On the other hand, a female child must identify with the Mother, seeing herself as subordinate to the Father/male—as *lacking* the phallus that grants authority in phallocentric culture. Thus, "[d]espite social changes since Freud's time, the Oedipus complex still symbolically depicts a status quo operating within western patriarchal society," *but* "the Oedipal trajectory is not a natural course of individual development. It results from social manipulation. . . . What appears as instinctual actually results from an oppressive behavioral pattern within bourgeois society" (Williams 2014: 13–14).

In cinepsychoanalysis, horror is often understood as sharing in the work of fantasy more broadly "to enable the return of the repressed and thus to engineer sublimation, and social consensus" (Powell 2005: 21). In terms specific to the family, Williams writes of the tension between civilization and individualization, as "civilization relies on repression, often molding individuals in ways detrimental to their individual potentials. But repression never totally succeeds. Repressed factors return in distorted forms, often violently reacting against agents of repression such as state or family" (2014: 13). Williams traces this return of the repressed through the Bush-Reagan years, during which the so-called family values movement sought unsuccessfully to restore patriarchal structures, including the nuclear family, yet for reasons as much economic as social (e.g., the need for two-wage-earner households that necessitated women's education and professionalization), the white, patriarchal—or, as Williams terms it, "traditional"—nuclear family had lost its battle for hegemony. By the 1980s, as revealed in that era's popular slasher genre (*Nightmare on Elm Street, Friday the 13th, Halloween*), society had reached a state of "unconscious patriarchal hysteria trying to hold back contradictory tensions, especially those involving changing gender roles" (Williams 2014: 19). Kimberly Jackson picks up Williams's argument in analyzing twenty-first-century family horror films, arguing that where we now find ourselves is a postpatriarchal/postfeminist moment which, "[l]ike the various other 'posts' used to characterize contemporary society, . . . does not imply that we have gotten beyond patriarchy but rather that it is no longer a functional model for describing social relations, yet it is so deeply entrenched we cannot envision an alternative" (2016: 1).

Both Williams and Jackson note that in the late 1960s, following second-wave feminism, films such as *The Exorcist* ascribed the threat to the nuclear family (upon which construction of binary gender and maintenance of the patriarchal status quo rests) to women and children. By the late 1970s and early 1980s, however—the beginning of those Bush-Reagan years—the father comes to bear the blame for the breakdown of the nuclear family. "As the father is the anchor for the traditional nuclear family and the larger patriarchal structure that it supports," argues Jackson, "the weak or mad father represents a threat to the entire social order" and leaves a power vacuum which increasingly in late-twentieth- and twenty-first-century horror comes to be filled by "feminine surrogates, who are often portrayed as both nurturing and protective, as violent and destructive" (2016: 8, 10), as female characters assume the role of both "victim" and "attacker."[7] But just as Carol Clover's Final Girl was not actually a feminist development—she was, instead, a reification of masculine heroism in a female body that existed to defeat the monstrous male-feminine killer in slasher film—Jackson argues that the mother-and-child heroes of twenty-first-century family horror, although on the surface they may appear "empowering" and "liberating," in fact serve to reveal how

> the individual stance that women are allowed to adopt in contemporary Western culture comes with enormous pressures. . . . "To a much greater extent than men, women are required to work on and transform the self, to regulate every aspect of their conduct, and to present their actions as freely chosen. . . . [T]he partial social revolution accomplished by [second-wave feminism] has thrust women into a kind of 'double jeopardy' in which they are exposed to what they perceive as the demands of the feminist world—to achieve in the public realm— even as more traditional demands on women—to shoulder the bulk of work in the family, to present themselves as desirable sex objects—remain in place." (Jackson 2016: 12)

Pointing to "invisible systems of power and privilege" (Jackson 2016: 13)— for example, misogyny, heteronormativity, racism, ableism—that structure experience of the world for all of us, Jackson looks at twenty-first-century horror film and asks: "How will family identities need to be renegotiated based on the new positions of mothers and fathers, women and men? What versions of feminine identity are sustainable in the twenty-first century? What will happen to the children, especially the girl children, who must carry the burden of an uncertain future" (2016: 19)? My attempts to answer those questions seek at those "established truths" that still underpin binary thinking about gender. Again, I maintain that it is only in tracing a line of flight from the gender binary that we will find an escape from the postpatriarchal/postfeminist moment—and with that escape an opportunity to (re)create functional families that do not manipulate members into socially proscribed roles for gender and sexual orientation, among other things, but instead free members to live liberating lives that fully maximize their individual potential.

Thus, we must give up the fiction of a preexisting order into which we come to fit our differentiated, egoistic "selves." We must see instead the potentialities of *a* person, not an individual Subject to be scripted into the social order (or allowed/encouraged to opt out of it). The family must become the place where those potentialities are lived, as "family" comes to mean not a contained unit but rather a series of connections and assemblages with which we become as the family-assemblage forms and re-forms throughout our lives. I am calling this "the post-human family," a family evacuated of the subjective tyranny of the great social delusion that lies in perceiving the hegemonic gender binary and/or heteronormative society as the preexistent reality into which individuals either do or do not fit, when in fact hegemonic culture is nothing more than a culturally constructed, agreed-upon fiction masquerading as reality.

Deleuze describes "a life of pure immanence, neutral, beyond good and evil, for it was only the subject that incarnated it in the midst of things that made it good or bad" (2005: 29). In horror, monsters exist in this interstitial space, between, and therefore beyond, human and nonhuman; the monster is thus purely immanent until our egoistic minds label it good or evil. Film matters because on Deleuze's direct, visceral level, in which the brain *is* the screen, film allows us to *experience* difference; it extends our partialities beyond what is "like" us or "close" to us. The more we imagine difference as affirmative rather than frightening—the more our imaginations allow us to experience ourselves as becomings rather than beings—the more just and inclusive could be the society we create. For schizosophic difference, what Deleuze called *pure difference*, is the "horizon that cannot appear in its own terms but is implied in the very possibility of . . . an other and their relations . . . that bind each 'thing' to every other and to the whole of existence without, however, linking them to an organic or metaphysical wholeness or unity" (Grosz 1994: 208–9). It is in the effort to remain within the openness of the in-between, within the "spacings" and "intervals" which, if anything can be said to, define difference, that schizoanalysis resists closed readings of horror films, focusing instead on the never-finalized processes via which such films are experienced, and the affect(s) they might have on viewers.

The chapters to follow will demonstrate a theorization of filmic technique (or expression) that works in tandem with filmic content (or narrative), a theory that embraces the potential for the cinematic experience to change viewers, including changing how we see ourselves in relation to difference, sexual or otherwise. The maternal is an important vantage point from which to approach our postpatriarchal moment because the maternal is where we find most undeniable the sexual difference our postfeminist society still denies by focusing on *sameness* as the basis for equality. (From a patriarchal standpoint, I will argue, as Ann Hall has, that even reproduction has been about denying difference and reproducing sameness—yet the embodied maternal experience of reproduction is never the same for women and does not produce subjects but *individuals*.) By focusing less on representation and more on expression, schizoanalysis's embodied approach to film viewing may also create more space for the responses of viewers from marginalized or minoritarian communities.

It is worth noting here again that this book ranges broadly in the films it schizoanalyzes. Cleanly separating films along generic lines is less important in Deleuzian film theory than seeking out films that exhibit schizoid elements; hence, the scope of films within this book incorporates films with both fantastical *and* horror elements, such as *Mad Max: Fury Road* and *Ex Machina*. Rather than concerning myself with genre, I have been concerned with choosing films whose content and expression is either primarily molar or molecular, while also maintaining focus on the maternal.

There are, of course, many horror films dealing with the maternal that I have chosen not to include. For instance, *Rosemary's Baby* is a classic example of maternal horror, yet I have chosen instead to analyze the *Twilight* films because the *Twilight* franchise presents intriguing tension between molarity and molecularity, and therefore reveals more than *Rosemary's Baby* can about our ongoing struggle to (re)define the maternal in a twenty-first-century, postpatriarchal society. In other words, some excellent maternal horror films do not figure into this project simply because they are not from the right era to exemplify the politics of reproduction in postpatriarchal, postfeminist society.

The importance of this project lies in part in the interstitial moment in which we find ourselves, in which shifting gender roles have nullified the patriarchal order, yet, as Jackson says, an alternative to that order has yet to emerge. A main contention of mine in examining the maternal in horror film is that feminism needs to be aware of how sexual difference remains under-theorized, leaving very real people to struggle with the politics of reproduction, whether we are talking about queer, transgender, or single parents; women's reproductive rights; co-parenting; or racialized economic inequality. The films in this book reveal the contested place of the maternal in a society that, clinging to egalitarian feminism and other notions of equal rather than equitable treatment of minorities and marginalized communities, still denies sexual difference. Because like Deleuze I believe film has the power to change its viewer, I intend this book to show us a way out of the postpatriarchal, postfeminist limbo in which we find ourselves, by embracing schizosophic theories of difference as difference-in-itself. Until we embrace this radically affirmative philosophy and learn to love our own monstrosity, no longer seeking to reproduce static subjects deluded into accepting the gender binary as a truth beyond question, the liberative potential of a post-human family will continue to exist only in fiction.

2

Mother (of) Monsters

My aim in this chapter is to demonstrate the schizoanalytic approach to feminist horror film analysis I described in the previous chapter—an approach that will lead us, I hope, to new and better understandings of the gendered work of horror film. Because my response to the *Alien* franchise's contemporary prequels *Prometheus* and *Alien: Covenant* is what launched me on my current project, I will use the *Alien* films as my gateway to explore, through a schizosophic lens, the politics of reproduction in contemporary horror film.

As a feminist, it has often been difficult for me to justify, even to myself, why I enjoy horror films. It is not only that horror takes joy in torturing and killing women (although it certainly does). It is also that many horror films serve to reify the hegemonic status quo, privileging the able-bodied, white, middle-class, cisgender, heterosexual male as the cultural identity par excellence, to the exclusion of all Others. Nevertheless, while I recognize that horror films monstrous-ize and victimize women (as well as persons of color, individuals with disabilities, and members of the LGBTQA+ community), and while I acknowledge, along with Carol Clover, that it can hardly be considered feminist for the sole female survivor of many horror films to be empowered only by renouncing femininity for masculinity, it has long been my contention that some horror films—and I would count the original *Alien* franchise among those—do in fact disrupt the hegemonic gender binary, employing that "monstrous philosophy" Rosi Braidotti describes. For one thing, there is the open-ended nature of horror. Jack Morgan points out that, whereas both comedy and horror transgress social norms (including the male-masculine/female-feminine gender binary), only comedy ends on an "upswing," with rights put wrong, lovers reunited, and villains punished or exiled; horror, by contrast, allows for no such restoration: bodies, once torn asunder, cannot be put back together, and the killer, as every horror fan knows, can never be permanently defeated (Morgan 2002). Hence, as Morgan says, comedy, like the Bakhtinian carnival, is a bordered space, one with an established beginning and end. These borders make comedy a safe space for norms to be transgressed, since once the carnival ends, the social order will be restored. On the other hand, horror is *not* a contained space, but rather acts as what Deleuze and Guattari call a rhizome, a heterogeneous, unbounded system without beginning or end.

The connection between horror's rhizomatic nature and its potential progressiveness will be returned to before this chapter ends. For now, it should be reiterated that, aside from its close cousin pornography, horror is the only film genre to base its success on the bodily reactions of its audience: for example, to say *Alien* "scared the shit out of me" is to say it is a good horror film. And it is this, the *affective* dimension of horror—the *embodied* rather than the spectatorial experience of the horror audience—that ultimately led me, a feminist fan of horror films, away from the traditional lens of cinepsychoanalysis, into schizoanalysis.

One goal of this book is to argue for including schizoanalysis in a field dominated by psychoanalytic criticism. Nonetheless, it is not my intention to denigrate the work of cinepsychoanalysts. Indeed, my own understanding of gender in the horror film is greatly indebted to Carol Clover's Final Girl and to Barbara Creed's castrated and castrating mother, both of which I will discuss in this chapter. Nevertheless, it seems the main conclusion we can draw from cinepsychoanalysis is that horror films are at best phallocentric, at worst misogynist. Even if Ellen Ripley, the sole survivor of *Alien*, ultimately (if temporarily) defeats the monster, Clover would say she has done so only by renouncing her femininity and "manning up." And when the alien monster appears, its very abjection (its filth; its slime; its deformity), regardless of its biological sex (or lack thereof), means it must be read, in psychoanalytic terms, as *feminine*.

As the previous chapter argued, this is because at the heart of cinepsychoanalysis is the dualistic definition of woman as man's Other, as defined by what she lacks: the phallus. In psychoanalytic terms, difference of any sort—difference from the ideal able-bodied, white, male, cisgender, heterosexual form Freud imagined as the universal *human* subject—is always negative. In Freudianism, the goal is *order*, the "appropriate" identification of the son with the father, the daughter with the mother, which prepares individuals for what Freud viewed as our biological destiny: reproduction. Against the difference-as-lack Freudian perspective, Deleuze and Guattari decried the notion of an Ideal Form and, indeed, the very possibility of a rigid identity such as that assumed by Freudian subjectivity.

In Deleuze and Guattari's radically affirmative schizosophy, one could never "be" a man or a woman, for to Deleuze and Guattari there are only becomings, the moment-by-moment constructions, deconstructions, and reconstructions of our identities. Although *I* may have been assigned female at birth based on my biological sex, *I* cannot be a woman, for the category Woman is not something "I" can be fixed or frozen into, since "I" am not the same "I" of ten years ago, or even ten minutes ago; "I" am constantly changing, constantly *becoming*, in response to the people, places, things, and ideas I come into contact (or "form assemblages") with. One of those "things" I can become with, according to Deleuze, is film.

In his Cinema Books, Deleuze posited that film viewers are not disembodied spectators dispassionately analyzing what images on film "represent." Representation, as was already discussed, is very much the stuff of psychoanalysis; the knife the psychokiller wields represents the phallus, for instance, and Clover's Final Girl survives by assuming masculine power when she appropriates the phallus in defense of herself (Clover 1996). Deleuze argued that sole focus on a film's content ignores the equally powerful aspect of a film's expression—not only the story a film tells but also the way it affects its viewer, through camera movement, editing, light and shadow, and sound and visual effects. According to Deleuze, highly affective films like horror films—those films that invoke an intense bodily response in viewers—have the power to make us *different people* than we were when we sat down to watch the film, for, as Powell puts it, as viewers we "feel and think the films directly on our nerve-endings, 'inside' with emotions and ideas, and on the surface of our skin in goose-bumps. Film alters our perceptions, extending and transforming mundane modes of consciousness" (2005: 201). Importantly, the alterations, extensions, and transformations we, as embodied horror film viewers, experience are not a matter of identifying with a character. Instead, they are a matter of what Deleuze called the *cinematic assemblage*—a matter of becoming *with* a film, of having our sense of ourselves as rigid, unified subjects with fixed, monolithic identities (white/black; male/female; straight/queer) disrupted as we are affected into becoming-camera, becoming-fire, becoming-alien, and—as the next chapter will explore—becoming-woman.

The *embodied* experience of the horror film viewer, as opposed to the detached analysis of the psychoanalytic spectator, allows us to appreciate both how a horror film works *and* what it says. Schizoanalysis breaks down the binary between content/expression, considering both at the same time, something cinepsychoanalysis, with its concentration on identification and representation, has thus far failed to do.[1] While experiencing a horror film, "the distinction between my body and the film's images is constantly blurred through the almost unmediated affects of terror, suspense, horror and anxiety" that assault viewing senses too rapidly to be assimilated, making the viewing of a horror film an *"intuitive experience,* full of immediate impressions that connect with the viewing body" (Rizzo 2012: 91–2). The viewer-film connection lies at the heart of the cinematic assemblage, and assemblages, by their very nature, resist binarism, for the elements of an assemblage cannot be isolated to be fixed, frozen, or analyzed. Assemblages are constantly forming and reforming, coming together and breaking apart. This, Deleuze and Guattari believed, is the very essence of what it means to be (becoming) human:

> Via embodied thought, the human machine forms assemblages with other humans; other life-forms; or more heterogenous machines such as time, space, and plane. It [the becoming-human assemblage] can also incorporate "spirit": the metaphysical plane of operations. Deleuze's use of the body develops its relational quality in the "linkages" of a "post-human-trajectory." (Powell 2005: 92–3)

A post-human trajectory—that sounds much like the content of horror film itself, as human bodies onscreen transform into animals, insects, aliens, zombies, cyborgs, mutants, vampires, and corpses. But schizoanalysis is not only about the *what* of horror films. It is also about the how, the *affective, embodied* experience of the horror film viewer. Since one of the linkages the post-human trajectory can form is with cinematic technology, schizoanalysis prompts us to accept the inherently ethological nature of film, which is why Deleuze considered the cinematic experience worthy of philosophical study in the first place: because *embodied viewings may prompt becomings.*

This is what cinepsychoanalysis has missed about the cinematic experience in its attempt to categorize and rationalize a chaotic, embodied process by centralizing representation and identification. The cinematic techniques so common to horror film—the rapid-fire cuts between killer, weapon, and victim while screams, groans, and musical instruments punctuate spurting blood, spilling entrails, and sizzling flesh—create a sense of horror in us not simply because they create sympathetic awareness of our own, or a character's, vulnerability/mortality. More importantly, these effects *affect* our witnessing bodies in deliberately visceral, disorienting ways. Rizzo picks up this argument from Powell, maintaining that what she calls "affective intuitive perception" (Rizzo 2012: 95)—the sort of perception Deleuze argued was vital to the schizo experience of becoming—requires the breaking down of borders and boundaries between self/Other, subject/object, or inside/out. By focusing on how horror films disrupt the viewer's fixed sense of *being* and create space for becomings through embodied viewing, schizoanalysis opens an avenue for understanding how horror film does that progressive work I began this chapter claiming it can do. Schizoanalysis gives us a way to theorize how horror films disrupt our sense of the body as "natural," as existing outside of time, experience, or culture. Horror films thereby force us, quite violently, to witness and experience our bodies as becomings, as "always open to change and always a part of larger assemblages" (Rizzo 2012: 158).

Of course, not every horror film *is* progressive; some horror films, including two discussed in this chapter, reify the hegemonic status quo. What is exciting about schizoanalysis is that, by considering both content and expression, it provides a more nuanced tool than cinepsychoanalysis for distinguishing those films that reify hegemonic beings (what I call molar films) from films which open up space for viewers' becomings (what I call molecular films). Moreover, because Deleuze and Guattari did not give credence to the gender binary, schizoanalysis also creates space for affirmative, qualitative sexual difference—for monsters that are not monstrous, no matter how far they may be from the hegemonic ideal; for biological males and females who can be understood in terms other than the binary construction masculine or feminine, or even Clover's cross-gendered combinations male-feminine or female-masculine; and for theories of gender that more adequately account for the inseparable effects of race, class, ability, and sexual orientation on the experiences of culturally coded, non-natural, *gendered* bodies.

The remainder of this chapter will demonstrate the schizoanalytic approach by considering the politics of reproduction in the *Alien* franchise. *Prometheus* and *Alien: Covenant*, as molar films, shift the focus of the original quadrilogy's narrative from the monstrousness of birth to the birth of the monster, and in so doing use reproduction for the phallocentric ends of excluding difference and reproducing sameness. By contrast, the original four films, for all that they have been said to represent male fear of the archaic, castrating mother, are molecular films, using the monstrousness of birth to disrupt viewers' rigid identities and prompt nonbinary becomings.

Becoming the Monstrous-Feminine

The original *Alien* film rewrote the rules of pregnancy so that both males and females could conceive—although, to be clear, no one wants to be the one carrying that little bundle of alien joy. In her seminal work *The Monstrous-Feminine*, cinepsychoanalyst Barbara Creed writes of the "attempt in *Alien* to appropriate the procreative function of the archaic mother, to represent a man giving birth . . . but here birth can exist only as the other face of death" (1993: 28). Creed reads *Alien*'s reimagining of insemination as suffocation, gestation as parasitic infection, and birth as evisceration as evidence of the female/maternal body's *abjection*:

> [D]efinitions of the monstrous as constructed in the modern horror text are grounded in ancient religious and historical notions of abjection—particularly in relation to the following religious "abominations": sexual immorality and perversion; corporeal alteration, decay and death; human sacrifice; murder; the corpse; bodily wastes; the feminine body and incest. These forms of abjection are also central to the construction of the monstrous in the modern horror film. . . . The abject threatens life . . . [and therefore] must be . . . propelled away from the body and deposited on the other side of an imaginary border which separates the self from that which threatens the self. (1993: 8–9)

To be sure, seeing *Alien*'s facehugger attached to the male astronaut Kane is an uncanny experience—and an intensely affective one. In close-up, we *feel* the facehugger's tail tighten around Kane's throat; we experience the haptic contrast between the alien's bony digits and Kane's silky-soft hair as the facehugger clings to the astronaut's skull. Later, when the alien fetus bursts through Kane's chest, we cringe at the sound of his sternum splitting apart; recoil from the warm stickiness of blood; and shriek as the chestburster is revealed in extreme close-up: a screeching, glabrous creature slimed with viscous fluid. Because abjection in psychoanalysis equates with the feminine, Creed argues that the monsters of horror film—including *Alien*'s facehuggers, chestbursters, Xenomorphs, and the eventual Queen—are also inherently feminine. I am not denying that horror films abjectify the feminine. I am, however, arguing that, if we disavow boundaries and borders and embrace assemblages, rhizomes, and becomings, abjection, though it certainly exists, need not be *negative*.

This claim is foundational to a monstrous philosophy of becoming. Creed, like Kristeva, recognizes that, from a phallocentric perspective, the true horror of the abject lies in its dissolution of borders and boundaries, so that what was closed becomes open (to decay and contamination). In Freudian psychoanalysis, what is closed, contained, and ordered aligns with the Father, with the masculine, with purity and structure; what is open, fluid, and natural aligns with the Mother, with the feminine, with darkness, chaos, and danger. To the phallocentric imagination, the darkest, most chaotic, and most dangerous of all femininity is, as Creed maintains, not the castrated mother—the mother the male child recognizes as "lacking" the phallus he, like his father, possesses—but the castrat*ing* mother, the archaic mother, the primordial, all-powerful, and therefore "phallic" figure in the infant's life. In horror, abjection plays into and upon the repressed "desire to return to the original oneness of things, to return to the mother/womb," which, Creed argues, is "primarily a desire for non-differentiation," so that the "desire for and attraction of death suggests also a desire to return to the state of original oneness with the mother"—yet because by this point the individual "has developed as a separate, autonomous self," returning to the mother becomes synonymous with death (Creed 1993: 28). In Creed's view, "the confrontation with death as represented in the horror film gives rise to a terror of self-disintegration, of losing one's self or ego—often represented cinematically by a screen which becomes black, signifying the obliteration of self, the self of the protagonist in film and the spectator in the cinema" (1993: 28).

From the psychoanalytic perspective, Creed is only able to view the erasure of boundaries between self/other as loss, death, or, as Rizzo puts it, *annihilation*. To the phallocentric viewpoint that must distinguish its subject-self from the body of the mother that has housed, birthed, and nourished it, nothing could be more horrifying than returning to an undifferentiated state, prior to or outside of subjectivity and identity (Rizzo 2012: 113)—in other words, returning to the maternal, which Freudianism views as binarily opposed to the paternal/patriarchal. Thus, Creed argues that *Alien* reifies phallocentric fear of the archaic, castrating mother as it sets its female hero up to literally "expel" the maternal from the narrative by slaying the mother-monster. Rizzo, on the other hand, argues from the Deleuzian perspective that "through the many scenes that deal with the breakdown of the human-alien distinction ... an explicit preoccupation with the defiling of borders is expressed that far outweighs the elimination of the abject at the end of the film" (2012: 114).

Rizzo presents a gorgeous meditation on the affirmation of qualitative difference vis-à-vis maternal abjection in the *Alien* quadrilogy. This chapter turns in a somewhat different direction, considering the "obliteration of self" Creed believes is "represented" when the cinematic screen is swallowed up by darkness, when borders breakdown and the subject/ego is reincorporated into the mother/Other—especially because Deleuze himself had theories about what it means when the screen goes dark, propelling viewers into what he called "any-space-whatever."

Importantly, no one in *Alien*, *Aliens*, or *Alien³* becomes-alien, although the alien, we might say, undergoes a becoming-host. In *Alien³*, the alien birthed from the dog is a Runner, not a Xenomorph, and has different qualities than the aliens birthed from humans. Nevertheless, in the host-alien assemblage, humans (and other organisms, such as the dog) remain "closed sets," that is, the alien grows inside the host, but the host does not grow *with* it, so there is no host-alien-becoming, only the host's inevitable destruction when the alien finishes gestating inside it. This is to be Ripley's fate as well. At the end of *Alien³*, as the alien fetus bursts from her chest, the already-dying Ripley clutches her offspring as she falls into the fire, destroying herself along with her monstrous child. Yet, beyond what we might see as reification of patriarchal order elaborated via the dangers of dissolving the human/alien boundary, the *Alien* quadrilogy also incorporates us, the viewer, into countless other dissolutions. The hacked-apart android Ash dissolves into a puddle of thick white liquid (experienced by the viewer as the sticky sour-sweetness of either breast milk or amniotic fluid); the infected/impregnated soldiers in *Aliens*—already on a "post-human trajectory" as their advanced, prosthetic armor and weaponry have them becoming-machine—are slowly dissolved into the Queen's cocoon-like womb; in *Alien*, the crew's voices over the radio often dissolve into static, while in *Aliens*, Newt's screams dissolve into a howling wind; in *Alien³*, the crash-landing of Ripley's ship dissolves the borders the all-male penal colony has erected around itself, even as light in the film consistently dissolves into the shadows of subterranean corridors lit by fire.

Again, what matters here as much as what dissolution means (what it represents, the abjection of the feminine-maternal) is the viewer's *experience* of each dissolution, for instance as we see and hear the alien's acidic blood melt the steel layers of a spaceship into goo. *How* do we "experience" these dissolutions? Through what Deleuze called *opsigns* and *sonsigns*—"'pure optical and/or sound situations' that break from the narrative drive" (Powell 2005: 77), such as when Newt's screams, though no one is around to hear them, become a howling wind; through *tactisigns*, "'a touching which is specific to the gaze'" (Powell 2005: 142), such as when we *feel* the stickiness of the fluid flowing from Ash's mouth; and through *chronosigns*, images "distanced from the sensory-motor actions of characters"—irrelevant to the diegesis, in other words—that "seek to present time itself directly rather than implying its presence" (Powell 2005: 160), for example in the many ponderous shots of the *Nostromo* floating in space, forcing viewers to appreciate the immensity of the universe, and geologic and cosmic time, as our sense of our world's "borders" dissolves.

Although we might tend to think of dissolution as liquefaction and therefore water-based, fire can also melt bone, tissue, and flesh. In fact, in *Alien³*, fire becomes what Deleuze called a "diagrammatic component," a "map[ping of] assemblages in their mutual operations, to meld form, style and content," which "may be an image, or an element of framing or editing" (Powell 2005: 23, 211). A film's diagrammatic component (or components) is its ultimate abstraction, the intensity or matter that somehow exceeds, and can be extracted from, the film's combined content and expression. An analysis of the diagrammatic component of fire in *Alien³*, for instance, eventually leads us back to self-obliteration and Deleuze's any-space-whatever. On the one hand, Ripley's self-immolation can be read psychoanalytically as a repudiation of the feminine-maternal: Ripley is already carrying the alien fetus when she crash-lands, and rather than allow her monstrous offspring to be weaponized by the military-industrial complex, she chooses suicidal/matricidal infanticide. On the other hand, if we consider how this final scene is *expressed*, we find a less nihilistic experience. As Ripley casts herself into the furnace, we do not see the flesh burn from her bones. Instead, as gentle instrumental music begins to swell and smoke and steam flow gently through the frame, gauzing the rose-orange firelight reflecting off the set's machines and catwalks, we are presented with a lingering medium-close-up of Ripley's face. Her expression is peaceful, resolute, free of fear. Positioning itself behind her, the camera then watches as Ripley falls backward with her arms spread—in slow motion, not as though she has jumped but as if she has simply leaned back, letting gravity take her. The camera then moves to look down on her from above, as she falls toward a lava-like CGI fire.

At this moment, we *hear* Ripley's sternum crack and the chestburster screech as it lunges forth—but though Ripley seems to gasp, we hear no scream as she clutches the alien to her breast, cradling it against her as our sense of falling into the red-orange flames alongside her is enhanced by the camera pulling upward. Ripley and the alien disappear into the fire; the camera cuts from the furnace's dying engine to the sun rising around the rim of the planet; the light of the sun expands, filling the entire screen, momentarily obliterating every other image in a wash of pure white light.

Creed describes (self-)obliteration as darkness, the screen going black. Thus, it might be tempting to read Ripley's suicide as the *opposite* of self-obliteration, as self-realization or self-determination—but that reading depends upon the binary of darkness/light, which Deleuze, unsurprisingly, rejects. In *Cinema 1*, Deleuze writes reverently of light, claiming filmic light and shadow interact in a sort of dance in which they "no longer constitute an alternative movement in extension and enter into an intense struggle which has several stages" (1986: 49), from "infinite opposition" (which is neither binary nor dialectic, since "light would be nothing, or at least nothing manifest, without the opaque to which it is opposed and which makes it visible" [49]), to contrast (i.e., stripes of light and shadow), chiaroscuro, and finally to colorism, or color as varying degrees of light intensification: "shimmering, glistening, scintillation, sparkling, a halo effect, fluorescence, phosphorescence," all the way to *"pure incandescence or blazing of a terrible light, which burned the world and its creatures"* (1986: 52, 53). For Deleuze, that last is the color red. Deleuze calls red "the noblest colour, which contains all others, and engenders a superior harmony as the whole chromatic circle" (1986: 54). He sees the use of fire and its "reddish glow" in film as the realization of Kant's dynamic sublime: *"the non-organic life of things* culminates in a fire, which burns us and which burns all of Nature" yet which simultaneously "unleashes in our soul a *non-psychological life of the spirit*, which no longer belongs either to nature or our organic individuality, which is the divine part in us, the spiritual relationship in which we are alone with God as light" (1986: 54).

For Deleuze, the light we "rise . . . towards" is in fact not Heaven but our "soul . . . rejoin[ing] the luminous part of itself" (1986: 54). Within Deleuze's conception of a "plane of immanence . . . entirely made up of Light," in which "things are luminous by themselves without anything illuminating them" (1986: 60), we cannot escape non-differentiation—the obliteration of subjective borders and egoistic boundaries as we lose our sense of self-as-molar-being and find ourselves without subjectivity or ego. Yet this obliteration of self is hardly annihilation; it is *life,* not *death.* Rejoining the luminous part of ourselves means becoming Deleuze and Guattari's Body without Organs, or BwO, a post-enlightenment body we can become (but never be) once we seek freedom from binaries, dualisms, and all other egoistic attempts to fix, freeze, order, and organize a subjective-self.

Fire plays such a role in *Mary Shelley's Frankenstein*, a film discussed in the next chapter, in the funeral pyre upon which Victor Frankenstein and his monster burn; and it plays such a role in *Alien³*, as Ripley escapes her binarily constructed, culturally over-coded body and becomes-fire, which becomes-light, which fills the screen (like darkness can) so that, as viewers, we find ourselves without reference to time or place, in Deleuze's any-space-whatever: "Any-space-whatever is not an abstract universal, in all times, in all places. It is a perfectly singular space, which has merely lost its homogeneity . . . so that the linkages can be made in an infinite number of ways. It is a space of virtual conjunction, grasped as the pure locus of the possible" (1986: 109).

In schizosophy, oneness is not sameness, just as the BwO is not empty but is full (of possibilities, of becomings). To evacuate the body of organs, to free an assemblage from the molar plane of hierarchical organization and allow it to become, is not to erase the differences between individuals, between organisms, between species, or even between ourselves as becomings. Schizosophy's radical affirmation of difference does not rely on claiming that underneath, we are really all the same, and therefore differences do not matter. Rather, Deleuze and Guattari insist upon difference which is always, and simply, *difference-in-itself*, not difference *from* a culturally constructed ideal. To get there, however, we must somehow free ourselves from the molar plane that has determined how we will experience our bodies. As was argued in the previous chapter, Moira Gatens's imaginary body helps us understand that our bodies are not natural; they are culturally written, so that we cannot know what it would be like to experience our bodies in a culture that coded race, ethnicity, ability, class, size, gender, or sexual orientation differently than it does. For even as we "perform" our gender, as Judith Butler says, those performances are in response to (either conforming to or rebelling against) cultural codes for how a man or a woman of a certain race, ethnicity, class, and so on, should look, act, think, and feel.

Between *Alien* and *Alien³*, Ripley experiences this cultural over-coding in ever more insistent ways. In *Alien*, Ripley could best be described as androgynous, less hegemonically feminine than Lambert, the only other female crew member, yet not overtly masculine like the male crew members. By contrast, in *Aliens*, her implied romance with Corporal Hicks as well as her caretaking of the orphaned Newt "feminizes" her so that Creed argues her eventual standoff with the alien Queen

> opposes two forms of mothering: Ripley's surrogate mothering in which there is no conception or birth and where the female body is unmarked; and Mother Alien's biological, animalistic, instinctual mothering where the maternal body is

open and gaping. . . . However, it is not so much that Ripley is an "antifertility mother" and that she and Mother Alien represent diametrically opposed principles of reproduction—instinctual and cultural—. . . but rather that Mother Alien represents Ripley's other self, that is, *woman's* alien, inner, mysterious powers of reproduction. It is the latter, the female reproductive/mothering capacity *per se*, which is deemed monstrous, horrifying, abject. Like Mother Alien, Ripley also transforms into an indestructible killing machine when her child—even though a surrogate offspring—is threatened. (1993: 46, 51)

Regardless of whether she has given birth to Newt, then, in *Aliens* Ripley is insistently read as *woman*, and therefore, in an admittedly skewed echo of essential motherhood, as monstrously maternal. In *Alien³*, Newt's death might serve to free Ripley from this cultural (over)coding, but in fact, *Alien³* dwells on the femaleness of Ripley's biological body more insistently than either of the previous films. Ostensibly, Ripley's head is shaved to protect her from lice, but the visual effect of this is to make her appear less "like a woman"—which is necessary for her survival, since the film insists that the presence of a biological female among the "YY chromosome" prisoners will awaken all of their repressed violent instincts, leading them to become rapists and murderers again. *Alien³* emphatically connects gender to biology (the YY chromosome, it seems, is responsible for the male prisoners' violent behavior) and emphatically imperils Ripley *as a woman*, subjecting her to an attempted gang-rape from which she must be rescued by a male prisoner. This, coupled with her alien pregnancy, serves to trap Ripley within the hegemonic gender binary, until the only way she can escape is by becoming-imperceptible.

What is being celebrated here, however, is not suicide (literal self-annihilation) as an avenue to becoming; schizosophy is far too affirmative for *that*. For Deleuze and Guattari, the dissolution of borders is not about annihilation but about possibility, about opening oneself to the full, fluid potentialities of becoming. Becoming-imperceptible is a "state of not being able to be recognized within any single category. Becoming-imperceptible is change that cannot be perceived" (Rizzo 2012: 112). The obliteration of self is necessary to becoming-imperceptible, but, like the BwO, becoming-imperceptible is not a state of being, not an endpoint; it is processual, a becoming. And just what are "becomings," one might ask? Becomings, Elizabeth Grosz explains, are "the movement or transformation of one 'thing' to another that in no way resembles it . . . not based on mimesis . . . not a question of symbolization or metaphoric representation but of the relation set up between" the one who becomes and what one is becoming

(1994: 174–5). Moreover, Deleuze and Guattari's argument that becomings "always involve substantial remaking of the subject" means that becoming cannot be reduced to what Grosz calls "an advertising slogan ('Become whatever you want to be')" (Grosz 1994: 174). Becoming is less willful—and, as Ripley's story shows, more violent—than that. Grosz writes, "One cannot become-animal"—or -camera, or -fire, or -alien—"at will and then cease and function normally. It [becoming] is not something that can be put on or taken off like a cloak or an activity" (1994: 174), because becoming means *becoming something else*, an irrevocable, although impermanent, transmutation.

Transmutation is the radically affirmative fate of Ripley in the original *Alien* quadrilogy. Once Ripley falls into the fire of Deleuze's "pure incandescence" and becomes-imperceptible, in *Alien: Resurrection* her BwO emerges from the any-space-whatever as the alien-human hybrid clone Ripley 8. At last, as a result of the genetic engineering that resurrected her (and her alien offspring), Ripley becomes-alien—which is not a matter of mimesis or identification but means, rather, that "through a series of encounters, [Ripley] enters into a process of transformation with the alien who is itself in a process of transformation" (Rizzo 2012: 110). In *Alien: Resurrection*, the dissolution of borders and boundaries evidenced in the first three films culminates in a profoundly molecular experience of becoming both for the characters onscreen and for viewers.

Alien: Resurrection may be the most disturbing and terrifying of the original four films. Visual effects technology brings the aliens to life more horrifyingly than ever before, and the viewer's sense of dread and suspense is heightened by our recognition of the aliens' becomings. For instance, as the mercenary crew attempts to escape up a ladder while the Xenomorph attacks from below, the Xenomorph, evidencing the same remarkable cunning that allowed it to escape its cell earlier in the film, spits acidic blood to melt the face of the mercenary Christie, nearly causing him to topple off the ladder. In another scene, as the mercenaries swim through a flooded kitchen, two Xenomorphs appear in the water, unexpectedly proving aquatically as well as terrestrially agile. These are *intelligent* creatures, able to adapt, respond, and strategize. Only Ripley's alien-like intellect, emphasized through the many lingering close-ups of Sigourney Weaver's watchful, not-quite-human expressions, allows her to defeat them.

Perhaps *Alien: Resurrection* is so affecting because its diagrammatic component is mutation. The opening credits play over morphing images of alien-human hybrids, complete with disgusting close-ups of hair, eyeballs, teeth, and flesh. The first scene takes us inside the laboratory as Ripley 8's chest is sliced open in a pseudo-Caesarean section that removes the infant Queen. In one scene that deeply affects me every time I watch it, Ripley 8 finds the lab where the "failed" Ripley clones have been kept alive for experimentation and is confronted by the inhumanity of science's attempts at creation before she humanely grants Ripley 7's simple wish to die. In an even more grotesque—and emotionally affecting—echo of this scene, at the film's climax Ripley 8 is forced to kill the hybrid Xenomorph, a.k.a. "The Newborn," which, with its overtly human eyes and facial expressions, has identified Ripley 8 as its mother. When Ripley 8 causes The Newborn to be sucked through a window out into space, we, along with her, experience one of the franchise's most extended and gruesome deaths. The Newborn's brains are sucked out by the vacuum of space through a hole in its skull; its entrails first spill out onto the floor and then are sucked back through its body while it wriggles and squeals; finally, its entire skeleton folds up to be sucked out through the narrow, broken window, stripping the flesh from its humanoid skull, which stares accusingly at us, the viewers, for half an instant before exploding. All the while, The Newborn has been screaming and crying, its alien voice containing the garbled-yet-still-recognizable word *mother*.

Ripley 8 survives this film, and the final scene in which she tells the female android call that she is "a stranger here [her]self" gives us to understand that Ripley 8 intends to forge a new life on Earth, which she has saved from the aliens. Of course, Ripley 8 is herself a hybrid, and thus we should expect that her mutation, her becoming-alien, will continue, with what results we cannot guess. It is the open-ended, *rhizomatic* nature of this horror film, that, as Rizzo says, partly makes the *Alien* quadrilogy so molecular. For rather than reconstituting "wholeness, completeness, or unity," Rizzo contends that the original *Alien* films "lend themselves to a Deleuzoguattarian understanding of 'becoming' where the body, subjectivity and identity are all understood as constantly changing, full of possibilities. . . . This is because in the *Alien* series identity and subjectivity are tied to the body; and bodies in these films are mutable and open to change" (2012: 108).

Mutable bodies, open to change: How else would the phallocentric imagination describe the monstrous-feminine, not to mention the monstrous-maternal? Yet schizosophy maintains that mutability, openness, and change are qualities to be cultivated, not resisted. Why, then, do films like *Alien* need to show us mutability and openness as "monstrous" to create space for affirmative difference, for becomings? Here again, schizoanalysis prompts us to consider the affect scenes of horror and abjection have on embodied viewers. Creed

says, "Viewing the horror film signifies a desire not only for perverse pleasure
. . . but also a desire, once having . . . taken pleasure in perversity, to throw up,
throw out, eject the abject (from the safety of the spectator's seat)" (1993: 10).
But the spectator's seat is *not* safe. The extreme affect of the horror film *changes*
the viewer in ways that cannot be "thrown up" or "thrown out." The cinematic
assemblage we have been made part of has altered us, become part of us, become
with us; we cannot "eject" it, even after the film is over.

Thus, while Creed, like Kristeva, argues that horror film has taken on
religion's ideological work of "purification" as characters confront "the abject
. . . in order to finally . . . redraw the boundaries between the human and nonhuman . . . separat[ing] out the symbolic order from all that threatens its stability,
particularly the mother and all that her universe signifies" (1993: 14), if we accept
that becoming/with the cinematic assemblage changes viewers, mutates our
mutable bodies, and prevents us from redrawing boundaries, it is not much of a
stretch to say that, far from disavowal of the maternal body, what molecular films
like the *Alien* quadrilogy offer are an embodied experience in which the viewer
becomes what to the phallocentric imagination is that most open, disordered,
boundary-less "thing": the abject maternal body; the monstrous-feminine.

Last (wo)Man Standing, or The Final Girl in Schizoanalysis

Why must becoming-imperceptible in the *Alien* films rely upon first becoming
the monstrous-feminine? I realize the importance of this question, and I intend
to take it up in the next chapter, with a discussion of Deleuze and Guattari's
disputed notion of becoming-woman. Where I want to focus now is on this
question: Even if we accept that abjection, because it dissolves borders and
boundaries, can open audiences to becomings, does the fact that most horror
films end with the death of the monster—with the expulsion of the abject
feminine from the patriarchal order—undermine horror film's progressive
potential? In the *Alien* films, this question feels particularly problematic, since it
is Ripley who must "expel" the mother-monster.

It is possible to read *Alien* as a guidebook for the woman looking to make it
in a man's world: surrender your femininity, sisters, for you will only survive if
you are willing to be more of a man than he is. This would follow Carol Clover's
theory in which Ripley, like all Final Girls, only survives by becoming female-
masculine (1996). Yet Clover's psychoanalytic interpretation of horror film's

Final Girl (the sole surviving female character who defeats the monster/killer) depends on adherence to the gender binary, in which strength and intelligence are coded masculine while terror and hysteria are coded feminine. Thus, in Clover's estimation, the Final Girl is merely a stand-in for the male hero, albeit an interesting one since it seems the teenage male viewer of slasher films (Clover's horror subgenre) wished to identify with the experience of masculine heroism in the body of a biological female. On the other hand, Teresa Rizzo proposes a nonbinary, schizosophic perspective that does not depend upon spectatorial identification with the Final Girl *and* in which the Final Girl's survival owes not to her repudiation of the feminine or assumption of the masculine but instead to her ability to *become*. That is, what makes the Final Girl different from her victim-friends is not her "masculinity" but her *perception*, or what Rizzo, following Henri Bergson, calls her "intuition," which allows the Final Girl to perceive threats her friends, regardless of gender, remain blind to.

Rizzo asserts that horror films' victims, whether male or female, are trapped within hegemonic identities, too caught up in trying to *be* society's idea/ideal of a man or woman to achieve self-awareness (2012: 92, 94). Although not the teenage victims of the slasher films Rizzo and Clover refer to, *Alien*'s adult crew nevertheless fits this description. Captain Dallas asserts his alpha male authority by insisting on tracking the alien alone through the ship's air shafts, resulting in his demise. Lambert, the only other woman on the crew, spends most of the film either screaming or crying, and when faced with the Xenomorph, is too terrified to even run, let alone fight. Parker throws his masculine weight around, belittling Ripley, and ends up becoming a meal for the alien he has sworn to kill. Ripley, by contrast, *intuits* danger and, by being both present and self-aware, adapts to dangerous circumstances. She is the only crew member to suspect the android Ash of having a sinister motive in allowing Kane and the facehugger back onboard. (Indeed, had it been up to Ripley, the crew would have survived, as Ripley alone insisted on following quarantine protocol.) And when the Xenomorph manages to escape the *Nostromo*'s destruction, Ripley has the presence of mind to use space itself as a weapon in defeating the monster.

The becoming of the Final Girl is not just a nonbinary way of analyzing characters. The Final Girl's becoming also has implications for the becoming of the horror audience. Extending the dissolution of binary thinking beyond the character of the Final Girl, Rizzo claims that "highly visceral films" like *Alien* destabilize our sense of being *outside* the film, inviting us into a cinematic assemblage hallmarked by "a state in which change is always becoming different from what one is, rather than in relation to [a molar or ideal] identity.... [Thus] the way the body is classified in terms of gender and sexuality is undermined. For if a body is always becoming other than what it is, then it is impossible to classify it into fixed categories" (2012: 102, 106).

Hence, perhaps the most significant difference between the original *Alien* quadrilogy and its twenty-first-century prequels is, simply, that *Prometheus* and *Alien: Covenant* have no Final Girls. Whereas in *Alien* Ripley suspects Ash from the moment he overrides the quarantine protocol, even before she knows he is an android programmed to obey the company's orders, Elizabeth Shaw, the (alleged) Final Girl of *Prometheus*, seals her own fate by reconstructing the evil android David, even after he all but confesses to infecting her partner Charlie with the alien parasite. Unlike the almost hypervigilant Ripley, Shaw remains oblivious to the danger the crew is in until the film's bitter end, when she finally realizes her beloved "engineers" stockpiled the alien parasite to wipe out the humans they had created. Even Shaw's one true act of Final Girl resourcefulness, when she reprograms the ship's surgical chamber to perform an emergency abortion of her alien fetus (resulting in one of the most affective sequences in the entire film, as we experience the Caesarean procedure at squirmy closeness, inside the surgical chamber with Shaw) turns out to be for naught; for in *Alien: Covenant* we learn that, after they escaped the engineers' planet, David infected his "dear Elizabeth" with the parasite again, using Shaw's (initially barren) womb to spawn the race of Xenomorphs that bring death and destruction to the crew of the colony ship Covenant.

Alien: Covenant picks up the story with Daniels, the direct predecessor, even in looks, of Sigourney Weaver's small-but-mighty Ripley. Daniels seems at first to possess the Final Girl's intuitive perception. She is the only character to question the rogue transmission and the sudden appearance of an uncharted planet that appears perfect for colonization; her intuition tells her this is a trap, while Captain Oram, like *Alien*'s Captain Dallas, insists he is making data-based decisions. Yet, in the end, Daniels turns out to be just another clueless victim. Duped into believing David is his lookalike android-double Walter, she does not realize her mistake until she is trapped inside her cryochamber with David preparing to realize his rape fantasy by depositing the alien eggs in the spaceship MOTHER's technological womb.

If horror film were to follow a progressive social trajectory, we would expect Ripley's legacy to be even more-nonbinary heroes in *Alien*'s twenty-first-century prequels. Instead, in *Prometheus* and *Alien: Covenant*, women have regressed from self-rescuing heroes to victims of the male-created monster. For—and this is crucial—the android David, more so than any alien, *is* the monster here.

Alien: Covenant drives this point home. The film opens on an extreme close-up of David's eye as he wakes up after being born (or activated). The ensuing dialogue between David and his creator, Dr. Peter Weyland, does more than establish the plot of both prequels; it also establishes that what these films are really about is David's rage at being seen as less-than-human when he believes he is better, more perfect, than his human creators, like the flawless Michelangelo sculpture from which he chooses his name. Forget *Alien's* tenuous plot device of an evil corporation bent on weaponizing alien life. *Prometheus* and *Alien: Covenant* are about (hu)mankind's search for our creators—here understood, in typically phallocentric terms, as having nothing to do with mothers.

On the one hand, it should be acknowledged that neither *Prometheus* nor *Alien: Covenant* demonstrates *Alien's* preoccupation with abjectifying the maternal body. The facehugger never appears in *Prometheus*, the Xenomorph does not appear until nearly the last sixty seconds, and in both films, insemination is rewritten from oral rape to infection by a water- or airborne virus (with the exception of Oram's death, to be taken up in the next section). Yet any promising feminist takeaway from this is muted by the films' depiction of the "Final Girl's" death at the hands, not of the man who creates the monster, but of the *male monster the man creates*—a startling triumph of parthenogenesis, male-only reproduction, which has finally succeeded where the original quadrilogy failed in expelling the maternal from the narrative.

Molar Beings, Molecular Becomings, and the Putting into Discourse of "Woman"

In concluding this chapter, let us establish why, in terms of their hegemonic content, films like *Prometheus* and *Alien: Covenant* also rely on molar expressions. Rizzo writes of the molar plane as imposing order on the disordered elements of the molecular plane; thus, molarity "fixes everything into hierarchical categories and produces identities and subjectivities" while molecularity "favours change, movement and processes, and . . . continually threatens to disrupt hierarchical orderings" (Rizzo 2012: 60). Simply put, molecular assemblages invite becomings, while molar assemblages reify hegemonic beings. Although most films incorporate both assemblages, a film is likely to skew toward one type of assemblage over another, with hegemonic content tending to be more closely associated with molar than molecular expressions.

Prometheus actually begins in a promising place for molecularity, with what Deleuze called *liquid perception*, with shots of lakes, rivers, waterfalls, and clouds (which flow across the sky like water). Water, according to Deleuze, is always engaged in becoming-imperceptible, that most becoming of becomings, as water is always changing, always flowing, but the changes in it cannot be seen by the naked eye. Images of water on film therefore invite the viewer to share in its fluidity. *Prometheus* seems bent on prompting these fluid experiences, as the camera plunges inside an alien's body as it liquefies, its DNA breaking apart. The alien—one of humankind's "engineers"—then falls into the river and dissolves, only to reassemble, to become something entirely new, on a genetic level.

After the opening titles, however, the molecular tone of *Prometheus* all but disappears. We join our main characters Elizabeth Shaw and Charlie Holloway in Scotland, where they discover cave paintings that seem to confirm their hypothesis that aliens engineered human life. The film then skips ahead to the year 2093 as we are taken onboard the vessel *Prometheus*, introduced to us through the perspective of David, who ultimately becomes the film's antagonist.

The opening of *Alien*, by contrast, is a study in what Deleuze called *camera consciousness*, as the camera, acting of its own volition rather than as the perspective of or on any character, slides and sweeps along the corridors of the *Nostromo*. Camera consciousness, perhaps even more so than light, is fundamental to Deleuze's cinematic philosophy. As Patricia Pisters notes, in Deleuzian terms, "the essence of cinema lies in the mobility of the camera and its emancipation of the viewpoint whereby cinema stops being spatial and has become temporal" (2003: 2): The "sole cinematographic consciousness is not us, the spectator, nor the hero," Deleuze relates; "it is the camera—sometimes human, sometimes inhuman or superhuman" (1986: 20). Unlike the eye/I of the shot/reaction shot formula, in which as viewers we understand which character we are supposed to identify with, camera consciousness destabilizes our sense of molar identity: We do not know who we are supposed to *be*, as we surrender to becoming-camera.

Alien makes significant use of camera consciousness, such as the scene in which Ash is analyzing the facehugger's DNA and the camera approaches him from behind, suddenly revealing itself (we think) to be Ripley—yet rather than assuming Ripley's perspective, the camera remains on the floor, at an angle, showing us Ripley's back as she interrogates Ash. In *Prometheus*, camera consciousness is almost nonexistent. Nearly every shot provides us with a character's reaction shot, telling viewers how we are supposed to think and feel in response to the dialogue or action. In fact, *Prometheus* is so determined to resist destabilization that viewers are often forced to take on the perspectives of characters via the use of suitcams that tell us whose eyes we are seeing through—a device *Alien: Covenant* will also employ. Forced to be, we are not allowed to become, and such enforced subjectivity complements the phallocentric content of both films, established in the previous section. Take, for instance, this exchange between David and Charlie in *Prometheus*:

> CHARLIE: What we hoped to achieve was to meet our makers. To get answers. Why they ever made us in the first place.
> DAVID: Why do you think your people made me?
> CHARLIE: We made you because we could.
> DAVID (*after a long pause in which the camera lingers in medium-close-up on his vanishing smile*): Can you imagine how disappointing it would be for you to hear the same thing from your creator?

Rendered entirely as shot/reaction shot between the actors, this dialogue, intended to explain David's motivation for infecting Charlie with the alien parasite, allows for no disorientation, no confusion as to whose position we should sympathize with (David's). For even as we abhor what he is about to do, the film seems determined to make us see David as complex instead of simply cruel. Whereas the aliens in *Prometheus* and *Alien: Covenant* have once again "regressed" to their natural, animalistic (and therefore, according to Freudianism, *feminine*) drive to (a) survive and (b) reproduce, David, both prequels go to great lengths to establish, is on a far deeper quest to discover and perfect his identity, and, in *Alien: Covenant*, to bring to life his own race of "perfected" creatures.

Although facehuggers, chestbursters, and Xenomorphs feature more prominently in *Alien: Covenant* than in *Prometheus*, even this film incessantly returns to David as the tortured anti-hero. *Alien: Covenant* maintains its molar expression even during the reenactment of Kane's death, in which the camera focuses not on the gruesome horror of Captain Oram's death but on David's gleeful reaction to witnessing the chestburster's birth. The affective potential of this scene is thereby flattened, sterilized of fear, disgust, or disorientation; the potential dissolution of viewers' borders and boundaries is exchanged for what seems to be the film's grim admiration of David's cunning brutality.

Of course, the analysis presented here may surprise those who have declared *Alien's* prequels feminist for featuring "strong" female characters. Yet the assumption that a strong (read: masculine) female character is necessarily an empowered (read: not-feminine) character itself remains mired in the gender binary—and here we once again bump up against the limits of the feminist project in a still-phallocentric world. Three decades ago, Alice Jardine asserted that determining "legitimacy," what "counts" or is "given value" in the Western imagination, has ever been the purview of the patriarchy, "which, historically, has determined the right to govern, the succession of kings, the link between father and son, . . . the ability to decide *who is the father*. . . . The crises experienced by the major Western narratives have not, therefore, been gender-neutral. They are crises in the narratives invented by men" (1985: 24). When feminism, in tandem with postmodernism, began to de-naturalize these narratives, revealing their phallocentrism, Western philosophers were forced "back to the Greek philosophies in which [those narratives] are grounded and, most particularly, to the originary relationships posited between" man and woman, "and all the dualistic oppositions that determine our way of thinking" (Jardine 1985: 24)—first and foremost being the patriarchal, heteronormative gender binary. According to Jardine, the postmodern deconstruction of those dualistic oppositions has "required backing away from all that has defined . . . the major topics of [Western] philosophy: Man, the Subject, Truth, History, Meaning," and has meant "above all a reincorporation and reconceptualization of that which has been the master [male] narratives' own 'non-knowledge.' . . . This other-than-themselves . . . has been coded as *feminine*, as *woman*" (1985: 25), a process Jardine terms *gynesis*, "the putting into discourse of 'woman' . . . , the valorization of the feminine, women, and her obligatory, that is, historical connotations, as somehow intrinsic to new and necessary modes of thinking, writing, speaking" (1985: 25).

On the surface, gynesis may sound like a step forward for women. Yet the primary problems Jardine points to in the gynesitic project are that, first, the *woman* gynesis produces is not a reality but a representation, and secondly, that this "woman" has not escaped the system of representation that still assumes Man to be the universal, ideal human form. From a theoretical standpoint, gynesis continues to figure women and the feminine primarily as vehicles for understanding men and the masculine rather than rendering women as individuals with worth and value unrelated to the dreams, philosophies, and desires of men. Moreover, the danger of gynesis as we see it particularly in film is that it positions us to still view "women" through the lens of the male imagination—which is how women have been taught to see ourselves, within the negate-ive binary system of representation and identification in which to be different is to be a degradation of the ideal (male) form. Gynesis, perhaps an early manifestation of the postfeminist mindset Kimberly Jackson described decades after Jardine's writing, ultimately perpetuates the gender binary, coding some things feminine, some things masculine, always, inevitably, reading men and women as binarily different: either phallic or castrated.

Thus, we find ourselves returning to my contention that if feminist film theory—and, I would submit, feminism itself—is to move forward, it must adopt a perspective other than one which reifies the gender binary. Jardine writes that reimagining the West's "master narratives" has meant "the transformation of woman and the feminine into verbs at the interior of those narratives that are . . . experiencing a crisis in legitimation" (1985: 25), but the problem is that the "'[w]oman,' 'the feminine,' and so on have come to signify those *processes* that disrupt symbolic structures in the West" (42), so that "[o]nly by participating in this elaboration may women remain aware of our position in the signifying chain," for even to "remain outside of magisterial discourse, rejecting it as phallocentric"—to opt out, in other words—would "only reinforce the central position of the discourse of power. The Masters do not care at all about what the slaves *believe* so long as the slaves *remain* on the exterior of the empire" (Jardine 1985: 44). As feminist film theory has discovered, pointing out the phallocentrism of horror film does not free us from the hegemonic gender binary that continues to tyrannize all people, regardless of biological sex, for whether it is masculinity or femininity being privileged, in a binary system that seeks to produce ordered, organized, molar subjects, difference will always be *difference from* some privileged ideal, never difference-in-itself.

This seems to be exactly what has happened for feminist film theory under cinepsychoanalysis, which, with its emphasis on identification and representation, relies on spectatorial theories of identification in which a "cinematic subject" is produced (Rizzo 2012: 17). This subject, problematically, continues to be, for the most part, the able-bodied, white, middle-class, cisgender, heterosexual male, imagined not only by theorists but, seemingly, also by many filmmakers as the universal film audience. Hence, all viewers who do not identify as white, middle-class, cisgender, heterosexual, able-bodied, and male would seem to always-already be excluded from the cinematic experience (Rizzo 2012: 21). Although cinepsychoanalysts like Creed and Clover made unquestioned strides toward introducing *women as subjects* into the phallocentric discourse of film theory, Rizzo rightly maintains that remaining within a binary, negate-ive perspective on sexual difference has ultimately led feminist film theorists to flatten the differences *between* women, resulting in the construction of a female cinematic subject who "turns out to look very much like a white, middle-class and heterosexual subject" (Rizzo 2012: 24).

The point is this. To recognize and deconstruct the phallocentrism of Western discourses, disciplines, institutions—the whole of Western culture, in fact—was a necessary starting point for feminism, and for feminist film theory. Nevertheless, molar systems of subjectivity—those, like cinepsychoanalysis, that continue to seek fixed, stable subjects with static, categorizable identities—have proven wholly inadequate to overturning or undoing systems of inequality and oppression. Even if we replaced phallocentrism with gynocentrism, we would encounter the same problems, only with male-masculinity reconfigured as lack or degradation; for so long as we remain attached to the phantasy of an ideal, idealized form, whatever that form is, difference will always be negative, difference *from* what one "should" be: the universal "human" subject.

What we need, particularly in this new era of rapid change and hybrid fluidity, is what schizosophy offers us: a radical unthinking of molar subjectivity, which, as embodied theories of horror film viewing show us, begins *with the body*—the body that is always changing, never natural, vibrating at various intensities of speed and slowness, forever in the process of becoming different from itself. Such embodied unthinking has already begun, of course, with theorists like Grosz, Braidotti, Rizzo, and Powell. My aim in this book is to push the embodied unthinking of the gender binary further in the field of feminist film theory, for the sake of both film theory and feminism itself.

As this book progresses, I hope to demonstrate how only by unthinking binary models of subjectivity and embracing radically affirmative, embodied philosophies of sexual difference can feminism become truly inclusive and address some of its most enduring and pressing problems, chief among those the politics of reproduction. Such unthinking will not come easily. When our very system of language, as Lacan said, forces us into subject positions ("I" am not "you") and when, as Althusser wrote, all of our Western institutions rely upon artificially freezing individuals into those fixed, unchanging subjectivities—including, as Rizzo has noted, the positions "he" and "she"—learning to dissolve borders and boundaries and to exchange our beings for becomings will require us to do no less than Ripley, ultimately relinquishing our need for egoistic subject formations as we fall into the pure incandescence of the plane of immanence, burning away our sense of self and Other as we become-imperceptible.[2]

Yet the rewards of this endeavor will be worth the effort. The postfeminist outlook would have it that films like *Prometheus* and *Alien: Covenant* are feminist for featuring strong female characters, wherein strength is still coded as masculine. Yet when one looks closer, we see that these films, in both content and expression, propagate phallocentric fear of the archaic, castrating mother *and* the patriarchy's demand that woman serve as man's mirror onto the world, reflecting not her own femaleness but the values of the patriarchy back onto itself. As Ann Hall puts it in her analysis of *Frankenstein*, that most fecund of reproductive texts, "the patriarchy, the masculine subject, denies indebtedness to the mother, proposes individualization, and reproduces sameness. No difference, that is, femininity, is allowed . . . [for] reproduction in patriarchy . . . is about relationships among men . . . It is about re-producing the masculine image. It is about control and perpetuating the status quo" (2010: 215, 220). Both Frankenstein and his monster, Hall writes, "are obsessed with power and self. It is ironic, then, that when Frankenstein dies, the creature takes his body to the North Pole, perhaps offering a vivid symbol for the quest for identity—the pursuit of a stable, static identity results in or can only be death, never life, with its constant change, shifts, and interrelationships" (2010: 221).

Change, shifts, interrelationships—this is becoming. *Prometheus* and *Alien: Covenant* transfer focus from the alien-as-monster to Dr. Weyland's monster, David, who, unlike his literary predecessor in *Frankenstein*, is physically beautiful, as well as cunningly intelligent (and entirely merciless). David is certainly obsessed with power and self. *Prometheus* and *Alien: Covenant* likewise seem obsessed with what Hall calls the patriarchal "search for . . . the other that will fulfill them, making them feel whole, complete, [that will] help them find the perfect identity . . . [But] that goal is impossible. Identity is always a misshapen, half-formed creature, full of desire, seeking completion" (2010: 214), for although "we desire succinct, rigid interpretations," Hall tells us that "what we live with are the unformed, misshapen texts and identities that are constantly being rewritten and reformed. . . . [T]his state of affairs"—this *becoming* "—is not entirely disconcerting, for [it] affords . . . the opportunity for new life, new ideas" (2010: 215). *That* is the radically affirmative message behind Deleuze and Guattari's schizosophy, which highly affective, molecular films like the *Alien* quadrilogy bring us closer to realizing: that as misshapen, half-formed creatures, full of desire, like the alien-human hybrid clone that emerges from the fire to become Ripley 8, humanity's savior and a mother-monster, each of us can remain open every moment of our lives to new possibilities, new combinations, new becomings.

3

Meet Your Makers

The emphasis of the films in this chapter is not on birth or the mother per se but on *creation*, the engineering, through various non- or extra-maternal means, of "perfected" forms of life. In *The Island of Dr. Moreau*, the titular Moreau attempts to genetically engineer a superior, nonviolent race by blending the (allegedly) pure souls of animals with the (alleged) rationality of humans. In *Mary Shelley's Frankenstein*, Victor Frankenstein seeks to construct a body beyond the reach of death, employing "philosophy" and "imagination" where science and religion have failed. In *Ex Machina*, a brilliant (male) programmer attempts to create the "perfect woman" via artificial intelligence (AI). Whether discussing mothers or makers, however, one fact remains obvious: *the female body stands not only as a contested site for feminism but also as an arena of mystery and terror for the phallocentric imagination.* Before turning to the films this chapter will explore, we therefore need to consider how women's bodies have, or have not, been theorized in the West, relying on Elizabeth Grosz's critique of that theorization as a means of exploring how the monstrous-feminine might come to mean differently if female bodies were to be understood in their specificity, rather than as the male body's Other.

Becoming-Woman: The "Universal Girl" and the Ever-Shrinking Man

As we have already seen, some feminists resist theorization of the female body precisely because *the body* has been used to oppress and repress women. In one view, "menstruation, pregnancy, maternity, lactation" are "regarded as a limitation on women's access to the rights and privileges patriarchal culture accords to men; in the other, in more positive and uncritical terms . . . , the [female] body is seen as a unique means of access to knowledge . . . a special insight . . . men lack" (Grosz 1994: 15). Whether invoked to highlight women's oppression (the view of egalitarian feminism) or to celebrate women's ways of knowing (the view of essential motherhood), Western conceptions of the female body seem to have accepted patriarchal and misogynist assumptions about that body as "more natural, less detached, more engaged with and directly related to its 'objects' than male bodies" (Grosz 1994: 15). Hence, women's bodies have not been theorized *as bodies* but only as that which differs, either through limitation or specialization, from the universal, male body. With respect to the female body's role in reproduction, Grosz argues that egalitarian feminists have sought to "free" women from the demands and confines of motherhood imposed upon women in binary culture, whereas essential motherhood has argued that pregnancy and maternity represent women's special, biological destiny—leaving women in the twenty-first century caught between two ends of an ideological spectrum that divides those women who identify as feminists from those who oftentimes reject the label because they believe feminism denies the importance of female or feminine experiences like motherhood. Thus, motherhood itself is often used to divide and conquer efforts toward women's collective action. In light of this divide, Grosz quite radically calls for feminist theorists to forego a "neutral or objective perspective on . . . sexual difference" (1994: 192), as egalitarian feminists have tried to do, arguing that men and women are the same and therefore should be granted equal rights and opportunities. Instead, Grosz wants us to seek out an inclusive, "sexually specific perspective . . . able to open itself up to, meet with, and be surprised at the (reciprocal) otherness of the other sex(es). Sexual difference entails ongoing negotiations between beings whose differences . . . are left intact, but with whom some kind of exchange is nonetheless possible" (1994: 192).

Denying sexual difference has not served to create equality between the sexes. It has, instead, left women in the double bind of being sexually different from men without being able to invoke that difference as a call for the *equitable*, rather than equal, treatment of women, whose bodies play a different role in reproduction than men's. Under the current binary system, to acknowledge women's sexual difference has been to "admit" that women are not the same as, and therefore are *less than*, men. But sexual difference exists, whether it is acknowledged, and Grosz's entire thesis hinges on the insufficiency of binary, phallocentric culture for reconciling this difference because said culture has no framework for understanding *the body*, which it automatically reads through gender. While de-naturalizing gender (demonstrating the distinction between gender and biological sex) may have provided a basis for understanding the social construction of gender, Grosz maintains that even corporeal feminists like Judith Butler have concluded that women's experiences of their own bodies have yet to be theorized with any specificity, as women's bodies continue to be defined by and through scientific and philosophic systems devised by men (Grosz 1994: 108).

Grosz is here pointing to what Deleuze and Guattari pointed to: the need for theories of difference as difference-in-itself, applied in ways that help us understand biological bodies of all types outside cultural expectations for what those bodies should *be* based on gender and other binary systems. A shift in philosophy must happen for this to occur; science alone cannot accomplish it. At this historical moment, despite dizzying advances in biomedicine, Grosz argues that, for men, the female body remains a mystery—an unknown/unknowable Other—because phallocentric culture still assumes the hu-man to be Man and hails His perfection against the abjection of the wo-Man's body: *his* sperm is not, like menstrual blood or vaginal fluid, "polluting," not just another form of excretion; *his* body, because it is not castrated, is not "wounded," "leaking," or "lacking." Deleuze and Guattari decried the possibility of theorizing affirmative difference so long as the primary metaphor of sexual difference was the metaphor of castration, of women's fundamental and irreparable "lack"; moreover, as Grosz points out, this Idealism of Form has racist, ageist, ableist, and homophobic connotations, as the human body is understood as "normal" and "healthy" only when it conforms to the ideal of whiteness, youth, ability, and heterosexuality denoted by the privileged middle class as the universal "nature" of humanity. Nevertheless, Grosz also highlights the danger of how difference might be theorized by neutralizing it (treating all bodies as *the same*, as Nietzsche's or Foucault's "blank page" to be written upon by culture) or by engaging in a form of gynesis, harkening back to "natural" (prelinguistic/precultural) Nietzschean instincts or Foucaultian pleasures that come, once again, to be associated with the feminine, with Woman (Grosz 1994: 157).

Even Deleuze and Guattari have been accused of falling prey to the gynesitic trap through their construct becoming-woman. If Jardine's objections to gynesis are, in the first place, that gynesis continues to treat woman as a representation of male phantasy and, in the second, that this representation is deemed necessary for furthering man's growth and knowledge, then becoming-woman would seem to place Deleuze and Guattari, like Nietzsche and Foucault, squarely within the gynesitic project. In *A Thousand Plateaus*, Deleuze and Guattari write:

> The question is fundamentally that of the body—the body they *steal* from us in order to fabricate opposable organisms. This body is stolen first from the girl: Stop behaving like that, you're not a little girl anymore, you're not a tomboy, etc. The girl's becoming is stolen first, in order to impose a history, or prehistory, upon her. The boy's turn comes next, but it is by using the girl as an example, by pointing to the girl as an object of his desire, that an opposed organism, a dominant history, is fabricated for him too. The girl is the first victim, but she must also serve as an example and a trap. (1987: 276)

Up to this point, Deleuze and Guattari seem to be prefiguring Jardine's critique of gynesis: The woman's "becoming" has already been "stolen" from her; the patriarchal construct of Woman has been coded onto the *fe*male body, to differentiate her from Man so that He will know both what He should not want to be (a girl) and what he should want (a woman). However, they go on to say

> the reconstruction of the body as a Body without Organs . . . is inseparable from a becoming-woman, or the production of a molecular woman. Doubtless, the girl becomes a woman in the molar or organic sense. But conversely, becoming-woman or the molecular woman is the girl herself . . . defined by a relation of movement and rest, speed and slowness, by a combination of atoms, an emission of particles: haecceity. . . . She is an abstract line, or a line of flight. Thus girls do not belong to an age, group, sex, order, or kingdom; . . . they produce *n* molecular sexes on the line of flight in relation to the dualism machines they cross right through. The only way to get outside the dualisms is to be-between, to pass between . . . . The girl is like the block of becoming that remains contemporaneous to each opposable term, man, woman, child, adult. It is not the girl who becomes a woman; it is becoming-woman that produces the universal girl. (1987: 276–7)

The universal girl is at the heart of what Jardine objects to in schizosophy, hearing in it "very little to do with *women*" (Jardine 1985: 215). To Jardine, becoming-woman is yet another masculinist appropriation of Woman's experience and what that experience represents, *for men*: the first loss of molecularity; the first "victim" as a molar identity is imposed upon the female body.

Jardine is right to call out appropriation of the very real oppression experienced by very real women (in different ways for women of different races, sexual orientations, socioeconomic classes, religions, national origins, ages) as the metaphoric vehicle via which men arrive at better understandings of either philosophy or themselves. Yet, in this case, Jardine seems determined to read Deleuze and Guattari in the most limited and limiting of terms, terms that overlook the revolutionary intent of schizosophy. In the molecular processes of becoming, "caught up in . . . osmosis . . . with de-anthropologized entities—for example, women, infants, animals, foreigners, the insane—in order to resist the dominant mode of representation presented by any majority," the "final stage [of which] is to become imperceptible—beyond any *percipio* [perception] as historically required for Man to master the world—or woman," Jardine sees only "a new variation of an old allegory for the process of women becoming obsolete" (1985: 215, 217). In other words, she construes Deleuze and Guattari's insistence that becoming-woman is the becoming that motivates all other becomings (Grosz 1994: 174) as yet again erasing real women from the textual or philosophic landscape, leaving us "only her simulacrum: a female figure caught in a whirling sea of male configurations . . . silent, mutable, head-less, desire-less, spatial surface necessary only for *His* [man's] metamorphosis" (Jardine 1985: 217).

And this critique would hold, were Deleuze and Guattari not speaking out against the very idea to which Jardine so thoroughly—and rightfully—objects: woman-as-representation, woman as "molar entity . . . defined by her form, endowed with organs and functions, and assigned as a subject. Becoming-woman is not imitating the entity or even transforming oneself into" a woman, Deleuze and Guattari argue, for "these indissociable aspects of becoming-woman must first be understood as the function of something else: not imitating or assuming the female form, but emitting particles that enter . . . the zone of proximity, of a microfemininity, in other words, that produce in us a molecular woman" (Deleuze and Guattari 1987: 275). Nor does schizosophy deny the importance of women asserting what Deleuze and Guattari call a "molar politics" concerned with the historic and ongoing oppression of women, women's issues, and the need for women's rights. However, they caution that

> it is dangerous to confine oneself to such a [molar] subject, which does not function without drying up a spring or stopping a flow. . . . It is thus necessary to conceive of a molecular woman's politics that slips into molar confrontations and passes under or through them . . . a becoming-woman as atoms of womanhood capable of crossing and impregnating an entire field, and of contaminating men, of sweeping them up in that becoming. (Deleuze and Guattari 1987: 275)

On the one hand, Jardine's reaction, like the reaction of many feminists, against Deleuze and Guattari's creation of a girl who is not *a* girl but a representation, in much the way gynesis creates a woman who is not *a* woman but a figure of phallocentric phantasy no less misogynistic than Freud's phallic mother, is understandable. Yet the becoming-woman Deleuze and Guattari argue for is an outright rejection of woman-as-representation, of woman as molar entity; "drying up a spring" or "stopping a flow" is the result of molar organization: the fixing or freezing of any specific woman into the monolithic category of Woman, denying her the possibilities of becoming. Becoming-woman, as Deleuze and Guattari stress, is not about men "imitating" or "taking on the form of" women, nor even only about *men* becoming-woman: "We do not mean to say that a creation of this kind is the prerogative of the man, but on the contrary that the woman as a molar entity *has to become-woman* in order that the man also becomes- or can become-woman" (Deleuze and Guattari 1987: 275–6). In other words, women must also become-woman because our bodies—and their molecular potentials—have already been "stolen" from us by hegemonic culture. Thus, women must also experience a deterritorialization of the molar identities constructed for us by phallocentric culture—identities which, as Moira Gatens's imaginary body makes clear, women project onto ourselves, inscribing our own flesh with (phallocentric) cultural expectations for what it means to "be" a woman, within a culture that carves women's bodies into pieces (thighs, breasts, stomachs, hips) and repackages them for us, digitally enhanced to impossible perfection (according to the male imagination) as ideals of beauty that define a woman's *worth*. Hence, becoming-woman may provide a line of flight that leads us away from what Grosz calls the molar Woman's "fantasmatic form" (1994: 176).

Why *becoming-woman*, though? Jardine was right to ask this, even if we disagree with her conclusion. Had Deleuze and Guattari turned to Woman as Nietzsche and Foucault did, as the phallocentrically ascribed, mysterious-yet-necessary Other, their becoming-woman would certainly fall within the gynesitic category. However, it is "women's subordinated or minoritarian status" in patriarchal culture that causes Deleuze and Guattari to so privilege becoming-woman as a line of flight from binary identity, not any "inherent qualities of women per se" (Grosz 1994: 177). Indeed, as Deleuze and Guattari write in *A Thousand Plateaus*, there "'is no becoming-man because man is the molar entity par excellence, whereas becomings are molecular'" (qtd. in Grosz 1994: 177). Moreover, becoming-woman, understood as a molecular process, involves the essential deterritorialization of molar identity, yet it nonetheless remains merely the gateway to becoming-imperceptible. Understood therefore as a line of flight from either masculine or feminine molar identities, the processes of becoming-woman involve "the breakdown or shrinkage of all identities, molar and molecular, majoritarian and minoritarian . . . whose end is achieved only with complete dissolution, the production of the incredible ever-shrinking 'man'" (Grosz 1994: 178).

The remainder of this chapter will turn to three films, two of which, in their molar content and expression, exemplify exactly what Deleuze and Guattari did *not* mean by becoming-woman. The third film, *Mary Shelley's Frankenstein*, although not without its patriarchal issues, provides a more molecular perspective on the monster man creates. In fact, Frankenstein's monster may reveal precisely the internal struggle between molar and molecular forces that allows us to finally trace a line of flight from becoming-woman to becoming-imperceptible.

Escaping (or Not) the Binary Machine

Noël Carroll has observed that horror film creates "fear" by "control[ling] and guid[ing] audience response" (1999: 149) to an "impure" and "interstitial" monster; because the characters onscreen react with horror and disgust to the monster, so, too, do we. However, as the previous chapter endeavored to show, not all horror films "control and guide" viewers' responses; those that do tend to be molar films and to rely heavily on the shot/reaction shot formula to script viewers into characters' perspectives. In molecular films, the camera breaks from this molar function, freeing viewers from adopting any subjective perspective on or of a character:

> A character acts on the screen, and is assumed to see the world in a certain way. But simultaneously the camera sees him, and sees his world, from another point of view which thinks, reflects and transforms the viewpoint of the character. . . . We will not say that the cinema is always like this—we can see images in the cinema which claim to be objective or subjective—but here . . . is a case of going beyond the subjective and the objective towards . . . an autonomous vision of the content. . . . It is a very special kind of cinema which has acquired a taste for "making the camera felt." (Deleuze 1986: 74)

Ex Machina is not of the class of this "special kind of cinema." Rather, its plot, and horror, relies on viewers adopting the worldview of Caleb, the young, able-bodied, heterosexual, white man who agrees to act as the "human component" in a Turing test with his boss Nathan's newly designed AI, Ava. The film opens with the camera (which we later learn is Nathan, spying on his unsuspecting dupe) observing Caleb through Caleb's computer as Caleb learns he has won a (rigged) contest and will be spending the weekend at Nathan's lavish, isolated estate. Having established this (not-objective) perspective on Caleb—sweet, innocent, awkward, brilliant but also clueless—we are then taken inside Nathan's compound-slash-mansion-slash-research facility through our "hero" Caleb's perspective, which is furthermore how viewers are introduced to Ava, who appears to us, fully exposed as a robot with only a woman's face, at the same moment Caleb sees her for the first time.

Caleb's growing suspicion that Nathan is a psychopath, Ava his helpless victim, builds dread and suspense for the viewer because the film relies on us knowing only what Caleb knows—which, it turns out, is what Ava *wants* him to know; the AI is manipulating Caleb for her own ends in the same way the film, by forcing viewers into Caleb's perspective on Ava, manipulates the viewer. Caleb often watches Ava through the research facility's cameras, while *we* watch Caleb watching Ava. His reactions tell us how we should feel about both characters—about Ava-as-love-object, Caleb-as-lover. This is not to say that the camera does not employ different angles, such as when the camera moves behind Caleb, showing us Ava from a long, low angle during their first conversation.[1] However, a low angle or even a tilted shot is not what Deleuze called a *deframing*—a "freeing" of the camera from subjective perspective—so long as the shot still corresponds to the point of view of a character. For instance, the much-vaunted I-camera in slasher films, which shows potential victims from the killer's point of view, does not constitute a deframing. We saw examples of camera consciousness (the camera *making itself felt*) in *Alien*; we will see examples of deframing in the next chapter, in the first of the *Twilight* films. In *Ex Machina,* however, even when we are not seeing his reaction, we are nearly always seeing the world through Caleb's lens. Again, we must, for the film to make us fear for the fate of the (apparently) star-crossed lovers. Moreover, even after the film shifts to a seemingly more objective perspective, showing Ava as she destroys her figurative father, Nathan, the perspective we are permitted remains what cinepsychoanalysis would call "the male gaze." For Ava is certainly that most gynesitic of projects, woman-as-representation, constructed by and for Man's imagination.

The repercussions of this are crucial given that *Ex Machina* seems to want to be read as a feminist text, in which Woman escapes the (metaphoric) prison masculinist culture has placed her in by turning femininity into a weapon as Ava plays her misogynistic captors for fools. *Ex Machina*'s primary diagrammatic component is the binary opposition of inside/outside. The film is edited so that the claustrophobic, subterranean scenes between Caleb and Ava, comprised of close, tight, stationary shots that, like Ava, prove unable to escape the confines of the set, are juxtaposed to extradiegetic shots of the rivers, forests, mountains, and sky that surround Nathan's estate, constantly reminding us, when we are with Ava, of everything that exists out-of-frame: the world she has been walled off from. Meanwhile, many of Nathan and Caleb's "profound" discussions about the meaning of life, their own brilliance, and the nature of AI take place either outside, in the snow and sunshine, or in front of the glass walls of Nathan's house, emphasizing the freedom they enjoy as men in a phallocentric society. In the film's most insistent illustration of this, when Caleb relates to Ava the story of "Mary in the Black-and-White Room," a story that (allegedly) illustrates the difference between human and machine consciousness, the camera zooms in slowly on Ava's face, then cuts from black-and-white flashbacks of her trapped inside the research facility to color-saturated fantasies of her outside, under the open sky. The implication that this is Ava's mind we are seeing into, not Caleb's, is reinforced by Caleb's shower-scene fantasy of being outside *with* Ava, while Ava envisions herself alone. At the end of the film, this is indeed the destiny she chooses, leaving Caleb trapped inside Nathan's compound while she takes her first steps on the path to freedom, now dressed/disguised as a woman.

Yet Ava, though she is the only one to survive, is not the only AI Caleb, or the viewer, has interacted with. Nathan's "domestic servant," Kyoko—a veritable sex slave—is also an AI, and at the end of the film, we learn that Nathan keeps a harem of discarded female robots which Ava makes use of to manage her escape, peeling the synthetic skin from these robotic "sisters" to cover up the skeleton that would make it impossible for her to "pass" as human (or woman). In the use Ava, a white woman, makes of these other, mostly Asian women, LeiLani Nishime speaks to the hegemonic, and binary, logic of the film:

> For most film critics, the story and body that matters here is Ava's. . . . By centering Kyoko, however, Ava's liberation is neither a story of men who foolishly underestimate the females they exploit nor a tale of the duplicitous nature of women, even robot women. Instead, we see the dependency of white female empowerment on the disposition of Asian bodies . . . [as] Ava chooses her new skin from a closetful of lifeless prototypes, so the skin of the Asian cyborg she wears is simply there for the taking. This fantasy of empowerment can be realized only in the absence of Asian people, especially ones who might

assert their own demands for recognition and self-possession.... [T]he pleasure of Ava's escape would wither in the face of the Asian robot's claim to her own skin. (2017: 35–6)

From a schizosophic perspective, we might ask whether Nishime is off-target—whether Ava might simply be engaged in becoming-woman as she assembles a new flesh from her discarded "sisters'" skins. The answer here would be an emphatic *no*. To discredit Nishime's argument would be to totally misinterpret both the nature of assemblages and the nature of becoming. Becoming, as the last chapter established, is a two-way flow. Just as the human and animal hosts of the *Alien* franchise do not become-alien, Ava does not become-woman, the *molecular* woman, by donning another's skin, in large part because Ava does not *assemble with* these other AI; she assembles herself *from* them, seemingly with no regard for what, or who, is exploited in service of her self-construction. Becoming is not about what one becomes, not about the endpoint; it is about the ongoing processes of deterritorialization that free us, like the schizo, from the tyranny of molar identity. Ava, although her body has no organs, is thus not *the* Body without Organs (BwO), nor does the ending move her closer to becoming the BwO, to becoming-woman, or to becoming-imperceptible. From start to finish, Ava, as literally the woman man creates, is a "closed set," the artificiality of which Deleuze located as the basis of all binary machines; for in a closed set, the "parts" are erroneously separated as distinct from what Henri Bergson called the whole:

> If one had to define the whole, it would be defined by Relation. Relation is not a property of objects, it is always external to its terms. It is also inseparable from the open . . . [for] through relations, the whole is transformed or changes qualitatively. . . . Sets are closed, and everything which is closed is artificially closed. Sets are always sets of parts. But a whole is not closed, it is open; and it has no parts, except in a very special sense, since it cannot be divided without changing qualitatively at each stage of the division. The real whole might well be . . . an indivisible continuity. (Deleuze 1986: 10)

As a machine, Ava has parts—but she is less machinic than mechanical, in the Deleuzian sense, because her parts do not appear to make up a whole, that is, she can change her mechanisms (her limbs and skin, through prosthetics; her hair, through wigs) without undergoing an actual transformation (or transmutation). Ava therefore is, from the beginning to the end of the film, always-already Woman, a *molar* woman, her becoming, like Kyoko's, like the other discarded

AIs', already stolen from her. These are, moreover, women as the phallocentric imagination would have them. Ava was designed from her would-be lover Caleb's "porn profile." Kyoko accords to Nathan's fantasy of the silent female domestic worker who performs her tasks, even sexual tasks, without complaint, without interiority or desire, as we see in her disturbingly automated, although technically proficient, dance sequence. Even Ava's "mind" was designed by, and for, men. She tells Caleb that she did not *learn* to speak, that she could *always* speak, which she realizes is "strange" because "humans *acquire* language" at the same time we acquire culture. In this, Ava speaks to the original over-coding of her "woman's" body by what Deleuze and Guattari call "the primitive territorial machine" that "codes flows, invests organs, and marks bodies" (2009: 144), which is

> a founding act—that the organs be sewn into the socius [social machine] . . . through which man ceases to be a biological organism and becomes a full body, an earth, to which his organs become attached . . . following the requirements of a socius. Nietzsche says: it is a matter of creating a memory for man . . . by means of a repression of biological memory . . . [for] an *other* memory, one that is collective, a memory of words (*paroles*) and no longer a memory of things . . . This organization, which traces its signs directly on the body, constitutes a system of cruelty, a terrible alphabet, . . . the movement of culture that is realized in bodies and inscribed on them, belaboring them . . . . It makes men or their organs into the parts and wheels of the social machine. . . . And if one wants to call this inscription in naked flesh "writing," then it must be said that speech in fact presupposes writing, and that it is this cruel system of inscribed signs that renders man capable of language, and gives him a memory of the spoken word. (Deleuze and Guattari 2009: 144–5)

From a certain gynocentric perspective, Ava's over-coded body might represent the cruelty of being inscribed by the social machine as this inscription is experienced by women: the stifling subjugation and objectification women experience in a patriarchal society, confined to the domestic or private sphere, imagined as either Man's sex slave or love object, valued only as a possession to be traded in the male economy between father (Nathan) and husband (Caleb). Read in this way, it might be tempting to see Ava's escape as feminist, the figurative death of the patriarchy serving to enable women's empowerment. But, in the first place, as Nishime points out this reading assumes viewers who do not identify with the experiences of people of color in the film—a white audience, in other words, who may be expected to applaud Ava's "liberation" without recognizing that it comes at the expense of the racialized female bodies she uses and then discards. Secondly, Ava's "liberation" does not liberate her from the territorialized, hierarchically organized, fixed-and-frozen molar identity into which she has been inscribed. Nor does the film attempt to liberate viewers from our hegemonic perspectives, leaving us to "read" Ava as heartless (if we continue in Caleb's phallocentric perspective) or triumphant (if we adopt Ava's no less binary gynocentric perspective). Apparently the film does not see, nor does it intend its (white, hegemonic) viewers to see, anything problematic in a white woman stealing the flesh from racialized Others because *Ex Machina* remains blissfully unaware of the specificity of *any* woman's body—of the impossibility of a woman, a *molecular* woman, slipping her body into the skin of another, which of course seals perfectly, seamlessly, to Ava's robotic frame; because of course, in the end, the binary machine that inscribes gender onto biological bodies views all women as the *same,* cut from the same cloth, beautiful and deadly and deceptive in exactly the same ways because we are *Women.*

Ava's escape is thus not a becoming-woman, not a line of flight leading away from hegemonic culture. If anything, Ava undergoes this process in reverse. Donning the skin she strips from the Asian robot, she solidifies herself as a molar Woman, organized according to binary logic (human/robot, male/female). By this logic, the experiences of women living in differently racialized bodies cease to differentiate them, so that the "liberation" of a white Woman can be hailed as the liberation of *all* Women because the differences between women have been erased, allowing experiences of racial difference to once again disappear from white, hegemonic minds. Although it lacks the racialized overtones, I cannot help but compare the molar ending of *Ex Machina* to the ending of the 1975 film adaptation of *The Stepford Wives*, in which Joanna, after spending the entire film fighting against the phallocentric gender binary that wants to steal *her* becoming, becomes trapped in a disorienting maze of dark corridors, at last finding herself confronted with her robot-doppelganger. Cornered, Joanna can only watch as the robot turns its empty eyes on her and, with a horrific parody of a smile, rises in its see-through negligee to strangle its human antecedent with a nylon stocking.

The final image of *The Stepford Wives* is an extreme close-up of the soulless, expressionless eyes of Joanna's robot-doppelganger, a "perfect" female creature created (like Ava) by men, here evacuated of agency or desire. The horror we feel as the Joanna-robot walks toward the camera in her pristine hat, dress, and gloves comes from knowing the *real* woman has been lost. In *Ex Machina*, in every sense of the word, there is no "real" woman under Ava's skin. The unknown/unknowable female body, the source of terror and mystery for the phallocentric imagination, has been erased from the filmic landscape, transformed into transparent plastic, glowing circuits, and sleek gears. Ava's robot-body, which the camera often lingers on, is knowable to, even programmable by, her male creators/captors, right down to her vagina, which has been designed to respond to (male) stimulation, rendering men in control at last of even the female orgasm. This is not the BwO, deterritorialized, open to endless becomings. Ava's body is and remains a molar entity onto which has been written, in Nietzschean terms, male fantasy, including the gynesitic fantasy that Ava's "escape" speaks to female empowerment—or that, since it leaves intact the racist, hetero/sexist gender binary, it is any escape whatsoever.

Law of the Father versus the Law of the Jungle

Despite the almost two decades that stand between them, *Ex Machina* and the 1996 adaptation of *The Island of Dr. Moreau* are intriguing films to juxtapose. The molarity of *Island's* expression, like *Ex Machina's*, guides viewers into the perspective of another white, able-bodied, heterosexual male hero, Edward Douglas. After an opening credit sequence which, like *Prometheus*, seems to set the stage for a molecular experience, destabilizing viewers' molar sense of self through a rapid-fire montage of dividing cells, roiling storm clouds, mutating animal and human irises, animalistic jungle "heat vision," and the union of sperm and egg, the film introduces us to Douglas, stranded in a vast blue ocean on a life raft with two other survivors following a plane crash. In voiceover (like the shot/reaction shot, another molar technique that guides viewers into adopting a character's perspective), Douglas relates how his fellow survivors "fought like beasts, not men" over the "last canteen of water" until they fell overboard and were eaten by a shark.

Eventually Douglas is rescued, by Montgomery, and brought to Moreau's island, we later learn because Moreau intended to harvest Douglas's DNA for his genetic experiments. Viewers are introduced to the results of those experiments when Douglas wanders into Moreau's laboratory. Through the bars of the animals' cages, we watch Douglas approach what appear to be human doctors surrounding a surgical patient—until the camera reveals to Douglas, and to us, a hybrid pig-woman giving birth to a humanoid infant with the aid of hybrid "doctors." The infant's protruding, serpentine eyes and feline skull are revealed in close-up, after which the camera cuts immediately to Douglas's reaction: horror, mingled with disgust. He flees the lab and attempts to flee the island, aided by Moreau's "daughter," the cat-woman Aissa, but their flight through the jungle brings them in the end only to "the Sayer of the Law," a goat-man who articulates to the other "beast people" (as Douglas calls them) the binary logic of Moreau's island. It is "bad" to want "to make love to more than one, every which way . . . ; to claw the bark of trees . . . ; to go on all fours . . . ; to jabber . . . ; to eat flesh or fish. . . . These are not the things that Men do," the Sayer of the Law declares, "and we are Men, because the Father has made us Men." Therein lies the explicitly hegemonic message of *The Island of Dr. Moreau,* as well as its primary distinction from *Ex Machina.* Whereas Nathan was the father of his AI in abstraction only, Moreau deliberately establishes himself as The Father on his island, with all attendant patriarchal (and imperialist) overtones.

The dualism of Moreau's island proves as fundamental as it is inescapable. Over dinner, Moreau and Douglas debate the nature of human versus animal, good versus evil, and—the ultimate question of patriarchal authority—God versus the Devil, as Moreau defends the purity of purpose that motivates his genetic experiments:

> MOREAU: The Devil is that element in human nature that impels us to destroy and debase.
> DOUGLAS: And what are you about on this island besides destruction and debasement?
> MOREAU: Well, I can tell you—no, please don't do that! *(to the crustacean-man Majai, when he puts his feet on the dining table)*

This short scene—rendered entirely as shot/reaction shot—reveals the dualisms within Moreau's dualisms. The film repeatedly contrasts the island's dark, dangerous, odious jungle to the Father's (i.e., Moreau's) "civilized" world, where classical music is played, Moreau's "children" (those hybrids apparently human-like enough to have earned the right to leave the jungle) recite Yeats and wear European-style clothes, and the "family" dines off the finest china. When the diminutive hybrid Majai violates Moreau's sense of etiquette by placing his feet on the tablecloth, Moreau instantly corrects him, reinforcing the film's anthropocentrism as well as its colonial subtext. The "good" hybrids are those who can play the piano like Majai, dance like Aissa, or read like M'Ling; the "bad" hybrids are those like Lo-Mai and Hyena who lack such "sophisticated" human sensibilities, preferring the law of the jungle to the law of the Father. The film reinforces viewers' acceptance of this binary differentiation by repeatedly using voiceover and shot/reaction shot to script us into the worldview of Douglas, who, after expressing unequivocal disgust for the hybrids when he is first introduced to Moreau's "children" (he calls them "Satanic"), by the end of the film has revised his position: The camera looks on as Douglas gazes down at the primate-man Assassimon with feelings we are meant to share, namely admiration for the "purity," "innocence," and "nobility" of "the beast."

For this is the perplexing molar use to which *Island* puts its hybrids: to redraw the boundaries between human and animal, reason and instinct, civilization and savagery (with all the self/Other colonial assumptions that binary implies) even as it presents a pseudo-critique of the uses to which "man" often puts "his" reason. Yet this critique does not question—in fact, it reinforces—binary thinking and hegemonic order as good, proper, natural (in the sense of being essential to [hu]man nature).

The primary diagrammatic component of *Island* is bars. We see Montgomery through the bars of a rabbit cage; mirroring this, Douglas first spies Aissa through a set of horizontal blinds. Light shining through those blinds forms striped shadows like bars, while the strong vertical and horizontal lines of the set's architecture—staircases, siding, posts, even the cabinetry and beaded curtains—reinforce this cage-like imagery so much so that, when Douglas throws open his shutters, we are hardly surprised to discover actual bars across the window. On Moreau's island, humanity is made possible only by caging one's "animal instincts." Moreau himself seems to doubt that this is possible; the cruelest of Fathers, he takes away his children's freewill, using electronic implants to shock them into submission at the first hint of threat to his patriarchal order. If, as Jardine, Kristeva, Creed, and even Grosz have maintained, the female body has long been theorized by the phallocentric mind as more "natural" than the male body, the Mother's "baser" or "animal" drives set against the superiority of the Father's rationality and logic, then it is impossible not to read Moreau's hybrid creations as feminized, with the "good" hybrids fighting to suppress the natural/feminine instincts which, when indulged, make them unclean, unfit for the Father's world. Nor is it possible to overlook the exaggerated racial and ethnic othering of the "beast people," whose skin, hair, and facial features mark them as not-white and not-European as much as fur and fangs mark them as not-human. Moreau purports to dismiss this, shrugging off as meaningless that he might have "fallen short of the human form . . . by the odd claw or hoof," yet the film returns insistently to this shortfall as Moreau's original crime against his creations, who, despite heroic struggles to resist their animal natures, will never share the Father's perfection as a (hu)man. "I want to be like you!" Aissa screams at Moreau; "will I never be like you?," while Hyena accuses Moreau of not truly being the hybrids' father because "we are not like you."

Hyena here speaks to Moreau's greatest failing as a creator. As Ann Hall has said, the goal of reproduction from the point of view of the patriarchy is to reproduce "sameness and the status quo"—Man in His own image. Moreau, in co-opting the *true* Father (God's) creative power, fails in "purifying" humanity. Rather, he pollutes it, for Moreau has forgotten *his* place in the patriarchy's "natural order": "There must always be a God Number One," Douglas tells Hyena. Moreau's insane hubris furthermore pollutes everyone around him, most notably Montgomery, once a "brilliant" scientist now "reduced" (according to Douglas's voiceover) to a glorified zookeeper. Although Moreau begins and ends the film as the archetypal mad scientist, Montgomery descends deeper and deeper into madness as the film progresses, becoming less and less like Deleuze and Guattari's schizo, more and more like the schizophrenic. The reason for Montgomery's insanity seems directly linked to his confrontation with the destabilization of the human/animal binary; he responds to this threat against the ego by turning to drugs, which become another kind of prison—this one for his mind: "[T]he immanent molecular and perceptive causality of desire fails in the drug-assemblage," Deleuze and Guattari observe in *A Thousand Plateaus*, as "addicts continually fall back into what they wanted to escape: . . . a territorialization all the more artificial for being based on chemical substances, hallucinatory forms, and phantasy subjectifications. . . . Drugs are too unwieldy to grasp the imperceptible and becomings-imperceptible" (1987: 285, 286). Montgomery, unwilling or unable to relinquish his molar sense of white, male, European self for the BwO, tries desperately to reclaim an ego, *any* ego, by the end dressing in Moreau's clothes and speaking in imitation of Moreau's voice while reigning over a veritable bacchanal among the hybrids. Rather than become-woman, become-animal, or become-imperceptible, he seeks in vain to redraw the sharp, egoistic boundaries between self/Other. And not without reason, for those boundaries prove to be the key to survival on Moreau's allegedly hybrid island.

Perhaps at this point the question to ask is why abjection in films like the original *Alien* franchise subverts the hegemonic order, whereas the same phenomenon in films like *The Island of Dr. Moreau* reinforces it. The answer lies again in the two-way flow between content and expression. Molecular films like *Alien* seek to affect viewers into becoming the monstrous-feminine in ways that destabilize hegemonic identities and therefore subvert the oppressive, repressive status quo. *Alien* frees us to become-camera, become-alien, become-hybrid, become-clone. *The Island of Dr. Moreau*, on the other hand, despite its profusion of "hybrids," makes use of almost no molecular techniques such as camera consciousness, montage, superimposition, deframing, and liquid perception, for the interest of this film is not in destabilizing viewers' molar identities but in re-solidifying them. The abject, the interstitial, the monstrous, understood in the film as that which goes against God the Father's (white, European, Christian, heterosexual, able-bodied, cisgender, masculine) order, is that which must be denied, rejected, and finally expelled so molar identities may be restored. Hence, the film invites viewers into no becomings. Just as tellingly, Moreau's hybrids never in any molecular sense become-animal.

Just as becoming-woman does not mean that one becomes *like* a (molar) woman or that one *imitates* a woman—becoming, again, is not mimesis—Deleuze and Guattari explain that we "become animal only molecularly. You do not become a barking molar dog, but by barking, if it is done with enough feeling, enough necessity and composition, you emit a molecular dog" (1987: 275). Deleuze and Guattari are not talking about shape-shifting, or, if they are, they are talking only about the hyphenate experience of shifting shape, about the "proximities between molecules in composition" (1987: 275) that occur in the interstitial space as one *becomes*.

Becoming-animal, then, like becoming-woman, is about the *process* of deterritorialization, not about what one becomes. Deleuze and Guattari describe becoming-animal as the next "link," after becoming-woman, leading toward becoming-imperceptible. Having destabilized our sense of molar identity through the molecular process of becoming-woman (via woman's minoritarian status), by becoming-animal we destabilize the anthropocentric view that contributes to—and perhaps even provides the foundation for—our egoistic sense of self, the eye/I that perceives and orders the world according to Deleuze's "great dualism machines," one of which is human/animal in which humans are superior and thereby allowed to use, abuse, and discard animals (and their environments) as we see fit. But just as becoming-woman is not about some quality women *represent*, becoming-animal is not an invitation to a "purer," more "innocent," or more "natural" state represented by animals. "Becomings-animal are basically of another power, since their reality resides not in an animal one imitates or to which one corresponds but in themselves, in that which suddenly sweeps us up and makes us become—a *proximity, an indiscernibility* that extracts a shared element from the animal far more effectively than any domestication, utilization, or imitation could" (Deleuze and Guattari 1987: 279).

In this sense, it is obvious that Moreau's creations do not become-animal. They do not "become" anything. As Ava's robotic female body is insistently over-coded with the molar identity of Woman, allowing her to seamlessly don the skin of any woman because women, after all, are interchangeable, defined solely as man's Other, so the "beast people's" bodies are over-coded with all the ways in which they are mankind's (not just *humankind's*) Other: impure, interstitial, feminine, monstrous, abject. Those who do not die or choose death, like Hyena, elect to remain on Moreau's lost island, allowing "nature to take its course" as they no longer have access to the serums Moreau provided to keep them from "regressing" to their animal states. The Sayer of the Law declares that they shall "be what they are," that is, no longer hybrids caught in the interstice between human/animal but fully their (molar) animal forms. Douglas—with his white, able-bodied, European male identity intact—is the only being to escape the island. In a final voiceover as he sails away, he reinforces the patriarchal superiority of wholeness as, over a montage of footage from wars and riots, he reflects on how often his "fellow man" reminds him of the "beast people . . . neither wholly animal nor wholly man . . . as unstable as anything Moreau created."

That instability—the dissolution of boundaries—seems to be what the molar logic of *Island* objects to most of all. It is hardly to be wondered at, then, that the film, rooted as it is in a binary, patriarchal worldview, resists all manner of becomings. Of course, to say that a film feminizes that which threatens the patriarchal order and casts the feminine threat out in order to make whole its subjects is not to say anything new; those are precisely Creed's, and Kristeva's, arguments. What I am saying, by contrasting the monstrous uses of "the feminine" in molar films like *Ex Machina* and *The Island of Dr. Moreau* to more molecular films like the original *Alien* quadrilogy, which no less abjectify the feminine monster, is that the more molecular films, by affecting viewers into an embodied human-cinematic assemblage, invite us to become with them: to become-woman, become-animal, become-alien. Cinepsychoanalysis provides an excellent framework for identifying the monstrous-feminine and for understanding why it is monstrous to the phallocentric imagination. But it stops there, with the contention that any film that monstrousizes the feminine or feminizes the monstrous works *for* the hegemonic order, inevitably reinforcing women's state of lack.

Schizoanalysis, on the other hand, provides a framework for understanding how the monstrous-feminine, that which dissolves borders and boundaries, can be expressed in ways that work *against* that order, since "[i]ndiscernibility, imperceptibility, and impersonality remain the endpoints of becoming" (Grosz 1994: 179). Indiscernibility does not refer to *sameness*; becoming-imperceptible does not mean flattening differences, but means, instead, freeing individuals from molar identities that permit only identification with or against an/other, rather than the opportunity to assemble with all manner of persons, places, ideas, and entities. Thus, Grosz maintains, becoming-woman may lose its problematic (from a feminist perspective) status of "radical otherness" as Deleuze and Guattari "produce a radical antihumanism that renders animals, nature, atoms, even quasars as modes of radical alterity" (Grosz 1994: 179). On the way to discovering a line of flight for the post-human family—a family freed from the tyranny of gender and other binary systems—the final section of this chapter will turn to that "radical antihumanism" in search of that most radical of alterities: the becoming-monster.

The Psychomechanics of Becoming-Monster

From the cinepsychoanalytic perspective, it is entirely possible to read in Kenneth Branagh's adaptation of *Mary Shelley's Frankenstein* a thoroughly binary message. After his mother dies in childbirth, young Victor Frankenstein determines to prevent this tragedy from befalling any other mothers (or sons) by finding a new way to create life out of "philosophy" and "imagination"—a parthenogenetic brainchild, in other words, akin to Athena bursting fully formed from Zeus's skull. Furthermore, as a new, "perfected" form of life—something women's wombs cannot create—Victor's creation will never die.

Julia Kristeva has written of phallocentric fear of the archaic, castrated/castrating mother as "essentially fear of her generative power" which "patrilineal filiation has the burden of subduing" (qtd. in Creed 1993: 43). In violation of this "proper" Freudian identification of the son with the father's world, Victor-the-son forsakes his physician father's ordered, rational domain of medicine for the shadowy world of illegal scientific research conducted in dark, secret chambers; reliant on the scavenging of "raw materials" from corpses and "strange" Eastern philosophies; and thereby redolent of the monstrous-feminine. For his attempt to assume the mother's generative power, Victor will be soundly punished. First, he descends into madness (which, since it disturbs order and identity, is gendered feminine). Then, after casting aside his creation, he is prevented, by the very monster he created, from marrying Elizabeth and rejoining the bright, rational world of the father.

Such a reading finds us in familiar binary territory: men should not want to be *like* women; if they forget this, death and destruction follow. This is a perfectly defensible psychoanalytic reading of the film. When, however, one approaches the film as a direct event, without welding such preconceived psychoanalytic notions onto it, a highly molecular experience emerges to subvert this hegemonic message.[2] What this chapter will demonstrate is how *Mary Shelley's Frankenstein* uses molecular expressions to insistently provoke in viewers that deep introspection of our internal operations Bergson claimed can make us aware of ourselves as living things constantly becoming, a necessary movement toward the molecular process of becoming-imperceptible. For this analysis to make sense, however, it is necessary at this point to reflect on why Deleuze found cinema so ripe for philosophic study.

Against the primacy of structuralism, of sign and signified, Deleuze insisted that language was less important for what it *represents* than for what it can *do*. Cinema, Deleuze writes in the conclusion to *Cinema 2*, though not itself a language, "brings to light an intelligible content which is like a presupposition, a condition, a necessary correlate through which language constructs its own . . . signifying units and operations" (1989: 262). This "inseparable-but-specific" correlate "consists of movement and thought-processes (pre-linguistic images), and of points of view on these movements and processes (pre-signifying signs). It constitutes a whole 'psychomechanics,' the spiritual automaton, the utterable of a language system which has its own logic . . . anterior to all linguistics" (1989: 262). In effect, Deleuze argues that the machinic nature of cinematic technology—image coupled to movement and sound, with which the viewer assembles—creates the capacity for cinema, as language's utterable correlate, to indicate "the highest exercise of thought, the way in which thought thinks" (1989: 263); moreover, as the viewer assembles with cinematic technology through our optic and auditory nerves, experienced not by the eye/I but by the *brain*, we are freed to be "dispossessed of [our] own thought" (Deleuze 1989: 263).

To be "dispossessed of our own thought" is the very essence of the schizo experience, the evacuating of a hierarchically organized, fixed-and-frozen, egoistic molar Self. Thus, Deleuze asserts that in its psychomechanical operation "there is something specific to cinema which has nothing to do with theatre," that is, with *representation*, for the specifically machinic nature of the cinematic assemblage is "automatism become spiritual art" (1989: 263), that is, cinema as *a thinking-machine that allows us to (un)think thought* via an "image of thought" which "inspires by its developments, forkings and mutations the necessity of always creating new concepts, not as a function of external determinism, but as a function of a becoming which carries along the problems themselves" (Tomlinson and Gatens 1989: xvi). What schizoanalysis of *Mary Shelley's Frankenstein* demonstrates is how the film's molecular expressions realize that "spiritual art" which, as Powell has said, can schizophrenize viewers, destabilizing our "external social projections"—our self-as-representation. Hence, we shall begin by tracing the lines of flight from molar identity provoked *in viewers* before turning to how those expressions interact with the film's content—a pivot that will bring us back to the politics of reproduction. I want to stress, however, that I am separating expression from content purely for the sake of analytic clarity. Content and expression coalesce in film and can never in actuality be divided, for content and expression are what Deleuze called *dividual*, parts forming a whole (the film) that transforms entirely should any part be altered or subtracted.

In sharp contrast to the primarily molar films this chapter has explored, the camera in *Frankenstein* is almost constantly in motion, acting not as a perspective of or on any character but as a cinematic consciousness. This consciousness is conveyed via montage, which "couples together any point whatsoever of the universe in any temporal order whatsoever . . . : slow or high speed shots, superimposition, fragmentation, deceleration, micro-shooting" (Deleuze 1986: 80–1), with montage becoming "the pure vision of a non-human eye . . . which would be in things. . . . This is the definition of objectivity, 'to see without boundaries or distances'" (1986: 81). From its opening moments, *Frankenstein* sweeps viewers up in its montages. We are taken aboard a ship buffeted by a storm; alongside dogs being killed by the Creature (Frankenstein's monster); and later into Victor's lab, where the camera races along metal tracks, spins around flywheels, sparks across metal rods, washes us inside the copper "womb," and finally drowns us in amniotic fluid as the Creature is born. The film as a whole is edited to move rapidly, almost irrationally, through the action, each unmatched cut destabilizing viewers' identification with any particular perspective as the camera continues to *make itself felt*, for instance spinning around Dr. and

Mrs. Frankenstein during the birth of Victor's younger brother; becoming rain cascading down a window; then cutting to a bolt of lightning striking a tree.

Combined, the film's camera consciousness and irrational cuts become what Deleuze calls *pure movement,* movement that is "extracted from bodies or moving things" (1986: 23). Pure movement moves us closer to thinking that Bergsonian whole rather than closed sets, which, as was explained earlier, are both a hallmark and a precursor of binary thinking. When we think *masculine* or *feminine*, for instance, we are thinking in artificially closed sets—we are not seeing the *whole* of phallocentric culture that brought those signifiers into being, nor are we seeing the individuals upon whose bodies those terms are inscribed, who, in their specificity as living things constantly becoming, could never be reduced to labels like masculine or feminine. The schizosophic experience of cinema's pure movement helps us unthink this binary thinking by allowing us to *think* the openness of what we try so desperately to keep closed. Because it "varies the elements of the set by dividing them up into fractions with different denominators—because it decomposes and recomposes the set—[montage] also relates to a fundamentally open whole, whose essence is constantly to 'become' or to change, to endure; and vice versa" (Deleuze 1986: 23). Importantly, what "decomposes and recomposes" the shot in montage is not our eye. Rather, the camera in montage "exceeds the limits" of the human eye, according to Deleuze, moving with agility and speed our eyes never could. Thus, composition and decomposition are accomplished by the camera, "sometimes human, sometimes inhuman or superhuman" (1986: 20). Films like *Frankenstein* that rely heavily on montage therefore short-circuit our human subjective perspective, destabilizing us into becoming-camera. But *Frankenstein* does not stop there. Pure movement is, rather, the overarching molecular expression that enables viewers to be swept up in the film's many other schizosophic elements.

Music is one of those elements, and it, in turn, sets the stage (so to speak) for the cinematic synesthesia, to be discussed momentarily, that perhaps best indicates viewers' becoming with the cinematic assemblage. In writing about cinematic music, Deleuze distinguishes between the music that was often played over or with silent films as they were projected in the theater and the cinematic score as we have now come to think of it, the audio of the audiovisual film. For the silent film, Deleuze maintains, music "found itself subject to a certain obligation to *correspond* to the visual image, or to serve descriptive, illustrative and narrative ends" (1989: 238). Interestingly, we could say that the inclusion of *popular* music in many sound-enabled films serves this same molar function, as anyone who watches romantic comedies, action movies, or melodramas knows. The cinematic score of the sound-enabled film, on the other hand, becomes "emancipated, and can take flight" (Deleuze 1989: 238) from the narrative; however, "the image and the music had themselves to form a whole" which is not merely "mixing" but which, rather,

> replaces external or illustrative correspondence by an internal correspondence; . . . the whole should be formed by the visual and sound which go beyond themselves in a higher unity. . . . [C]inema music must be abstract and autonomous, a true "foreign body" in the visual image, rather like a speck of dust in the eye, and must accompany "something that is in the film without being shown or suggested in it." (Deleuze 1989: 238–9)

Frankenstein's score rises to this order of "higher unity" that is felt within the viewer. When Justine is falsely accused of murder, for instance, the roar of the lynch mob and Victor and Elizabeth's panicked shouts soar into the increasingly frantic orchestral score, which builds in volume until it drowns out Justine's attempts to tell her friends what she saw by the lake. At this point, the music has an "illustrative" correspondence—it heightens the tension and confusion of the scene—but, the moment after the noose is forced over Justine's head and the mob flings her over the city wall, viciously snapping her neck, the music continues unabated, at its same frantic pace and pitch, while we watch her feet swing slowly above the heads of the crowd. This is the moment when the music becomes a "foreign body" in the film. The action is over—Justine is dead—there is every expectation that the music will soften or slow, yet it refuses to comply. It is a moment foreshadowed during the Creature's birth, as Victor races around his laboratory, turning on machines; and it is a moment echoed later in the film, after Elizabeth's resurrection, when she and Victor dance to music that becomes increasingly, stridently discordant while the camera swings wildly around the dancers.

What is the "something" in the film that is neither shown nor suggested to which these moments of incongruously swelling, soaring music might be speaking? Each moment centers on Victor, whose face the camera finds in the crowd in a jump-cut from Justine's swinging feet. In each, the cinematic score serves to *catch* the viewer, to carry us along wildly with the film, as the music becomes almost noise, like static, at times obliterating diegetic sound. Yet music rarely plays around the Creature; there is, for instance, no score at all during the scenes he spends in the woods before seeking out his revenge, only diegetic sounds like birdcalls, hoes striking frozen soil, branches creaking, and so on. Whereas Victor seems caught inside an endless torrent of racing thought, rushing breathlessly from one foolish decision to the next, seemingly unable to assume a perspective on himself or his world that would allow him to contemplate the disastrous potential of his actions, the Creature is observant and reflective, ultimately *introspective*, aware of what he is and who—and how—he is becoming. That Victor is a molar being, the Creature a molecular becoming, will have great resonance when we turn to the film's content. For now, it is enough to say that the film's musical score expresses this difference between the characters in a way that reverberates with viewers not by forcing us into subjective perspectives on or of the characters but molecularly by bringing us *inside* these characters' internal operations.

Because it brings us *into* the film, music is therefore also another means via which viewers are opened to the "spiritual automatism" of the film and come to be deeply affected by it, to the point of experiencing cinematic synesthesia. Applying phenomenological readings to film, scholars such as Julian Hanich have noted how certain films use the senses of sight and hearing to affect our senses of smell, taste, and touch (2009). The key to this synesthetic experience is the viewer's *engagement* with the film—our sense of being inside with, rather than outside of or detached from, what we see and hear. *Frankenstein* promotes this engagement in two important ways, the first, leading to the second, being *rarefaction*. After Mrs. Frankenstein's death, the camera soars over the set as Victor's father, covered in his wife's blood, stumbles down a giant, white marble staircase toward an empty marble foyer. The starkness of this scene is important, as it is repeated numerous times throughout the film, notably at the end when Victor, in a reversal of this scene, races *up* the staircase with Elizabeth's corpse in his arms. According to Deleuze, the cinematic frame contains elements that are "sometimes very numerous, sometimes of limited number. The frame is therefore inseparable from two tendencies: towards saturation or towards rarefaction" (1986: 12). In *Frankenstein*, the rarefaction of scenes serves to invite viewers into a kind of meditation on the image as that prelinguistic language or pre-signifying sign. Whereas cinepsychoanalysis insists on symbolic readings of images based on what they represent—for example, in the slasher film the killer's blade represents the phallus, while the wound the blade creates represents castration—Deleuze demands,

> And why is expression not available to things? There are affects of things, the "edge," the "blade," or rather the "point" of Jack the Ripper's knife, is no less an

affect than the fear which overcomes his features. . . . The affect . . . does not exist independently of something which expresses it, although it is completely distinct from it. (1986: 97)

In other words, both saturation and rarefaction—most often rarefaction in *Frankenstein*—can help viewers think beyond the preconceived notions psychoanalysis would map onto the film-as-a-text, allowing us to experience the affect of "things" directly.

Once we begin to experience the materiality of the image directly, viscerally, without the remove or detachment of symbolic analysis, we begin to experience what Deleuze called tactisigns, images that "reveal 'a touching which is specific to the gaze'" (Powell 2005: 142). Anna Powell observes how tactisigns like blood and slime in horror film serve to disgust viewers (2005: 142), yet tactisigns do not need to invoke disgust, revulsion, or terror to be affective; indeed, Deleuze wrote of the tactile perception of softness invoked by images of feathers. In *Frankenstein*, tactisigns begin with the sumptuous—a lace cuff, a velvet cloak—and proceed into the repulsive: the fur of a disembodied simian arm; thread sewn into skin; a steel rod plunged into the sole of a corpse's foot, at which point we have so thoroughly assembled with the film that our toes may curl in sympathy.

As the molecular expressions of the film compound upon one another, viewers, as Powell has said, lose the distinction between inside (being *within* the film) and outside (*watching* the film). Like the monstrous-feminine, the molecularity of the film effaces the borders between self/Other and destabilizes our rational, logical, symbolic readings via pure sensory experience—brings us, in other words, into "proximity" with the "microintensities" Deleuze and Guattari described in becoming-woman, becoming-child, and becoming-animal, all movements toward becoming-imperceptible. Yet what is perhaps most molecular about *Frankenstein* is its expression of *time*.

It may be useful here to recall that the primary reason Deleuze and Guattari dismissed systems of representation that depend upon stable, static identities is *time*, or in schizosophic terms, *duration*. As durational creatures, each of us is engaged in becoming different-from-ourselves every moment of our lives; therefore, as was argued earlier, Deleuze and Guattari did not see difference as negative or positive—difference *from* any alleged ideal—but simply as difference-in-itself, evaluated as "good" or "bad" by its impact on our relation to our self and between ourselves and others. When cinema became truly philosophical, according to Deleuze, was when it shifted emphasis from the "movement-image" to the "time-image" by using the film-image to reveal the present-pastness of duration, in which memory is always present even as the present becomes the past. In *Gilles Deleuze's Time Machine,* David Rodowick describes the time-image as existing in the fluctuation between the *actual,* or what is happening in the present, and the *virtual,* or what already happened in the past and what *might* happen in the future (1997). Both past and future can only be experienced *virtually,* not objectively, either through memory (the past) or imagination (the future). When film succeeds in conveying a "direct image of time," Deleuze claims, it becomes a "crystal-image," an image that reflects, in the literal sense of a two-way mirror,

> the most fundamental operation of time: since the past is constituted not after the present that it was but at the same time, time has to split itself in two at each moment as present and past . . . , or, what amounts to the same thing, it has to split the present in two heterogeneous directions, one of which is launched toward the future while the other falls into the past. . . . Time consists of this split, and it is this, it is time, that we *see in the crystal*. Except, Bergson adds, . . . the crystal constantly exchanges the two distinct images which constitute it, the actual image of the present which passes and the virtual image of the past which is preserved. . . . The crystal always lives at the limit, it is itself the "vanishing limit between the immediate past which is already no longer and the immediate future which is not yet.". . . . What we see in the crystal is therefore a dividing in two that . . . prevents it from reaching completion. . .
>
> Bergsonism has often been reduced to the following idea: duration is subjective, and constitutes our internal life. . . . But, increasingly, [Bergson] came to say something quite different: the only subjectivity is time, non-chronological time grasped in its foundation, and it is we who are internal to time, not the other way around. . . . Time is . . . the interiority in which we are, in which we move, live and change. (Deleuze 1989: 81–3)

As perhaps the apex of the molecular cinematic experience, the crystal-image gives us access to thinking ourselves as durational creatures engaged in becoming different-from-ourselves, *affected by ourselves* across time, never reaching completion. It is not that *Frankenstein* is told almost entirely in flashback that makes it crystalline; flashbacks, or "recollection-images" to Deleuze, can serve molar ends if the flashback is expressed in ways that force adherence to subjective perspectives. In *Frankenstein,* however, the film's pure movement, camera consciousness, even the internal correspondence of its musical score,[3] all of which occur *within the flashback*, conspire toward an overarching crystalline expression of which the flashback is itself a machinic part. The present of the narrative envelops the flashback, without interrupting it; as viewers, we may even forget that we are in a flashback—but this is no matter. What *does* matter is that when the film cuts sharply back to the present as Victor finishes telling his story to Captain Walton, the reminder that we have all along been *in* a flashback prompts us to reflect on the film, to contemplate it, to trace the "forkings" of time that led to the present.

The first fork: Elizabeth's parents die; she is adopted by the Frankensteins. The second fork: Years later, Mrs. Frankenstein dies giving birth to Victor's brother, William. The third fork: Elizabeth declines to go with Victor to Geneva. The next fork: Victor meets Waldman, who introduces him to his research on reanimation. The next fork: Waldman, while forcing vaccines onto frightened peasants, is murdered by the man whose body Victor later uses for the Creature. The next fork: The cholera epidemic provides Victor with all the "raw materials" he needs to complete his creation. Tracing time's forks, Deleuze says, gives flashbacks "an authenticity . . . without which they would remain conventional. . . . [T]he forking points are very often so imperceptible that they cannot be revealed until after their occurrence. . . . It is a story that can only be told in the past . . . : How have we arrived at this point? It is perhaps the question of all questions" (1989: 50).

The question of all questions: the very essence of duration. Asking *how we have arrived at this point* prompts deep introspection on ourselves as living things constantly becoming. Yes, we have been subject to forces beyond our control, such as the death of Victor's mother—yet how did we respond; with what have we formed assemblages in our lives, how were we affected by those assemblages (which we also affected), and why? The crystalline expression of *Mary Shelley's Frankenstein* is such that the ending, in which the Creature chooses to burn himself on his father's funeral pyre, becoming like Ripley imperceptible as the fire "unleashes in our soul *a non-psychological life of the spirit* . . . in which we are alone with God as light" (Deleuze 1986: 54), although a tragic ending, nevertheless reinforces the schizoid experience by leaving us, the viewers, open to reflecting on how Victor and his Creature arrived at their mutual fates.

What we discover in reflecting on time's forkings is that the Creature is not monstrous because he is impure or interstitial. He *becomes* monstrous after he is repeatedly *treated* as a monster. This is important, in the first place because it helps us understand that, unlike Ava, whose robotic body was already over-coded with the molar identity Woman, the Creature is not "monstrous" by virtue of being assembled from parts that include a murderer, nor will he prove noble or wise because Victor provides him with the brain of a genius. The Creature is, rather, a supremely molecular assemblage. He is born with all the infinite potential of the BwO, but immediately his becomings are stolen from him as his body is inscribed with a social identity—in this case, that of the Monster. This social inscription does not excuse the awfulness of the Creature's revenge, but it does shift our understanding of what the Creature becomes from what he *represents* (the Other, the ab-normal) to how hegemonic society, in its treatment of difference, creates its own monster(s).

The Creature's molecular nature, which, like the girl's, is "stolen" from him by hegemonic society, also shifts the narrative of Victor Frankenstein. Victor is not punished as Moreau was for tampering with the natural order of things; the Creature is not born with the intention of killing or harming him. Instead, Victor seals his fate by contributing to the creation of the Creature-as-murderer through his cruelty and callousness. Gazing up at the naked, newborn Creature, caught in chains hanging from the ceiling of his laboratory, Victor appears overcome with horror by its "imperfect" human form. He makes the decision then and there to abandon the Creature, seeking to retreat into the patriarchal order he originally defied—a retreat emphasized by the dreamlike montage as he flees from the Creature. The montage furthermore disorients the viewer into experiencing not Victor's confusion and terror so much as the terror and confusion of the newborn Creature, thereby creating space for us to experience Victor's rejection from the Creature's perspective: as an utter lack of humanity toward a living being who is not evil, but merely *different*.

It is crucial that hereafter the film shifts focus onto the Creature for extended periods of time, allowing us to also trace the forkings of how he, along with Victor, arrives at his ultimate end. Ostensibly everything we see occurs inside Victor's flashback, as he narrates his life to Captain Walton in the present; however, as there is no way for Victor to know what his creation experienced after he fled from it (nowhere within the diegesis does the Creature narrate his own story to his father), the narrative in these sequences acts as the nonhuman camera does, providing us a perspective on the Creature that is neither Victor's nor the Creature's. Hence, it seems even narratively a subjective view has been superseded by that "autonomous vision of the content" to which Deleuze refers (Deleuze 1986: 74). Alongside the Creature, we experience the cruelty of the people who beat him and chase him from the city solely for his "monstrous" appearance; we experience the loneliness of the forest he wanders into, bathed in perpetual twilight; we experience the tender love of the family he secretly protects; we experience the joy of companionship as he finds acceptance and sympathy with the blind grandfather; we experience the hurt and sorrow that turns to rage after the family, inscribing onto his body the hegemonic binary goodness=beauty/evil=ugliness, casts him out. Even the crimes the Creature commits are not rendered in terms of good versus evil by the film. In the most schizosophic sense of ethics as ethology, what makes the Creature's revenge "monstrous" has nothing to do with whether the Creature *is* a monster (and therefore "evil") but with how the Creature's actions *affect* himself and others, which is ultimately to bring about his and their destruction.

None of this is to say that a phallocentric reading of *Mary Shelley's Frankenstein* does not exist. It does. What matters is that, unlike the *Twilight* films we will turn to in the next chapter, the film's insistently molecular expressions successfully rupture this message, dislocating our identification with hegemonic or even human characters, an identification that would be required for the molar message to be believed. This is not a matter of reading against the grain or even of queering the film, although the film's molecularity does invite queer and/or otherwise non-hegemonic viewing experiences more affirmatively than films like *Ex Machina* or *The Island of Dr. Moreau*, which, from a minoritarian perspective, could be experienced as affirmative only through resistance to the "master narrative." *Mary Shelley's Frankenstein*, on the other hand, resists its *own* master narrative. For within the text there is another text, a specifically minoritarian text, *a monster-text* uttering itself with and through the film, encompassed by the hegemonic viewpoint that would read Victor as the (albeit flawed) hero, his creation as the monster. *Encompassed* is a term of art for Deleuze in writing about cinema. As his translators Hugh Tomlinson and Robert Galeta explain, "Deleuze uses the term 'englobant' as a noun. The verb 'englober' has the sense of 'to include, embody, bring together into a whole.' We have translated this term as 'encompasser'" (1989: xviii).

As a dividual whole, then, the molecular expression of *Mary Shelley's Frankenstein* cannot be separated from the moments when the film tries to put forth a hegemonic perspective on its content. Take, for instance, the conversation between Victor and the Creature inside the Creature's ice-cave, which throws into question the nature of the Creature's assemblage (whether it is molar or molecular):

CREATURE: What kind of people is it of which I am comprised? Good people? Bad people?
VICTOR: Materials. Nothing more.
CREATURE: *(picking up wind instrument)* Did you know I knew how to play this? In which part of me did this knowledge reside? In this mind? In these hands? In this heart? And reading and speaking—not so much things learned as things remembered . . .

If we take the Creature at his word, Victor is to be excused of all blame except for the original patriarchal sin of assuming the archaic mother's generative power—for if, being assembled from raw materials that include the body and heart of a murderer, the Creature was always destined to become a killer, then it hardly matters that Victor abandoned him, nor how society treated him.

Yet by this point we have seen the monster engage in a process of becoming that is far more molecular than a "regression" into murderous instinct, à la Moreau's hybrids. The Creature's body is not Ava's over-coded, always-molar body, unable to escape what it is. What the Creature cannot escape, despite all his efforts, is the hegemonic society that despises his difference, beginning with the father who rejects him for being "hideously deformed" (according to Victor's journal). The Creature seems to understand this. Moments after the above exchange, he mocks Victor's hegemonic, binary beliefs:

CREATURE: Who am I?
VICTOR: You . . . I don't know.
CREATURE: And yet you think I am evil.

Good/evil, human/animal, normal/abnormal—these binary constructs cannot explain the Creature. The Creature recognizes this; he understands the complexity of his own internal operations. He mocks Victor further for his dualisms when Victor hesitates over reanimating the corpse of Justine, his childhood friend, to be the Creature's bride: "Raw materials, remember?" the Creature chides. While the Creature knows this is not true—this is not *any* woman's body, it is *a* woman's body, *this* woman's body, *Justine's* body; its specificity matters—Victor remains too wedded to the concept of molar identity to share this realization. Therefore, when Elizabeth dies, Victor does not hesitate to hack off her head and sew it onto Justine's body.

Here the phallocentric imagination's failure to acknowledge the molecular woman's body does not result in a seamless molar assemblage, woman to Woman, as in *Ex Machina*. When Elizabeth sees the sutures attaching *her* hand to Justine's body, the horror of what Victor has done washes over her while, in close-up, we watch that hand trace the sutures that crisscross her face and neck. Does Elizabeth immolate herself because she adheres to the hegemonic view that, in losing her beauty, she has become monstrous? Perhaps—although her reaction to the Creature both before her death and after her reanimation (she never recoils from him, and indeed seems almost fascinated by him) serves to throw this reading into doubt. Perhaps we could say the reanimated Elizabeth chooses death over her new life as the only avenue available to her for rejecting Man's relentless inscription of her body, which has now been stolen from her in the most literal sense by the man who was supposed to see her and her body as more than spare parts that could be re-assembled and still called "Elizabeth." Perhaps in the fire that consumes her and the Frankensteins' ancestral home, she is giving voice to the same complex interiority the Creature declares to Victor, asserting that he has "love in [him] the likes of which you can scarcely imagine, and rage the likes of which you would not believe." Thus, the monster speaks for the humanity hegemonic culture seeks to erase in its minoritarian subjects, flattening the specificity of their experiences into categories of difference measured against the hegemonic ideal.

I have always been deeply affected by the Creature's decision to take his own life, driven as this choice seems to be in part by remorse for his actions (the Creature weeps over Victor's body), in part by an irreparable loneliness. "I am done with man," he declares to Captain Walton, declining an invitation to return "home" with the crew. For the Creature, there is no home, no place in hegemonic society. Perhaps the only person who could have understood him, his creator, has died. Yet, for all his beauty and brilliance, it is not Victor's death that troubles me; it is the Creature's. The monster's journey is the journey I, as a queer woman, empathize with. His becoming is the one we see stolen, over and over, by the hegemonic order. Importantly, there is no sense that the Creature commits suicide out of self-loathing, even if he regrets his actions; he has not accepted, in other words, the molar identity of Monster that hegemonic society inscribes onto his body. Even so, death seems to be the only way he can escape that over-coded body.

As with Ripley's self-immolation in *Alien³*, the Creature's death is rendered peacefully. He kneels calmly beside Victor's body as the flames surround him, his expression one of tranquillity. From the way the scene is expressed, it is difficult not to feel that the light the Creature "rises towards" is his "soul . . . rejoin[ing] the luminous part of itself" (Deleuze 1986: 54). Yet there will be no resurrection for the Creature as there was for Ripley—no further becomings. The end of the film is therefore troubling because it tends toward nihilism, the opposite of Deleuze and Guattari's affirmative schizosophy. Nowhere do Deleuze and Guattari advocate self-destruction or even the complete deterritorialization of self that would allow us to act as agents in the world; instead, they promote "micro-destratifications" (Grosz 1994: 173) that lead us to the BwO, freeing us from the molar identities foisted onto us by hegemonic society, identities that rely on the false wholeness of artificially closed sets. The BwO is not closed. It is open to the molecular becomings that undo oppositions and dualisms and free us to experience life's flows, vibrations, and intensities. Becomings are about *life*, radically and affirmatively. Hence it must be said that from a schizosophic perspective, the Creature's death is not a becoming-imperceptible.

Nevertheless, the film, in its immanently molecular, crystalline expressions, does do for viewers what the monster of horror has traditionally done: it strikes at our vulnerabilities. What makes *Mary Shelley's Frankenstein* such a schizosophic film is that it does not cast the monster out for serving this function. It instead affects viewers into mourning his loss as much as, if not more than, Victor's. Counter to the patriarchal quest to restore wholeness, to reproduce sameness, the film does not seek to protect viewers against the destabilizing of molar identities. Rather, it insistently opens us to contemplating the codings, inscriptions, and territorializations that steal from the Creature his becomings—and which may have stolen from us our own molecular bodies. Therefore, it seems possible that, in helping us trace a line of flight away from the tyranny of hegemonic culture, becoming-monster might be the next evolution of becoming-woman.

4

It's a Monster (Baby)

What unites the two wildly different film franchises in this chapter is motherhood. Both Selene, the vampire heroine of *Underworld*, and Bella Swan, the vampire heroine of *Twilight*, become monsters—and mothers. Schizoanalyzing these films reveals the tension between molar and molecular forces in both franchises; these tensions furthermore reveal the lengths to which hegemonic culture must go to suppress the becomings of monsters *and* mothers (not to mention viewers). For it is again not only their monstrousness that makes Selene and Bella dangerous to the patriarchal order. It is also their procreative powers, their wombs, as the pregnant body schizosophically emerges as that which effaces and erases patriarchal borders between self and other.

Barbara Creed has written of the womb as "horrifying" because it represents non-differentiation, the absorption of self in/to an-other, yet she goes on to say that the very "mutable nature" of the body, particularly the female body, likewise threatens the patriarchy, which seeks to fix and freeze its subjects into unchanging identities (1993: 49–50). As Creed notes, horror films have exploited patriarchal fears of this "mutability" as the pregnant body is rendered terrifying and/or grotesque. Yet, as earlier chapters argued, the mutability of the pregnant body—its becomings—is *celebrated* in schizosophy, upheld as that which breaks down borders, boundaries, and binaries, in much the same way the vampire does.

If tracing a line of flight from molar identities might be more useful to the twenty-first-century feminist project as a becoming-monster than a becoming-woman, this chapter submits that the monster-we-become might be particularly powerful when it is a vampire. Indeed, vampires hold a special place among late-twentieth and twenty-first-century monsters. Valorized by Anne Rice's *Vampire Chronicles* (upon which the films *Interview with the Vampire* and *Queen of the Damned* are based), further popularized by the late-1990s television show *Buffy the Vampire Slayer* and its spinoff, *Angel*, and finally immortalized in pop culture by the book and movie phenomenon *Twilight*, vampires have metamorphosized from gruesome revenants into the seductively sophisticated aristocrats of the monster world. Vampires, as Deleuze himself noted, destabilize binary order, for vampires are a curious breed of schizoid monster, always-already destratified, deterritorialized; undead, vampires exist in the borderless space between human and corpse. Vampires thus embody a molecularity that cannot be fixed into molar categories: the living *or* the dead. Moreover, that vampires are capable of reproducing makes them even more threatening to the (white) patriarchal order. Kimberly Frohreich has argued that because the perhaps most famous vampire, Dracula, "mixes blood with white European women and uses their bodies to 'reproduce' other vampires. . . . [Bram] Stoker's novel illustrates Western European anxieties regarding Eastern European immigrants and the potential loss of supposed racial or ethnic purity" (2013: 33). The *Underworld* films deal explicitly—one could say obsessively—with the purity of bloodlines and the mixing of races. Yet this chapter argues that the *Underworld* films, although not without their (increasingly) molar elements, nevertheless present a more molecular experience, one truer to the vampire's potential for queering nature, than do the thoroughly hegemonic *Twilight* films, which, after a valiant struggle against molecularity, ultimately succeed in transforming the vampire into a molar being.

Let us pause here, however, to absorb the caveat that not all female monsters, even if those monsters are rendered heroically, challenge the patriarchal order. The female vampire is no exception; that a woman *is* a monster in film does not mean she *becomes-monster*, in the schizosophic sense, particularly if she is (hyper)sexualized, made yet another object of the male gaze. Of course, female vampires are not new to fiction; Joseph Sheridan LeFanu's *Carmilla*, with its female vampire antagonist, predated Bram Stoker's *Dracula* by two decades, and more recently Harry Benshoff has written of the lesbian vampire film, in which the female vampire serves the doubled function of the (already-queer) monster in subverting the love story between the heterosexual protagonists. Nevertheless, *Twilight's* Bella and *Underworld's* Selene are female vampires of a different nature, in no small part because both *become mothers*. Hence, while Rosi Braidotti finds a progressive thrust in the original *Alien* films leading from "the 'new female monsters' engineered by late post-industrial technosocieties" to "the heroic subjects who are most likely to save humanity" (2002: 209), a defining feature of *Alien's* Ripley is that *she is not a mother*. In *Aliens*, we learn that Ripley has a daughter back on Earth, yet that daughter has grown up and died without her mother's presence while Ripley, cryogenically preserved, was lost in space. Ripley may adopt a surrogate daughter in Newt, but as Newt dies in the crash that begins the third film, and as Ripley 8 can hardly be said to "mother" the alien offspring she delivers in *Alien: Resurrection*, it seems women in the twentieth century could become heroes only insofar as they were not mothers.

So what about when women become monsters, who then become mothers? There is an argument to be made in both *Twilight* and *Underworld* (to differing degrees) that each heroine's power, Bella's and Selene's, is neutralized via motherhood. Nevertheless, these vampire-heroines remain heroic monsters, and importantly for this project, monsters who have achieved miraculous births and resurrections. Both characters become, if not Holy Virgins, simultaneously goddesses and the god who dies and is born again, more powerful. It will be the project of this chapter to demonstrate phallocentric culture's attempts to use motherhood to erase their monstrousness, declaim their heroicness, and somehow untangle their femaleness.

The Blood ~~Is~~ Gives Life: Evolution in *Underworld*

Fluidity could be called the primary diagrammatic component of the first two films in the *Underworld* franchise, *Underworld* and *Underworld: Evolution*. Rainfall is almost constant throughout these films, particularly the first: raindrops slide down windows; splash up from vehicles and pavement; soak hair, skin, and clothes. *Underworld*'s camera regularly zooms in on close-ups of beakers filled with multicolored liquids; light pools like water on leather outfits; silver nitrate bubbles out of bullet wounds; and important battle scenes, including the film's climactic fight, take place in flooded tunnels, where water showers off the barbs of a silver whip. As will be discussed shortly, this liquid perception extends into the morphing of the Lycan characters. And, naturally, as these are vampire films, there is blood, captured in crimson close-up, echoed in the scarlet carpets and ruby drapes of the Vampire coven's mansion: blood bursting out of flesh pierced by fangs, gliding down the edges of swords, puddling around corpses, shimmering inside crystal goblets.

Both Kristeva and Creed have written of phallocentric culture's fear of blood's "impurity." Blood is associated with women through both menstruation and childbirth; passage through the birth canal is seen as "contaminating" the (male) subject with bodily fluids, excrement, and placental blood, or what Creed calls "traces" of being inside, undifferentiated from, the mother (1993: 49). Blood and fertility, blood and impurity, are thus conflated in the female body, and Creed rightly draws a connection between the phallocentric abjection of the maternal body and horror film's play on phallocentric fear of impurity, of contamination and contagion (1993: 49–50). But there is another side, a schizosophic side, to this monstrously feminine abjection, hinted at, as Creed quotes, in Kristeva's take on the nonbinary—or, we might say, hybrid—nature of blood as simultaneously "vital" and "impure," a "fascinating semantic crossroads . . . where *death* and *femininity, murder* and *procreation, cessation of life* and *vitality*" coalesce (qtd. in Creed 1993: 62), much as they do in the figure of the vampire.

Contamination and contagion through and of the blood are taken a step further in the *Underworld* series. Alexander Corvinus, the "original immortal," became so after his blood mutated in response to a devastating medieval plague, making him immune to disease and old age, capable of rapid healing and self-regeneration. Corvinus passed this mutation on to his sons through *his* blood, so that when Markus was bitten by a bat, he became the first Vampire. William, bitten by wolf, became the first Lycan. On the one hand, as cinepsychoanalysis would argue, the monstrous results of *man's* blood being (pro)creative should not be overlooked. Yet "contamination" by the Vampire or Lycan virus, although monstrous, is in fact *desirable* in the *Underworld* franchise. These are not films in which a plucky band of humans slay the monster hordes, for while vampires and werewolves may be monsters, they are the only characters that matter in *Underworld*; the films center around those monsters who become heroes in ways that have little or nothing to do with the human world. Having developed the technology to produce synthetic blood, Vampires, according to Selene, try not to kill humans, presumably so they can live undetected but also, she tells her lover Michael, because "you do not want that on your conscience"; hence, humans do not even play the limited role of prey in these stories. Moreover, it seems only those humans who are already in some way different can withstand the bite of a Vampire or a Lycan. In most cases, rather than Turning into an immortal, the weaker, lesser mortal races are simply killed by the Vampire or Lycan virus.

Lucien, the leader of the Lycan clan, is the first to see the (pro)creative possibilities of this contaminated blood. Following centuries of war between the Vampires and the Lycans, Lucien in the first film is seeking to evolve the Lycan race by using the blood of the mortal Michael Corvin, a direct descendant of Alexander Corvinus, to transform his werewolf pack into all-powerful Lycan warriors. Yet at this point man's parthenogenetic quest to genetically engineer a "superior" race is interrupted, as it is *Selene*'s blood/bite which transforms Michael into the first of his kind: a hybrid, "neither Vampire nor Lycan," with strengths and characteristics of both.

In *Underworld: Evolution*, Selene's evolution will begin, when she drinks the blood of Alexander Corvinus and develops powers, such as resistance to daylight, unique among Vampires. However, it would not be fair to say that Selene becomes a hybrid. Her evolution therefore lacks the procreative overtones of Michael's evolution, which returns us, ultimately, to the politics of reproduction.

Miscegenation has almost from the genre's inception been a concern of the vampire narrative; again, Frohreich, who also writes of the *Underworld* series, has gone so far as to claim the true horror of Bram Stoker's *Dracula* lay in its nineteenth-century audience's fear of "mixing" white, Western European blood with the blood (and culture) of immigrants (2013: 33). In fact, one reason the scarcity of actors of color in the *Underworld* series is so troubling is this racial implication; in *Underworld*, it seems, racial difference can be addressed only in the realm of fantasy, in the context of the Vampire/Lycan binary. Nevertheless, the obsession of the Vampire elder Viktor—Selene's surrogate father and immortal sire—with maintaining the "purity" of the Vampire bloodline ultimately makes Viktor both the first film's antagonist and, more importantly, antiquated in the *Underworld* universe. Viktor's obsession with purity started the Vampire/Lycan war, for after Viktor learned his daughter Sonya had taken Lucien, a Lycan, as her lover, he had her executed—not, he tells Selene, as punishment for her sexual transgression (although the manner of Sonya's execution, immolation by sunlight, would seem to suggest otherwise) but because it was his duty to protect the Vampire bloodline from "the abomination growing in her womb." Lucien, on the other hand, has recognized, after centuries of fighting a losing war, that to remain "pure" is to eventually go extinct. Evolving through the "mixing" of bloodlines is the key to survival; change is necessary for the continuation of the species.

In their meditation on fluidity, the first two films highlight the desirability of this evolution. Morphing, what Anna Powell describes as "the fluid technique of computer-generated becoming" (2005: 91) as solid matter "flows" from one "state" into another, contributes to the films' overall molecular experience, yet we should note that morphing and transforming are not affectively synonymous in film. The werewolves in *Twilight* have a wolf-form, for instance, but any affective experience of their human-to-wolf transformation is prevented by computer-generated effects that make the change instantaneous, too quick to be perceived. *Underworld* and *Underworld: Evolution*, by contrast, center for viewers the embodied flow of human-into-monster. When we first see a Lycan transformation, we watch as ripples move beneath the skin of a Lycan man; in medium close-up, we watch as his human nose elongates into a snout, his teeth grow into fangs, and his limbs and torso extend into the body of an enormous, furry beast which, already-hybrid, exists somewhere between wolf and man. (In *Twilight,* by contrast, the werewolves' wolf/human bodies remain visually distinct.) Sonsigns like snapping tendons and breaking bones add to the molecular experience of the Lycan's transformation, affecting viewers into experiencing the dissolution-of-form necessary for a human body to become a monstrous body. When Michael initially transforms into a Lycan, the camera goes so far as to plunge *inside* him, revealing tissue, artery, organ, and muscle as internal human anatomy morphs into the anatomy of a Lycan.

Once the camera moves inside a character, boundaries between inside/outside, between open and closed, have quite literally been dissolved. Michael's hybridity only expands from this point on, visually emphasized by his uniquely liquid-black eyes, Lycan torso and claws, and Vampire fangs. It is the queering of Michael's male-masculinity through hybridity that likewise "queers" his relationship with Selene, rescuing *Underworld* from being yet another heteronormative Romeo-and-Juliet love story—for Michael and Selene are *partners* in every sense of the word. Despite how powerful Michael is, his power does not diminish Selene's: He needs her to teach him the limits and possibilities of his new hybrid form, and when he is killed by the Vampire elder Markus, it is Selene's blood, newly evolved from the blood of Alexander Corvinus, that brings him back to life.[1] Both *Underworld* and *Underworld: Evolution* are punctuated by mutual saves as Michael and Selene fight for and alongside one another, in an equitable partnership undefined by rigid gender roles. It is therefore no surprise that their love affair begins with a glorious sex scene, over which light flows like water. Skin to skin, Michael's body and Selene's rise and fall together, to the accompaniment of orchestral music that sweeps the viewer up inside it, until the screen dissolves on a close-up of Selene's extended fangs and preternaturally blue eyes.

Far from being punished for this sexual encounter (or conflicted by it, as Bella Swan is by her sexual desires in *Twilight*), in *Underworld: Evolution* Selene wins the day. In the film's climactic battle, Michael and Selene fearlessly defend one another, both proving capable of what Carol Clover calls the Final Girl's "self-rescue." Michael kills William Corvinus, the original Lycan, while Selene slays Markus, the original Vampire. Having thus dispatched the Vampire/Lycan binary, as well as the representatives of the purity-obsessed patriarchal regime, Michael and Selene, our hybrid lovers, share a passionate embrace in the sunrise, which also serves to confirm Selene's escape from the phallocentric gender binary; now, she is immune to the sunlight that was used to destroy Viktor's rebellious daughter. In a final voiceover as the camera pans across the destruction of her (phallic) ancestral castle, Selene delivers what sounds very much like the rallying cry for a nonbinary reality: "An unknown chapter lies ahead. The lines that divided the clans have now been blurred. . . . All that is certain is that darkness lies ahead. But now, for the first time, I look into the light with new hope."

Then come the sequels.

If fluidity is the diagrammatic component of *Underworld* and its sequel *Evolution*, solidity would be the diagrammatic component of the franchise's twenty-first-century installments, *Underworld: Awakening* and *Blood Wars*. Liquid perception, whether it be rainfall or blood or morphing, is replaced in the cinematic assemblage by images of steel, concrete, stone, and iron. In *Underworld: Awakening*, alleys between skyscrapers, corridors inside the AntiGen laboratory, even the levels of a parking garage form a maze that traps and confines the once-fluid Selene; in *Blood Wars*, the marble halls of the Eastern coven's mansion become a literal prison where our vampire heroine is first caged, then paralyzed. At the same time solidity is privileged over fluidity, the films' expressive balance begins to shift from molecular to molar elements. These more recent films focus more on action than affect, particularly during fight sequences. Hence, the highly stylized battle between Selene and the Lycan Marius in *Blood Wars* may see Selene impressively back-flipping from frozen waterfalls and sliding across ice to retrieve a fallen sword, yet the fight lacks the claustrophobic feeling of Selene, in *Evolution*, fighting a chained Lycan at close range inside a tunnel, with the camera cutting rapidly between close-ups of her wide eyes and the Lycan's terrifying fangs, while ear-splitting gunfire and inhuman growls assault viewers' auditory nerves. Moreover, molar techniques such as voiceover, perhaps necessary in the original films to help viewers identify with Selene, a character we would normally dismiss as a monster, serve to more emphatically tell viewers *what* to think about the heroes and villains of these films, forcing us into an identification with Selene's perspective that remains uncomplicated by more freeing molecular elements. In fact, the twenty-first-century *Underworld* films have drifted so far from fluidity that when we rejoin

Selene following a brief prologue in *Awakening*, we discover that she has been literally frozen in place for the last twelve years, cryogenically imprisoned by the evil corporation AntiGen. During this time, she also unknowingly gave birth to Eve, a hybrid child conceived with Michael before their capture.

As Selene's pregnancy and its attendant possibilities for becoming occurs off-screen, it seems to follow that *Awakening* and *Blood Wars* spend little narrative or expressive energy on "evolutions" of any kind. The morphing that proved so affective in *Underworld* and *Evolution* has in these films been replaced by molar transformation; when shape-shifting occurs, it happens swiftly and is accompanied by fewer sonsigns than in the original two films. Even Eve, the hybrid child, does not morph on-camera. Eve may be visually distinct from a human once she transforms into her hybrid state, with liquid-black eyes, Lycan claws, and Vampire fangs, but since her transformations occur in the blink of an eye, it remains essentially a *dis*embodied process; certainly, viewers are given no opportunity to assemble with the experience of becoming-monster. Nor does Selene visually change in any significant way throughout the films. Rather than evolving or adapting, Selene is focused on *escaping* from this brave new world in which she finds herself, for blood, the source of power and change in the first two films, has become dangerously impure again. Through a series of events the films never fully explain, humans have discovered the existence of Vampires and Lycans. Departing from the Gothic surrealism of the original films, real-world-style news coverage conveys this backstory, along with a montage of humans "cleansing" the "diseased" races from the population. The genocide is necessary, we are told by the leader of AntiGen, because extermination is the only way to stop the Vampire/Lycan contagion from spreading. There is no cure for becoming-monster.

In the opening of *Awakening*, Michael and Selene are captured attempting to flee a burning human city. When Selene wakes inside her cryogenic cell, we also discover that the Vampire/Lycan binary Michael's hybridity seemed to disrupt, and which Michael and Selene's hybrid child would seem to have the potential to dissolve, has resolidified. Lycans, not humans, control AntiGen and have been secretly experimenting with Eve's blood to create a race of super-Lycans capable of conquering both Vampires and humans. As Selene plunges deeper into the maze of Vampire and Lycan politics, in which both races are now vying to genetically engineer "purer" warriors from Eve's hybrid blood, her attempts to escape are mirrored by the many images of mist, fog, vapor, fumes, and dust that permeate both films. Only these gaseous elements stand a chance of seeping between the resolidified, binary borders Selene and Michael fought so hard to free each other from.

It would be satisfying, therefore, to see in Selene's fate at the end of *Blood Wars* a becoming-imperceptible. Slain by the Lycan Marius, Selene is sunk beneath the icy waters of the Nordic clan's magically restorative pools. The next time we see her, she appears onscreen as a blur of white light—a phasing of atoms that evanesces among the invading Lycan forces, slaying at incredible speeds, eventually leading the Vampires to victory over their ancient (racial) enemies. Selene's ability to "phase," to breakdown her molecules and reform in another place at will, is credited to her passage through the Otherworld, from death back to life. However, like her monstrous pregnancy, this journey occurs off-screen. Selene as she (re)appears to us is visibly unchanged, aside from a few white streaks in her hair; she may now be able to breakdown her own solid form, but the film stubbornly resists inviting viewers into this dissolution, so unlike our embodied experience of falling into the fire with Ripley at the end of *Alien³*. Moreover, the phasing effects, like the morphing techniques in *Awakening* and *Blood Wars*, are rendered so that Selene remains mostly a solid being. As viewers, we never experience any dissolution alongside her.

The end of *Blood Wars*, then, leaves off with Selene as an evolved creature, yet evolution here has lost the force of a verb: evol*ving* foregone for evol*ution*, *being* substituted for *becoming*. Selene may have traveled beyond death to secure her new power, but by the end of *Blood Wars*, it is clear this power comes at the sacrifice of any meaningful relationship with her child—which is why it is important not to accept the postfeminist stance that Selene be declared a victor. Once a fugitive for slaying Viktor to save Michael, Selene tells us in the film's final voiceover that she has now been granted a seat on the council of Vampire elders—yet this political and martial power comes at the cost of the more personal victories Selene achieved in the first two films. Michael is dead, killed by the Lycans; there will be no resurrection for him this time, no happy family reunion. The queer potential of his relationship with Selene follows Michael into his grave, while Eve simply vanishes from the narrative—and the screen.

Selene never interacts with her daughter in *Blood Wars*. Any tenuous, tender connections she and Eve forged throughout *Awakening*, while Selene was focused on saving not the world but her child, are rendered moot by the end of *Blood Wars*, when Eve reappears silently to join Selene in a decidedly non-maternal reunion. By this point, Selene has died and been reborn (her own voiceover tells us) into an entirely different character from the mother Eve fought to save in *Awakening*. Eve herself has grown from a frightened, confused child, raised in a laboratory and unable to protect herself, into an independent young adult. She returns to Selene, alone and unaided, as a monster on equal footing, no longer in need of any "mothering." Thus, Selene must ultimately be "freed" to pursue her political destiny by having the demands of motherhood placed behind her, for while Eve remains part of the narrative, *Awakening* insists on reading Selene's warrior instincts through a more "basic" maternal instinct to protect her offspring, preventing her from fighting for any larger (that is, political) cause. That Selene's rebirth in *Blood Wars*, like Eve's birth in *Awakening*, takes place off-screen is also telling. Giving birth and being born are messy, bloody affairs. *Awakening* and *Blood Wars* sterilize birth (and rebirth) for viewers, and in so doing negate the monstrously feminine hybridity of blood, which contains both death and life. Blood, too, gradually solidifies in these films, "drying up" (as Deleuze and Guattari say of molar elements) any two-way flow between characters—for blood offers more than immortality in *Underworld*. It also contains *memory*.

Much is made of these blood-memories in the first two films. After being Turned by Lucien in *Underworld*, Michael experiences his Lycan sire's horror at being forced to witness Sonya's execution. In the same film, Selene uses her blood to awaken Viktor so he will witness Kraven's betrayal through her memories. In *Evolution*, Markus drinks Selene's blood to uncover the map to his brother William's prison, buried in Selene's all-but-forgotten human past. These blood-memories are conveyed through liquid-like flashbacks, with blurred edges, monochrome filters, and fluid-yet-fragmented montages (image flowing into image, flowing into image). Such hallucinatory effects prevent viewers from experiencing the flashbacks as part of the linear narrative, so that blood-memories in the first two films have as much in common with what Powell calls "dream sequences" (2005: 175) as flashbacks.

Psychoanalysis mines dreams for symbols and archetypes in the same way cinepsychoanalysis seeks out representations in the waking fantasy of film. Schizoanalysis, on the other hand, is more interested in the filmic flashback or dream sequence's affective potential, as both can serve to disrupt viewers' sense of linear time and ourselves as fixed-and-frozen beings. In *Underworld*, these dreamlike flashbacks' distortion of linear time serves a somewhat different function than the flashbacks of *Mary Shelley's Frankenstein*, which revealed to viewers time's forkings as Frankenstein and his Creature reached the present moment. Flashbacks in *Underworld* and *Underworld: Evolution* are more akin to the schizosophic concept of *duration*, the recognition that the past not only influences the present but, through memory, *assembles with* the present, through our consciousness. Memory, Deleuze and Guattari argue, thereby ruptures fixed-and-frozen ego formations as it prompts us to experience and reflect on ourselves as Bergson's living things constantly becoming (Powell 2005: 158). Powell even connects duration explicitly to creation and evolution, arguing, as David Rodowick, Elizabeth Grosz, and Teresa Rizzo have, that duration makes us mindful of the endless evolution-of-self that occurs throughout our lives, and which moreover disrupts any static identity we might attach to, as well as the processes of molar organization that seek to territorialize our bodies by freezing us into beings, rather than becomings.

Awareness of duration—to recall that we are not now as we always have been but are constantly becoming different-from-ourselves—can, as Rodowick and Rizzo argue, open us up to affirmative experiences of difference. For once we recognize the futility of ascribing to ourselves an identity that is in every moment changing, right down to the cells dividing in our bodies, we have been set on a path toward becoming the Body without Organs (BwO). Flashbacks in *Underworld* and *Underworld: Evolution* go a step further by opening viewers to the experiences of an/other's duration. In these films, through the flow of blood-memories, a character experiences, viscerally, what the other has seen, heard, tasted, touched, and smelled. Such embodied assemblage exceeds the boundaries of empathy or identification, offering the chance for becoming-with.

Although flashbacks all but disappear from *Awakening* and *Blood Wars*—when they are used, they are far less distortive or disruptive, serving mainly to remind viewers of events we may have forgotten from past films, and with the exception of Michael's death, are even constructed out of prior footage—*Awakening* initially offers an exciting alternative to blood-memories, as Eve and Selene turn out to share a psychic link. At certain points, Selene experiences the present moment as though she is inside Eve's body, looking through Eve's eyes. While Selene and Eve, as mother and daughter, share consciousness, the dynamic, creative power of maternal blood is once again brought to the forefront. Selene and Eve may now be separate, no longer sharing a body, yet they are linked; the border between mother/child, self/other has been tantalizingly blurred. Unfortunately, through means that are never explained, this bond has been severed by *Blood Wars*, leaving Selene now physically and psychically separate from her daughter.

The increasing molarity of the *Underworld* films exposes once again the limits of the monstrous-feminine within the gynesitic project. While the postfeminist view might have it that Selene provides a progressively feminist narrative, in truth the end of *Blood Wars* only succeeds in bringing us back full circle to *Alien*'s Ellen Ripley. Selene's power, like Ripley's, depends upon her freedom from (if not outright rejection of) the maternal-feminine, after which she (re)gains agency and realizes her (political) destiny. In almost forty years, it seems we have managed to return only to our original conclusion: that in the phallocentric world, the still-binary masculinist world, the only path to empowerment for women is to become more like men. Sadly, in a world that still denies sexual difference, women may have succeeded in becoming-monster, but they have not yet managed to simultaneously become mothers.

Prey Becomes Predator: Molecular Ruptures in *Twilight*'s Hegemonic Narrative

Under no circumstances would I argue that the *Twilight* books or films represent a feminist text; in nearly every respect, *Twilight* oppresses and represses both female and queer agency. Nevertheless, I maintain that there is a *potentially* monstrous text within the *Twilight* film franchise, one that, ultimately unsuccessfully, attempts to trace a line of flight from a hegemonic series of films determined to operate as a contained, unified master narrative. This section will demonstrate how schizoanalysis can help us *think* that monster-text's potential as viewers become-prey with Bella, who desires becoming-vampire. That is, without excusing any of the film's misogynist content, in an embodied experience of the films we as viewers may find ourselves sympathetic to the fragility of Bella's human body as her bone snaps under the lightest pressure of James's foot; at the same time, we may be awed, perhaps even seduced, by the vampires' alignment with natural forces as perilous as they are strange and beautiful. Like the natural world it often meditates upon, vampires in the first *Twilight* film are depicted as a primordial force, incorporated into arcane, uncontrollable sources of power humans remain separate from, other-than, and subjected-to. In an embodied experience of the film, we experience with Bella the desire to become-vampire, a desire that insistently disrupts the film's intended patriarchal narrative.

At the outset of this section, it seems important to point out, as has Fleur Diamond, that the *Twilight* saga as a whole is a product of a phallocentric culture in which, despite decades of feminist activism, "young women today still struggle with the myths of an institutional heterosexuality in which 'female desire' is in some sense oxymoronic" (2011: 43). In our postfeminist society, women are exhorted to be desirable *to* men while at the same time we are conditioned to desire being *like* men, in terms of jettisoning traditionally ascribed "feminine" attributes in order to enjoy the economic, political, social, and sexual freedom traditionally reserved for white, heterosexual, able-bodied, cisgender males. Contemporary norms of gender identity and (hetero)sexual relations, Diamond argues, have conflated heteronormativity with misogyny, a heterosexist position in which, as was argued previously, women are always defined, negatively, as different *from* men via lack: the "phallic/castrated" binary, as Diamond puts it (2011: 43). Thus, we must consider what the *Twilight* saga reveals about the impossibility of female agency—sexual, maternal, political, or otherwise—in a still-binary, still-phallocentric culture. Moreover, the crisis of that very culture may be revealed by schizoanalyzing the films' struggle to maintain their heroine's submission to male authority once Bella comes to share Edward's monstrous power.

From a content standpoint, Stephenie Meyer's book series hinges on teenager Bella Swan's desire to become immortal and the resistance of her vampire boyfriend to granting that wish. In the films, Bella's desire for immortality is characterized as a desire to spend eternity with Edward, while Edward's refusal is predicated upon his desire to save Bella's immortal soul from eternal damnation. In the books, this dynamic is perhaps more nuanced, as Bella's quest for immortality is more blatantly motivated than it is in the films by a desire for eternal youth and beauty. Hence, while we should not posit a feminist victory in Bella's obsession with her *looks*, the books do grant her slightly more agency than the films, in which her entire future rests on whether she will be loved by Edward. Nor do the films explore the books' murkier subplot of Edward's desire to keep Bella mortal because that is how he prefers her: the warm, soft, blushing virgin Beauty to his immortal Beast, in danger every moment of falling prey to his (blood)lust.

The films choose not to explore these elements, sublimating both Bella's (admittedly skewed) desire for the hegemonically feminine "empowerment" of youth and beauty and Edward's murderous desire for her blood into long, lip-biting stares brimming with teenage angst. In the films, Bella's longing to become immortal is hopelessly conflated with her sexual desire for Edward, who insists he will only Turn—and have sex with—her *if* she marries him. Operating from the books' regressive, abstinence-only stance, the films thus return us to a prefeminist landscape in which Edward asserts patriarchal control over female sexual agency. His self-professed "old-fashioned" morality insists Bella remain a virgin until she is wed, the phallocentric imagination once again conflating the "purity" of a woman's body with her soul's worthiness to enter the Kingdom of God.[2]

For much of the *Twilight* saga, Bella is caught between the vampire who (rightly, the films portray) wants to protect her virginity and the werewolf Jacob Black who refuses to take no for an answer—again rightly, the film tells us, for in a further disavowal of female agency, even if she won't actively consent, the films make clear that Bella *wants* Jacob to seduce her. Nor can Bella's desire for the carnal pleasures Jacob freely offers be easily separated from her desire to possess the phallus itself, to know the penetrative pleasure of having a "pair of her own"—fangs, that is. Within such a conservative narrative, the only way to solve Bella's psychosexual crisis is for her to marry—and in *Twilight: Breaking Dawn*, she does. Were the films to end there, with the wedding, the phallocentric, heteronormative message of *Twilight* might be tied up with a neat bow, the franchise unworthy of inclusion in a volume such as this. Yet the films forge ahead, into deeper waters, where once wed Bella's abstinence is rewarded with a night of rough sex that leaves her physically battered—and hungry for more.

Before turning to the *Twilight* films' expressions to look at the moments of molecularity that threaten to rupture the films' primarily molar expressions, in order to contextualize those molar-versus-molecular tensions we must remain focused for the moment on the content of the final installments of the series' five-part sequence, *Breaking Dawn: Part 1* and *Breaking Dawn: Part 2*. By the end of *Part 1*, *Twilight* is in very deep waters indeed. What could have been consensual sexual pleasure on Edward and Bella's honeymoon assumes overtones of domestic violence as Edward, echoing abusers everywhere, repents once he sees Bella's bruises and vows not to touch her again while she remains human. The solution to this seems obvious—alone on their private island, Edward could easily Turn Bella—except Bella's sexual awakening complicates any such straightforward march to a monstrous happy ending. Now that she has been penetrated, the film seems to say, Bella no longer desires to penetrate. Instead, she wishes to remain human, to continue having sex with Edward while she desires him more than blood. Submission to patriarchal control, herein portrayed as the marriage bed, therefore seems to have "cured" Bella of her series-long desire to become a vampire. And her willing subjugation to Edward's monstrous power appears to be rewarded with a different type of happy ending when Bella-the-virgin discovers she is about to achieve the pinnacle of female accomplishment in a patriarchal narrative and become Bella, the wife-and-mother.

Except. Horror here interrupts the comic ending of the conservative marriage plot as the fetus turns out to be a monster, sucking the life from its mother as it consumes Bella from the inside out. Unlike *Prometheus*'s Elizabeth Shaw, who unhesitatingly terminated her monstrous "pregnancy," Bella immediately and categorically rejects the idea of abortion. This decision pits her against Edward, who wants to destroy the fetus to save Bella's life. Throughout the last half of *Breaking Dawn: Part 1*, viewers watch as Bella visibly wastes away, yet this is no *Rosemary's Baby*, for Bella, unlike Rosemary, is more than willing to carry "the monster's seed." The film's convoluted anti-abortion message is finally brought to fruition when Bella is martyred in childbirth, her faith that her baby would be more miracle than monster proven true, putting even the ever-faithful Edward's doubt to shame.

This is still Bella's story, though, and the messy, bloody birth of the vampire child (to be discussed shortly) is hastily ushered off-screen for the main event: Bella's (re)birth as a vampire. At this point the film's patriarchal message—unintentionally, we should note—begins to fracture, revealing tensions long present in the film franchise. For although Bella's "maternal instinct" appears to mute the bloodlust she was warned would be insatiable for the first few months of her undead life, Bella is nevertheless now a monster, and as a newborn, even more powerful than her husband.

Although Bella's new, immense vampiric power will be directed in the series finale toward the "proper" feminine goal of protecting her offspring, the lengths to which *Breaking Dawn: Part 2* must go to contain and restrain Bella's monstrousness only serves to highlight how unstable the franchise's hegemonic, phallocentric message has become. The cracks within this message are obvious from the first film, once we step back to schizoanalyze them. For the more the franchise seeks to create molar identification between female viewers and its female protagonist, to convey the series' essentially anti-feminist message to a primarily female audience, the more the final film must somehow make its newly empowered heroine female-feminine enough to remain within the phallocentric gender binary. Only by submitting to her husband, in other words, will Bella earn her happy ending. Yet this containment of the monstrous-feminine proves no small task, since Bella has by this point succeeded where nearly every other female monster has failed: She has become both mother and monster.

The beginning of this section asserted that Bella becomes-prey in the franchise's first, and most molecular, film. *Twilight* has its molar elements, to be sure: popular music, voiceover (lifted almost verbatim from the books), and heavy reliance on the shot/reaction shot formula. Yet, in the first film, these molar expressions are intercut with moments of molecularity all the more affecting for their incongruity. From the opening moments of *Twilight*, humans, both male and female, are depicted as prey, the weaker species, while vampires, both male and female, are aligned with the harsher, stronger, more ancient forces of nature. The franchise's first film, with its insistent images of mountains, forests, waves, waterfalls, and all manner of dense green fauna, uses nature to both highlight and soften the vampiric threat. For while nature can be terrifying and deadly, it can also be awe-inspiring, more than beautiful—divine.

The film opens with Bella's voiceover (a molar technique) playing across footage of a deer being chased through the woods—later, we learn, by Edward, who subsists on a diet of animal rather than human blood. As Bella is conflated with the deer, Edward is insistently conflated with a predator, specifically a bird of prey. His room in the Cullen mansion is nest-like, with a window that opens straight onto a tree; he runs and climbs with the swiftness of flight; and when he first meets Bella, a stuffed owl stands behind him in the scene, its piercing black eyes mirroring close-ups of his. Yet the predator/prey binary is often confused within this first film. As Edward insists to Bella that he has killed people, while Bella insists she "doesn't care," the camera shows Bella pursuing Edward, perched bird-like above her in a tree, higher up into the limbs, a cat cornering her prey; he wants to kill *her,* Edward insists, while Bella, against all reason, insists that he "won't hurt [her]." The scene, unable to resolve this crisis without also undoing the lion/lamb, predator/prey binary it has been constructing, instead dissolves into mist, trapping Bella and Edward between two slabs of rock as they declare their love for one another. We then soar up into the clouds with the camera, which seems to have taken flight out of the narrative and into the cosmos, into a whiteness, a blankness, a perpetual light with no beginning or end.

Is this a becoming-imperceptible—an any-space-whatever? What we as viewers are meant to make of this scene is difficult to say. The first film stubbornly denies any character the opportunity to become-monster: "monster" here still equates with "evil," and a binary is drawn between evil vampires like the nomad James, who lives by his own code and enjoys killing humans, and "good" vampires like the Cullens who, in some sense, are more human than humans, so committed to remaining within the mortal world that they pretend to be perpetual teenagers, endlessly repeating high school in different towns. In fact, one way in which the franchise molarizes its vampires is by fixing and freezing

Edward into an eternal seventeen-year-old, one who, unlike the vampires we will meet in the next chapter, seems to have stopped aging emotionally as well as physically at the moment of his Turning. Edward certainly does not change from one film to the next. Tellingly, neither does Bella.

A stark shift in expression takes place between the first and second film, one that directs *New Moon* away from *Twilight's* molecular elements. In *Twilight*, the camera frequently comes unmoored from the action, spinning wildly through the towering trees of the Pacific Northwest; circling characters; gliding across mountains or streams; at times simply soaring into the sky before swooping down to "find" Bella and Edward amid the vastness of the forest or next to a mighty river. Such shots represent a *deframing*, a term Deleuze used to describe how the camera, divorced from any perspective of or on a character, may soar and spin of its own accord, providing perspectives and angles unrelated to the diegesis. According to Deleuze, deframing reveals "an absolute aspect by which the closed system opens on to a duration which is immanent to the whole universe, which is no longer a set and does not belong to the order of the visible" (1986: 17). To understand this, we must realize that a part of every frame incorporates the out-of-frame, the whole to which we understand these characters to belong; deframings are those moments when, for no narrative purpose, the camera spins and soars in such a way that viewers become aware of the whole to which we are (inter)connected, of the out-of-frame as more than backstory, world-building, or context—as a "more radical Elsewhere, outside homogenous space and time . . . introducing the transspatial and the spiritual into the system which is never perfectly closed" (Deleuze 1986: 17).

By *New Moon*, gone are these sweeping visual shots, as well as the melding of nature with narrative, the green and vegetative closeness that in *Twilight* felt almost claustrophobic, as though we might become-plant by dissolving (decaying?) into (inside?) the earth. *Twilight,* director Catherine Hardwicke's potentially monstrous text, disappears inside *New Moon's* resolutely molar expressions. Even the moments that should be molecular, such as Bella's descent into depression or her hallucinations of Edward, are over-coded by popular music, expository dialogue, and voiceover. These molar techniques do more than force us into subjective perspectives on/of the characters. Most importantly, they block us, the viewer, from experiencing disorientation or dissolution, or any deterritorialization of our molar identities that might set us on the path to becoming.

Hence, it follows that the one becoming in *New Moon* that should be obvious, Jacob's becoming-animal, is treated as a sudden and surprise CGI reveal—an instantaneous transformation, with no opportunity for viewers to assemble with the metamorphosis as there was in the original *Underworld* films. For Jacob never becomes-wolf; even the close-ups of Bella reflected in his distinctly wolf pupil tell us that Jacob is still Jacob, still possessed of, and by, his human subjectivity. Jacob therefore remains a wolf/man, a divided binary being, his transformation not so much a becoming as an enforced nuptial of the human and monstrous that Jacob takes scant pleasure in.

Although *New Moon* adamantly closes off possibilities for viewers' becomings, there are molecular elements in both it and the franchise's third film, *Eclipse*. Unfortunately, these are too marginalized to significantly affect viewers. Both films forego Hardwicke's nuances of deframing and camera consciousness for traditional steady-cam shots, minimal close-ups, and more popular music than score, sound effects, or silence. Nonetheless, at a few key moments that presage the molecular tension of *Breaking Dawn: Parts 1* and *2*, molecularity does deterritorialize these primarily molar texts. The many shots of the werewolf pack without their shirts, for instance, suggest the smooth hairlessness of the werewolves' human skin; evoke warmth; and create a haptic experience for the viewer, such as when Bella is cradled against Sam Ulee's bare chest or when she presses her fist against Jacob's bare abdomen. The heat of the wolf/men contrasts with the cold hardness of the vampires' ice-white skin, a hapticity reinforced in *New Moon* as Edward's face fissures into black lines that mirror the lines on the marble floor while he and Felix fight in the Volturi's lair, or in *Eclipse* by the snow-covered mountaintop where Edward finally faces down Victoria.

Primal elements like earth (stone), water (including rain and snow), and fire are also evoked in both films. The prologue to *Eclipse* is perhaps the most molecular scene of the film: As raindrops slide across the opening titles, the shot suddenly dissolves into a rain-soaked city street; the camera stalks a mortal boy, Riley, down a flooded alley, swooping suddenly down at him, then circling, finally chasing him to the nighttime wharf, where a blurred image—a vampire, moving too fast to be seen—bites his palm. Yet just as the swooping, circling, and chasing turn out to be not the camera freed from any character's viewpoint but Victoria, water, although continuously present around Riley and his army of newborn vampires, even in the form of snow, never becomes a diagrammatic component on par with the fluidity of *Underworld* and *Underworld: Evolution*. Instead, *Eclipse*, like *New Moon*, refuses to surrender its wholeness to the fragmentation necessary for viewers to assemble with the film in a becoming-monster. Both films employ molar techniques like a popular music soundtrack, voiceovers, and heavy reliance on shot/reaction shot to tyrannize our viewing experience, ensuring static adherence to a forced interpretation of a predetermined hegemonic narrative where no one, ultimately, changes.

In the final two films, *Breaking Dawn: Part 1* and *Part 2*, these molar techniques do not so much lose their power as prove increasingly incompatible with the content, for in these final films the potential monster-text in the *Twilight* narrative once again makes its (unintentionally) subversive presence known. *Twilight*, *New Moon*, and *Eclipse* could be described as straightforward teenage romances with supernatural elements spliced in for novelty, but *Breaking Dawn* is more emphatically un-real, like the final book divorced from what Diamond calls the "semi-social realism" of the earlier films. Bella has now graduated from high school and is soon to enter fully into the vampires' world. *Part 1* begins with clouds rolling across a red sunlit sky; the camera then swings down at a slow-yet-dizzying angle onto—it takes our brains a moment to process what we are seeing—a roof, covered by a tarp, being pelted by rain. The door of the house bursts open; a sheet of paper flutters to the ground; and Jacob Black runs out into the rain, tearing off his shirt as he transforms into a wolf. The camera tracks back to Jacob's father, Billy, as he looks down at the wedding invitation Jacob has discarded.

Jacob's becoming-wolf is more fully realized within this film than any other. The camera enters Jacob through his wolf-eye, immediately distorting our vision with colored filters and blurred edges that disorient us as the forest flashes by, creating a sense of the wolf's speed. Later, after Jacob learns of Bella's pregnancy, the camera remains in first-person perspective as we look at the world through his wolf's eyes. Superimposed over the speeding forest, we see rapid-fire images of Bella, Edward, and the Cullens dissolving into rapidly dividing blood cells, interspersed with flashes outside of Jacob's wolf-mind as his pack howls and races through the forest. Their (human) voices mix into a disorienting cacophony—*"Jacob Jacob Jacob Jacob Jacob"*—which, in the mere simplicity of only repeating Jacob's name, leaves the wolves wolf-like, while at the same time affecting viewers into the strong telepathic and emotional bond the pack shares. Without words, in a series of red-and-blue filtered, fragmented images, Jacob-wolf conveys the crisis of Bella's monstrous pregnancy to his pack, as well as the personal pain these events have caused him. The howls and urgent voices of his brother- and sister-wolves echo his anguish.

Disappointingly, the film soon reverts from simple-yet-sophisticated image- and memory-based telepathy to a conversation among the wolves, rendered from a medium close-up perspective on the CGI wolves with the actors' digitally deepened voices echoing slightly throughout the dialogue, as if to indicate how they would sound inside each other's heads. Here the film once again blocks viewers' experience of becoming-wolf, as Jacob speaks as Jacob, Sam as Sam, anthropomorphosis muting the becoming-wolf that briefly allowed us to experience Jacob's heightened-yet-simplified wolf-perspective. The film, in other words, artificially reinforces the *wholeness* of Jacob's character, refusing to allow for the monstrous experience of Jacob's becoming-wolf—because like the vampires themselves, Jacob and the werewolves turn out to be fixed-and-frozen characters, forever young, forever unchanging, if undying.

Of course, there is another monstrous "becoming" the franchise must address: Bella's becoming-vampire, which is preceded by Bella's becoming-mother after a pregnancy that, unlike Selene's, does take place onscreen. Paradoxically, given the possibilities for becoming this monstrous pregnancy could offer embodied viewers, what occurs as the *Twilight* films progress is a more and more determined resistance to becomings of any sort, a more and more insistent reterritorialization of the molecular plane by molar expressions that, as Rizzo says, "oppress" and "restrict" viewers' interpretations. Molar expressions such as those in *New Moon* and *Eclipse* force viewers into a hegemonic perspective of/on characters and events, preventing the "unique cinematographic perception" molecular expressions create by shifting between objective and subjective perspectives in ways that deterritorialize the viewing experience (Rizzo 2012: 62). This molarity becomes so insistent in the later *Twilight* films because the hegemonic content of these narratives requires a fixing and freezing of subjective perspectives. If viewers are to celebrate Bella's capitulation to patriarchal control, masquerading as it does in the guise of a romance, then we must accept her worldview as the correct one. Obviously, such a hegemonic perspective assumes an audience willing and able to identify with Bella's white, middle-class, heterosexual, cisgender perspective; this in and of itself excludes the perspective of any viewers who do not identify as such. Moreover, even for the films' seemingly intended audience (of white, middle-class, heterosexual, cisgender women), these molar expressions become increasingly muddled by molecular elements once Bella becomes pregnant.

The morphing denied to the werewolves in *Twilight* is instead reserved for Bella's embodied transformation into a mother—and later, into a monster—in *Breaking Dawn: Part 1*. CGI allows us to experience the wasting-away of Bella's body as the vampiric fetus consumes her from within. In one memorably affecting scene, the camera moves down Bella's naked back as she is helped into the shower, lingering on the scaffolding of ribs and knobs of spine beneath her graying flesh; the bones in her face stand out just as sharply as she gazes in the mirror at Edward with hollow, sunken eyes. The transformation of this vital young woman into what could almost be compared to Cindy Sherman's "pregnant senile hag" is made no less grotesque once the vampires discover that the only way to sate the fetus's hunger, and thereby prevent Bella from starving to death, is by feeding Bella blood. Viewers cannot help but feel their gorges rise as the camera zooms in on thick red liquid moving slowly up a straw, coating Bella's lips and teeth and tongue as she declares that the blood "tastes good."

Here is the paradox the *Twilight* saga cannot resolve. Rather than being eroticized, as Kelly Oliver tells us the pregnant female body often is in romantic comedies, Bella's pregnant body is abjectified—yet this monstrous pregnancy is not meant for viewers to reject. We are clearly not meant to side with Edward or Jacob, both of whom want Bella to abort the fetus; this is again not *Rosemary's Baby*, in which we root for the monstrous fetus to be destroyed, the mother's life to be saved. *Breaking Dawn* means for viewers to side with Bella in her decision to sacrifice her own life to save her "little nudger" (as she calls the fetus in the books), resulting in an irreconcilable collision of essential motherhood with the monstrous-feminine, as the film's anti-abortion message struggles against abjectification of the maternal body that plays *on* phallocentric fears of the alien womb that houses an/other, rather than playing *to* the male gaze through eroticization.

Ultimately, *Breaking Dawn: Part 1* cannot reterritorialize its molecular aspects. The birth of the vampire child is undoubtedly the most affecting scene of the entire franchise. Bella's labor begins with the horrific sound of her spine snapping as her body twists unnaturally in response to a contraction. Sound is evacuated from the scene, and the familiar, molar shot/reaction shot formula is replaced by an increasingly fragmented series of images, all seen through Bella's fading vision. Light glints off a scalpel in close-up; blood drips from its blade as an emergency Caesarean section begins. We hear the razor-sharp steel slice through Bella's abdomen, then the stomach-turning sounds of tearing flesh as Edward bites through the placenta, all while Bella remains screamingly unanesthetized. Even the expected joy when the baby is delivered alive is short-circuited as Bella dies and Edward drives a syringe filled with his vampiric "venom" straight through her sternum, into her heart.

Bella's resurrection is rendered via elements no less molecular than her daughter's birth. The camera sweeps across a bloody sunrise over the mountains before spiraling slowly down onto a rarefied shot of Bella's emaciated form lying spread-eagle on a gurney. The sound of a slowing heartbeat begins to echo as we witness, in close-up, Bella's hair increasing in highlight and texture, becoming more lustrous than it was before. The camera moves inside of her at this point, showing Edward's venom as it races through her veins, knitting together bone and tissue, after which we watch her corpse-like skin morph into a perfectly snow-white complexion while her skeletal body plumps into vital ripeness. As the heartbeat fades, the transition from human to vampire is conveyed through a montage of flashbacks from Bella's past, superimposed by drops of blood, all the way back to her earliest memory of herself as an infant in her mother's arms. While that final memory no doubt echoes the sentiment of essential motherhood—to become a mother herself one day has been Bella's destiny, just as it is every woman's, since the day she was born—the hegemonic takeaway is ruptured again by the fact that Bella is now a mother *and* a monster. The final image of the film drives this home, zooming in on a startling close-up of Bella's blood-red vampire eyes.

Again, we cannot assert that these molecular elements add up to a feminist recuperation of the *Twilight* films. They do not. Rather, our concern should be with what these molecular ruptures within a determinedly, almost desperately molar franchise reveal about the ongoing postfeminist confusion surrounding the politics of reproduction in a postpatriarchal world—a confusion inherited by the very twenty-first-century adolescent women *Twilight* targets. Bella's refusal to abort her child under any circumstances is rewarded when she gets what she has wanted the entire series: not (only) Edward, but the vampires' eternal youth, immortal beauty, and superhuman strength, speed, and agility. But now, the franchise's final film faces a second conundrum. How can Bella, possessed of all this newfound monstrous power, be rescripted into the gender binary in such a way that she remains happily submissive to the patriarchal control literally immortalized in the Cullens' white, upper-middle-class, heterosexist nuclear family?

Breaking Dawn: Part 2 struggles with this. Tactisigns like close-ups of dust and fibers or tiny details in artwork no human eye could discern incorporate viewers into Bella's becoming-monster, allowing us to experience her new vampire senses. The changes to Bella are more than cosmetic; although her crimson irises may be the most visible indication of her undead transformation, her movements and expressions have also become cat-like, decidedly aggressive, as she sets out on a hunt with Edward. In a striking reversal of the first film's metaphoric coincidence, *Bella* is now the predator. She scents and stalks a helpless deer, shifting eerily between towering trees with movements too swift for our eyes to follow; her awesome power and monstrous aggression are further revealed when she fights and kills the mountain lion that attempts to usurp her prey.

But here molar expressions begin to predominate once more, reterritorializing the molecular elements that have threatened to open viewers, and Bella, to becoming-monster. Rather than meditate on the horror of its heroine ripping apart an animal to drink its blood, the scene shifts immediately from Bella grappling with the mountain lion to her walking calmly out of the forest with Edward, her eyes now golden to indicate her abstinence from human blood. Just as her bloodlust is immediately recast into heterosexual desire for her husband, so too is Bella's monstrous power, like Ripley's, like Selene's, immediately redirected to the "proper" maternal role of saving her offspring when her baby is threatened.

Breaking Dawn: Part 2 does more than retreat from any "semi-social realism." Like *Blood Wars*, the film plunges its viewers into a vast and only loosely explained ocean of vampire politics. A host of hitherto unknown vampires flood the narrative as the Cullen family prepares to defend its newest member from the Volturi. Though Bella and Edward remain focused on the domestic, not the political, as they seek to protect their child, the film again begins to lose control over its hegemonic message as the final fight commences. The battle itself is not that affecting—horror elements are mostly dispatched in favor of action elements, like those in the more recent *Underworld* films—but the climax does play with *time* in a remarkably affecting way, especially for first-time viewers familiar with the books. Watching the film in theaters when it released, I witnessed viewers screaming and gasping as beloved characters like the patriarch Carlisle Cullen were, noncanonically, killed off. It is not until the battle "ends" that viewers discover this "present" has been virtual: a vision of a *possible* future conveyed by the precognitive vampire Alice to the telepathic vampire Aro, to show him what *would* happen if he chose not to alter his course and leave the Cullens in peace.

For the duration of Alice's vision, the real and the imaginary, the actual and the virtual, are impossible to extricate from one another, or in other words, are *indiscernible*. In terms of the time-image, according to Deleuze "indiscernibility makes it difficult for both characters and spectators to distinguish past and present" (Powell 2005: 162), or in this case, the (possible) future from the present. As viewers, we therefore have opportunity to contemplate *time itself* as it relates to our duration, to our ability to imagine ourselves across time (in the past and in the future). As was argued in the previous chapter, if I am able to see my self-in-the-present as different from my self-in-the-past and/or to see my choices in the present as creating many possible selves in the future, my sense of myself as a whole, static, molar being is necessarily disrupted, the potential for becoming created as I experience my own *duration*—for according to Deleuze, *change* is intrinsic to duration's very meaning: "it [duration] changes and does not stop changing" (1986: 8).

What is perhaps most disappointing about the determinedly molar ending of the *Twilight* saga is, therefore, its reterritorialization of the indiscernibility experienced by viewers in this extended, embodied experience of time-as-duration. Bella now has an eternity to spend with Edward and her daughter; all the characters we thought lost in the battle turn out to still be living, and even the love triangle between Edward, Bella, and Jacob is resolved with a happy ending. Bella could now *become* anything, engaging endlessly in becoming different-from-herself—but rather than become-imperceptible, Bella is reterritorialized, fixed-and-frozen into a molar being quite unlike Deleuze's idea of the molecular vampire. Alice's final vision, in which she sees a forever-young Bella and Edward greet their immortal teenage daughter and her immortal monster-lover Jacob Black, tells us plainly that Bella will not "become" anything. Like the other vampires in *Twilight*, Bella has simply stopped, for all eternity, at the moment of her transformation, evermore to remain eighteen. The solidity of the vampires' identities is expressed visually through their impenetrable flesh, which sparkles with diamond hardness in the sun or fissures like stone when torn, somehow spilling nary a drop of blood, only rock-like powder and dust. In fact, the *Twilight* saga ends up being so staunchly molar that, in its finale, text, what Deleuze calls a "lectosign," displaces image entirely, allowing the books upon which the films are based to literally have the final word—an invocation of semiotics as ultimate control over the viewer, forcing us to "read" the film(s) as its (their) author/makers intended.

The commercial success of the *Twilight* saga is undeniable. According to the Internet Movie Database (IMDb), the final film alone raked in more than $800 million globally. Clearly—and, from a feminist perspective, troublingly—viewers responded positively to *Twilight's* hegemonic narrative and apparently felt satisfied by the franchise's distinctly molar conclusion. Yet perhaps, as Diamond observes, Bella's "happy ending" could only be achieved in the fairytale-style ending the franchise presents: "Bella obtains her desire at the expense of any involvement in the world," when "the main characters are removed from the social semi-realism of the earlier novels, withdrawing into a kind of vampire Elysium" (2011: 52). Cinematically, this withdrawal is expressed through the vivid colors of Bella and Edward's secret meadow, which fade to gray as the pages of a book appear, flipping forward in stark black and white to the last word of the books, *forever*. Perhaps in our world, the postfeminist world, the still-binary-and-phallocentric world, the gynesitic Western imagination cannot countenance a hero like Bella, both a mother and a monster, neither castrated nor castrating. Perhaps, in that sense, it is not Bella who has failed us, as feminists, but *we* who have failed her, and all the young people of her generation, by continuing to resist our own becomings.

The Post-human Resistance

Creed has written extensively of the patriarchy's need to "ensure the break, the separation of mother and child" (1993: 38). Using examples like *Psycho* and *Carrie*, Creed argues that when this separation does not occur, we may read it not so much as a patriarchal "failure" but rather as maternal "*refusal*" to submit to the demands of the patriarchy—woman's refusal to be ordered, in other words, as a molar subject, *Wo-man*, for the benefit of the patriarchal system (1993: 38). That horror film insistently portrays maternal refusal of patriarchal order as monstrous tells us much about the potential for becoming-monster that viewers of horror film might experience, when and if we allow ourselves to be deterritorialized by a film's molecular elements. Like the monstrous-feminine, the schizosophic viewer refuses to submit to binary categorization, to conform to hegemonic culture, or to freeze oneself into an over-coded molar being. Indeed, Rizzo argues that "the kind of sexual difference that emerges from the processes of becoming are always monstrous—even when there is no literal monster" because the molecular, like the monstrous, "involve[s] the crossing and defiling of boundaries and affective connections between heterogenous terms" (2012: 119).

What becomings create, in other words, is what Deleuze and Guattari call *a thousand tiny sexes*, a nonbinary model in which, as we each engage in the endless process of becoming different-from-ourselves, we cannot be separated into two distinct, binarily opposed sexes. If every biological male is always engaged in becoming different-from-himself, he cannot be fixed or frozen into the molar category Man, for he is always-already being deterritorialized by molecular assemblages that dissolve such molar categorizations, and furthermore every man, like every woman, is different not only from himself-over-time but also from every other man, who is also engaged in becoming different-from-*him*self-over-time. Moreover, as Rizzo argues, the binary oppositions that often intersect with gender identity (black/white, dis/abled, heterosexual/queer) dissolve along with binary gender under schizosophy's affirmative, qualitative model of sexual difference that, like the monstrous, disrupts molar identities or categories, including "subcategories" like race and sexual orientation. Like Deleuze and Guattari, Rizzo does not argue that these molar categories serve no political purpose, nor that we should ignore differences between individuals based on race, class, disability, ethnicity, sexual orientation, and so on. Schizosophy in fact argues quite the opposite. Yet Rizzo maintains, as do I, that when the stability of molar categories is disrupted by molecular assemblages that prompt viewers' becomings, the hegemonic, majoritarian power inherent to all binary oppositions inevitably weakens. Why is it, then, that, as viewers and as individuals, we resist becomings?

As we move into the final chapter of this book, let us pause a moment on this question, for it may help us understand why decades of progressive social movements like feminism have not resulted in the equitable, inclusive society we desire. Instead, despite a very real wish to undo oppressive sociopolitical, socioeconomic, and sociocultural systems, feminists in the twenty-first century find ourselves stuck at an ideological impasse in which we are finally beginning to realize how far from equal the rights of men and women truly are, and how far we still have to go if we want to imagine, let alone create, systems and structures that no longer rely on a white, patriarchal, heteronormative worldview. At the heart of this impasse may lie an unwillingness to radically unthink ourselves as ordered, distinct, stable subjects, for whether psychologically innate or culturally ingrained, what Powell calls "our inbuilt mental tendency to impose stable structures" (2005: 104) on an ever-changing world that is anything but stable is understandable—and extremely difficult to jettison. Doing so requires us, like Nietzsche's man at midnight, to walk right up to the edge of the abyss, perhaps even to fall over, and then, as Deleuze and Guattari say, to climb back up, not in the sense of reordering or rebuilding ourselves, but rather in the sense of allowing our molar identities to dissolve into the BwO as "we become with the world, by contemplating it. . . . Becoming plant, animal, molecular, becoming zero" (Deleuze and Guattari 1994: 169).

Gender, like race, functions in our society as a category of organizing difference. From politics to economics, the gender binary has real-world effects; nearly all religious, economic, political, and educational institutions we live by were designed by and for wealthy white European men, who have benefited most from patriarchal (and racist, and ableist, and heteronormative) oppression. If we truly wish our social institutions to become more equitable and inclusive, social progressives long ago recognized that we must be willing to transform the ideologies that underpin these institutions. Yet divorcing gender from the body did not accomplish this for feminism; it has not sufficed to claim that women are the same as men, and therefore deserve equal rights. On the other hand, reembodying gender—embracing sexual difference as difference-in-itself, without privileging maleness or masculinity, or femaleness or femininity—offers a line of flight from merely demanding minoritarian rights in a majoritarian world. Deleuze and Guattari call the schizo *free* because, as a BwO, the schizo no longer seeks to solidify their becomings, to organize themselves into categories of molar identity constructed by a society more interested in maintaining its own structures of power than in forwarding the potential of any individual. The schizo is free because they are open to duration, to endless changes; to nomadism, the crossing of borders and boundaries and the free exchange of ideas; and to becoming, the dynamic assemblages and two-way flows that allow us to "become with the world" and all forms of life within it: plant, animal, mineral, and yes, human. Becomings destabilize identity and disrupt every social structure that depends upon identification, classification, opposition, and separation. It is therefore not surprising that, personally and politically, we might find becoming dangerous, easy to resist in comparison to the seeming safety of a solidified identity such as that offered by the immortal heroes of *Twilight*.

The popularity of the *Twilight* franchise and other molar, hegemonic films reflect as much about the culture that consumes as the culture that produces them. Schizoanalysis does not see films as mere propaganda; the schizosophic cinematic assemblage is not the same as the psychoanalytic cinematic apparatus, in which ideology is reinforced via identification and representation, for whether molar or molecular, films operate ethologically to incorporate viewers into planes of perception and reflection that are either transcendent (molar) or immanent (molecular) (Rizzo 2012: 63). Hence, viewers' largely positive responses to the *Twilight* films, if their commercial success is any indication, speaks to adolescent women's ongoing need to solidify a "safe" and "acceptable" feminine identity in a postpatriarchal, postfeminist world, just as the tendency to declare the latest *Underworld* films "empowering" to women speaks to the ongoing fantasy of a safe and acceptable maternal identity in a postpatriarchal, postfeminist world. No matter how freeing becoming sounds, it is difficult for any of us to want to become-monster when monsters are what have traditionally been outcast, expelled, rejected. It is likewise difficult to know how to go about living as a woman, or a man, in a world that binarizes, flattens, or monstrousizes sexual difference.

Bella Swan fades out of our world because there is no room for her in this one. To truly become-monster would mean to escape Deleuze's "great social delirium," to embrace the reality of molecularity and imperceptibility on a plane of immanence in *this* world, for our own sake as well as for the sake of freeing all life around us to enjoy a world that is more, and more truly, equitable and inclusive, as we queer "nature" and denaturalize "identity." This is not to say a future of total non-differentiation lies before us. The molar and the molecular are always acting upon one another, reterritorializing and deterritorializing one another; furthermore, schizosophy embraces rather than flattens or denies difference. We may always need to differentiate ourselves one from another. But if we are able to see ourselves, and everyone (and everything) else, as Bergson's "living things constantly becoming," difference stops being majoritarian versus minoritarian—stops being oppressive and restrictive and becomes affirmative and inclusive, opening us to contemplating our own, and everyone (and everything) else's, potentials.

If a child is anything, it is infinite potential. Yet gender begins to operate upon children in our binary society from the moment their biological sex is known. Who this child will be, what it will wear, who and what it will desire, what will interest it, and how it will feel and think are all assumed almost unconsciously based on the binary opposition male/female. Interpolated into this binary from birth, if not earlier (thanks to sonograph technology), we may find binary gender all but impossible to denaturalize. The family, as both Tony Williams and Kimberly Jackson, drawing from Freud, have argued, has exerted powerful psychological influence over the construction of binarily gendered individuals, because gender is a category of organizing difference patriarchal society needs the family to maintain, again for the sake of society, not for the sake of the family's members.

The rise of the heroic and sympathetic monster in the twenty-first century has coincided in many ways with the rise of new, alternative family structures, from co-parenting (in which single males and females use reproductive technology to combine sperm and egg, thereafter living, and parenting, cooperatively but separately) to mommunes (in which single mothers combine financial and emotional support in communal living situations that reduce the poverty and isolation many single mother households face). Williams and Jackson have shown how changing gender roles threw the white, middle-class, patriarchal nuclear family into crisis in the 1960s and 1970s, with horror films responding by monstrousizing threats to the nuclear family. Jackson has gone on to show how, in our postpatriarchal moment, the most common resolution to these threats has been to "empower" mothers and children to survive without the father—although the expulsion of either men or women from society is hardly the answer feminists are after. The next and final chapter will explore how new models of monstrous families might decenter and denaturalize binary identity, perhaps suggesting what role the family could play in helping us to embrace the ever-in-flux, never-finished assemblages, potentialities, and transformations that characterize the dynamic world of the post-human.

5

The Post-human Family

Each of the films in this chapter offers viewers an experience of cinema as Deleuze's "direct event" primarily molecular in both content and expression. In so doing, these films return us to the volatile, monstrous, and imaginary body, offering up a potential line of flight from the hegemonic gender roles the traditional nuclear family helps to (re)enforce. By this point, it should be clear that the pressure placed on heteronormative, phallocentric thinking by decades of increasingly vocal and visible social justice activism has brought us to a moment where current cultural gender norms are, for many of us, inherently dissatisfying. In this postpatriarchal moment, social progressives, including feminists, have begun looking for new ways of being, or becoming, beyond or without the gender binary—yet it is worth asking here again, at the conclusion to this book, why an actual line of flight from the gender binary is necessary. Why, that is, would it not suffice to revalue femininity on par with masculinity and, in divorcing gender from the body, to allow for gender identities that assume multiple combinations, if not outright "free variation" (Clover 1996)?

The answer brings us back to the need to reembody, rather than disembody, sexual difference. The work of corporeal feminism has been groundbreaking in its attempts to denaturalize gender, that is, to demonstrate that gender is a social rather than a biological construction and to separate gender from the bodies it codifies as masculine or feminine. Yet to disembody gender has also in some way been to deny the powerful influence gender exerts over *the body* that is written into, and onto which is written, cultural expectations of binary gender. Moira Gatens calls this our *imaginary body*: the body that lives, feels, and experiences itself according to cultural expectations for race, age, gender, sexual orientation, dis/ability, and so on. Freeing as it might seem to allow for more varied gender "performances," so long as the gender binary exists, the tyranny it exerts over us will mean that there is an inevitable association of maleness with masculinity, femaleness with femininity, even though those gender roles do not reflect—and may in fact obscure—the lived experiences of our bodies.

To disembody gender might mean allowing men to "act like" women, and vice versa, but what remains is the binary construction male/female, masculine/feminine. The actual experience of bodies always engaged in becoming different-from-themselves will therefore always be lived at some remove, muddied by gender norms, engulfed by the inevitable normal/abnormal, superior/inferior, majoritarian/minoritarian oppositions that arise from such dualisms. Moreover, our concern will always inevitably come back to the limiting question of what a body can *be* rather than the expansive notion of what a body can *do*. We can see this even in Patrice Diquinzio's "paradoxical politics of mothering" (in which, to quote her again, "some persons, including some women, will have little or nothing to offer in caring for children, and some persons, including some women, will want little or nothing to do with it" [1999: 249]), which must of necessity remain paradoxical, and therefore unable to truly free us from the cultural idea/ideal of Motherhood, so long as the politics of reproduction remain mired in binary thinking about gender and negative conceptions of difference.

In other words, reimagining the gender binary as more open or inclusive, or even as gynocentric, would still leave us trapped in a binary machine that negates and nullifies individual potential because it negates and nullifies *difference*. What I have been arguing throughout this book is that we, like the schizo, need to recognize the great social delirium that is "gender" and trace a line of flight from the tyranny of this binary system. Doing so involves not a rethinking but, as I submitted in the introduction, an *un*thinking of gender that begins with (re)embodying sexual difference affirmatively as difference-in-itself—with putting ourselves back inside our bodies, once the molar identities (man/woman, white/black, straight/queer, dis/abled) that have stolen our becomings have been deterritorialized. Only then, as we embrace the limitless possibilities and expansive openness of the Body without Organs (BwO), will we be free from the reactive forces that treat difference as dangerous and change as undesirable, instead discovering how to live and love ourselves (and everyone and everything else) as living things constantly becoming.

Consider, for instance, horror's turn to the monster-as-hero, which perhaps reflects a widespread and growing desire for a line of flight from hegemonic culture. The monster-as-hero allows us to imagine escape from a biological human body that, as Elizabeth Grosz has said, is never *natural*, since our bodies are always experienced through the culture that represents and inscribes it, the body, with meaning. Grosz is not suggesting, nor am I, that bodies *are* gendered, *naturally*, but rather that it does not suffice to attempt to live our lives as un-gendered, gender-less, or even cross-gendered in a binary society which, from the moment of our conception, inscribes onto our bodies the meanings of binary gender and the model of difference-as-lack. As perhaps the greatest evidence of this, Grosz questions why Freud would call the pre-Oedipal mother phallic rather than all-powerful if *phallic* merely signified the mother's ability to grant or deny the infant's wishes. "Something more is at stake here," Grosz argues, and since the child must abandon attachment to the mother in order to become its own autonomous Self, she goes on to say that *something* is nothing less than the patriarchy itself: "Aristotle . . . believed that the mother provided the formless, passive, shapeless matter which, through the father, was given form, shape, and contour. . . . In short, the conditions under which patriarchy is psychically produced is the constitution of women's bodies as lacking" (Grosz 1994: 60) as the male child must identify with the father who provides *form, shape, and contour*, the female child with the *formless, passive, and shapeless* mother.

One of the primary issues with psychoanalysis (and cinepsychoanalysis), then, is that, in explaining why psychoanalytic subjects become masculine or feminine—by revealing the powerful drive to distinguish the phallic from the castrated in a system wherein social privilege is written onto the biological body, which must be binarily sexed even if it is actually intersexed—psychoanalysis fails to explain "how this occurs (because . . . it is unable to see that its own pronouncements and positions are masculine)" (Grosz 1994: 60). Within this blindly phallocentric mindset, although the body has been (mis)taken for natural—as "innately psychical, sexual, or sexed"—the body is in fact "indeterminate and indeterminable outside its social constitution as a body of a particular type. . . . This implies that the body which [psychoanalysis] presumes and helps to explain is an open-ended, pliable set of significations, capable of being rewritten" (Grosz 1994: 60–1).

This chapter submits that the monster is one avenue via which horror film, in its most molecular expressions, has sought to open and rewrite the biological body from which gender cannot be adequately or easily divorced so long as that body is imagined as natural. There can be no "free variation" of gender in a society that automatically assumes male bodies will be masculine, female bodies feminine, and moreover assumes heterosexual relations between these binarily sexed bodies to be the norm. It is not just that women in phallocentric society are defined by what we lack or, as Kristeva would say, by our abjection—by the leaking, oozing, seeping female body. It is also that, from a medical, physical, and biological standpoint, bodies themselves have been understood only through the Western, white, heterosexual, able-bodied male imagination, which assumes itself to be the universal, normal, natural human body—the universal, normal, natural human experience. When we speak of *the body*, in other words, what we mean is the body as men understand it.

This phallocentric viewpoint holds true even despite the social progress made by the feminist cause, as feminism has perhaps continued to focus too much on changing attitudes toward masculinity and femininity without questioning the binary construction of biological sex and the naturalization of the body as *sexed*. And so, a more radical solution to the gender binary seems called for. For within such a system, in which our bodies from birth onward are caught up in both gender *and* biology, what possibility could there be for affirmatively experiencing a nonbinary, unnatural body except to make that body monstrous, and in turn to make the monster the hero?

Queering Creation

Released in the early 1990s, both *Bram Stoker's Dracula* and *Interview with the Vampire* reveal a post-AIDS preoccupation with blood as Julia Kristeva's "fascinating semantic crossroads" of life and death. Both films also queer creation, resisting the "idealiz[ing] of heterosexual sex as the origin of life" (Oliver 2010: 771). The politics of reproduction in these films have been denaturalized by the monstrously molecular power of blood, through the two-way flow (blood is drunk; blood is given) in which vampires are born to makers who become both, and neither, mother and father to their offspring, while the monster, by *Interview with the Vampire*, finally takes center stage as hero.

Bram Stoker's Dracula, released just two years before *Interview with the Vampire*, in many ways prefigures Neil Jordan's film, although of the two, Francis Ford Coppola's *Dracula* remains more molar, at least in terms of content—for in *Dracula* the monster is still that which must be destroyed. Nevertheless, Gary Oldman's Prince Vlad/Count Dracula is certainly a sympathetic character. The tragic story of his beloved Elisabeta's suicide—the impetus for Dracula to curse the Judeo-Christian god that would damn her soul—both opens the film and pervades it, as Dracula discovers Elisabeta reincarnated in Mina. Even Van Helsing, that spokesperson for truth, righteousness, and patriarchal order, expresses admiration for Dracula.

Unlike Frankenstein, who believed his Creature to be a monster based on what he *was*, Van Helsing tells Mina he only wishes Dracula destroyed because of what he *does*. Lestat, on the other hand, may be as much of a killer as Dracula, but by *Interview with the Vampire*, the compassion we are encouraged to feel for Dracula's "humanity" becomes an all-out sympathy for the devil.[1] Lestat is a true anti-hero, and his non-dualistic outlook on life—his resistance of those "higher values" of human society—is put into productive tension with Louis's search for a "higher power" and his dualistic, good-versus-evil outlook. "You've damned me to hell," Louis accuses his maker Lestat at one point, to which Lestat adroitly responds, "What if there is no hell, or what if they don't want us there—did you ever think of that?"

In fact, Lestat's ambivalence about the nature of good and evil more thoroughly destabilizes the human/monster binary than Dracula's tragic love story can. While the awful things Dracula does (driving Renfield mad, imprisoning Jonathan, murdering Lucy) could be understood as a skewed attempt to reclaim his lost love in Mina (a very human motivation), Lestat embraces his monstrousness with a relish that complicates the patriarchal, binary structures Louis clings to in his afterlife. "God kills indiscriminately," Lestat reasons, arguing that "no other creatures" are more like god than vampires; this sentiment will be echoed by Armand, who tells Louis they are "nothing if not vampires" and swears, in response to Louis's insistence that there must be a "source" of vampirism, that in 400 years he has "never learned a secret nor seen a vision that would damn or save [his] soul." The sort of vampire one becomes is not predetermined by what one *is* (a damned soul), in other words, but instead by what one chooses to feel or do. Louis finally accepts this when he turns down Armand's offer to teach him how to "live without regret." It is not only that Louis, unlike Armand, has recognized the role memory, including regret, must play in a vampire's long-term survival. (More to be said on this in a moment.) It is also that Louis has accepted that a vampire *is* a molecular creature, living *and* dead, in/human. Louis, like Lestat—perhaps *because* of Lestat—survives his transformation because he can live in that slash, existing within the complexity of what it means to "be" a vampire. In this way, *Interview* almost entirely reverses the molar/molecular tension of the twenty-first-century *Twilight* films, in which molecular ruptures never entirely destabilize the films' molar expressions or hegemonic content. In *Interview*, the falsity of molar expressions is routinely exposed, most notably as Louis's sermonizing voiceovers (a molar technique) are subverted by the logic and actions of Lestat, that most molecular of vampires.

It is also true that both *Dracula* and *Interview* end rhizomatically, without the closure that should be offered by "destroying" the monster. The films thus leave viewers open to contemplating what we have felt/experienced once the film has ended, for as Anna Powell has said, "perception and reflection vibrate in us at different speeds" (2005: 202). Dracula may die at the end of Coppola's film, but he also appears to have been redeemed, by love; the question remains of what will happen now to his redeemer, Mina, as does the question of what will become of Louis and Lestat. Nonetheless, it is important to note that Dracula's death restores order in a way *Interview* does not, perhaps because *Interview* has divorced itself almost entirely from those "higher values" and binary assumptions (human/monster, good/evil, hero/villain) *Dracula* cannot quite cast off. Perhaps this is because *Dracula*, like *Mary Shelley's Frankenstein*, remains fettered to its master narrative—a text from the Victorian era that still drew sharp distinctions between the human and the monstrous, rejecting difference as dangerous.

This may be, too, why *Dracula* still figures vampirism as contagion—a likely nod to what Kimberly Frohreich has observed of the original novel's xenophobic roots.[2] In *Interview*, by contrast, no explanations are offered for what vampirism is or for how it spreads; the domains of science and religion do not figure into Anne Rice's world. Yet—and here we return to the politics of reproduction—desire is a key component of creation in both films, in which desire itself is queered, made the key to creation (not phallocentric re-production) as it is in schizosophic becomings: desire as Deleuze and Guattari's *productive force*, in other words. There is Dracula's desire for, and seduction of, Lucy and Mina, but there are also, importantly, Lucy's and Mina's desires; and while it could be said that both women are punished for desiring, desire itself is expressed in such a way that viewers find ourselves swept up in the film's macabre erotica, feeling the silkiness of the red satin robe that billows around Lucy's nearly naked body or the satin-softness of the wolf's fur beneath Mina's glove. The camera, acting as Deleuze's superhuman perspective, brings us inside the labyrinth with Mina as she chases an entranced Lucy through the storm; onto the granite slab with Lucy where Dracula, in hybrid form as a beast-man, copulates with her; into the ring of candles Mina and Dracula, now the young-again Prince Vlad, waltz among. The simplistic conclusion that women are punished for desiring is therefore complicated by the desire we, as viewers, experience as the film's molecular expressions affect us into being *inside* the film.

Queerness is foregrounded even more explicitly as the driving/desiring force behind creation in *Interview with the Vampire*. Lestat desires Louis; Louis desires Lestat; from their mutual desire, Louis is "born to darkness," and later, so is Claudia, becoming the vampire couple's "child" (as well as Louis's beloved, if not his lover). In this queer family, love is complicated in the same way good and evil are complicated, figured more as choices (between kindness and cruelty, between forgiveness and revenge) than as a by-product of nature, relation, or partiality. Just as in *Dracula*, viewers are affected into *Interview*'s chaotic ecstasy of creation through molecular expressions that add up to what Deleuze called *saturation*. Both *Dracula* and *Interview* brim with sonsigns (howling wind and wolves, pounding hoofs, chiming bells, soaring orchestras); opsigns (opulent costumes, decadent wallpapers, crowded sets, superimposed memories and flashbacks); and tactisigns (gauzy curtains, lace ruffles, crystal chandeliers, blowing snow, blue flames, silver blades) that overwhelm the viewer, creating that cinematic synesthesia which again lets us know we have lost our stable, spectatorial sense of being *outside* the film.

Interview with the Vampire goes further even than *Dracula* in creating a sense of "being-with" the characters, as the camera insistently "makes its presence felt." Whether it is circling characters during dialogue; moving with Louis and Lestat through a crowded ballroom; backing away from Louis as he bursts through a doorway; or pacing through the rainy streets of New Orleans with Louis as he discovers Claudia, still human, in the plague quarter, the camera in *Interview* achieves that *imperceptible* fluctuation between objective and subjective viewpoints that Teresa Rizzo claims so successfully destabilizes any molar viewpoint. In fact, rather than bringing viewers into the perspective of/ identification with a character, in Jordan's film "the character has become a kind of viewer. . . . He is prey to a vision, pursued by it or pursuing it, rather than engaged in an action" (Deleuze 1989: 3). This is what Deleuze calls *pure movement*, movement unrelated to characters or objects; he gives the example of the camera "leaving" a character only to "rediscover him" (1986: 23), as, for instance, when the camera, sweeping slowly in over San Francisco Bay, moves through the crowded modern streets and up the side of a building to discover Louis in the window, or when the camera appears to be Lestat looking down at Louis for the first time, until the camera moves, leaving and then finding Lestat in silhouette as he moves to the balcony to watch Louis depart.

The film's dividual score contributes as well to the sense of being-with the characters, as "all the sound elements, including silence, form a continuum as something which belongs to the visual image" (Deleuze 1989: 241). In *Interview*, there is not necessarily a "unity" between sound and image so much as a "perceptual relinkage" (Deleuze 1989: 279) between the two. This dividual sound-image, such as when the echoing of Louis's footsteps on the Paris cobblestones become Santiago's footsteps mimicking his or when the orchestral score pulls us up above the river with Louis and Lestat as Louis is first bitten, creates a *closeness* that does not equate to identification yet "does enable the viewer to be in alliance with a character. Whereas the transcendental subject of the [cinepsychoanalytic] cinematic apparatus sees everything from a distance, being-with a character engenders a felt quality" (Rizzo 2012: 33) that, in its destabilization of the self/Other binary, means "[b]ecause we are with them [characters] we cannot judge them at a distance, however, nor are we being encouraged to . . . adopt their point of view. A life of pure immanence, for Deleuze, is free from judgment and exists 'beyond good and evil'" (Rizzo 2012: 141). To put it simply, being-with characters allows us to relate to them, which, as will be explained below, is quite different from *identifying* with them.

Importantly, for schizoanalysis, an embodied theory of film viewing that allows for differences *between* viewers without flattening those differences into universalizable categories like Man or Woman, being-with a character does not suggest that films affect us through mimesis. That is, we do not imitate the characters *represented* onscreen. Rather, as Daniel Stern has posited, we *attune* with the characters' internal feelings in a process Stern calls "attunement behavior" and which, far from being unique to the cinematic experience, is something children learn early in life, as we learn to *relate* to others, not to behave like them (Rizzo 2012: 146). Although Rizzo, in discussing Stern, does not make this connection, I am reminded of Deleuze's discussion of the Actors' School in *Cinema 1*, in which he describes actors achieving an internal state that allows them to convey, through behavior, what their character is feeling/thinking. Rizzo, in turn, applies the concept of attunement behavior to explain how viewers become with characters in the affective, embodied experience of film viewing—again, quite a different experience than identifying with representative characters.

As a molecular technique that frees viewers from molar perspectives and hegemonic identifications, then, being-with a character emphasizes the "rhythm and energy that results from particular camera and editing techniques" experienced as "sensations [that] could be described in dynamic and kinetic terms, like surging, explosive, . . . bursting and drawn out . . . where the viewer emerges, not as a subject but as a haeccity or an individuation without subjectivity" (Rizzo 2012: 146). If the value of becoming-monster is that it forms a link in the chain toward becoming-imperceptible and thus the BwO, then a cinematic assemblage that encourages viewers to experience our haeccity or *thisness*, in which "things are luminous by themselves without anything illuminating them" (Deleuze 1986: 60), would seem to be more important than attempts to *identify with* the monster—or even the monster's queerness, vis-à-vis *Interview*'s homoeroticism. This hopefully answers what might seem to be a logical objection to the becomings prompted by a primarily molecular cinematic assemblage, since from a minoritarian perspective, it might seem more worthwhile for horror to present us with molar films that force viewers into the monster's perspective, if what we want is to celebrate the monster's difference. We must recall that becomings, including becomings-monster, are always molecular. The point is not for viewers to *be* a vampire, as a molar entity, or to be forced into assuming the vampire's perspective; indeed, we may rightly take issue with much of what Dracula, Lestat, and other movie monsters do. The point, rather, is for us to experience the minoritarianism of the monster as we "pass between" subjective and objective perspectives, deterritorializing the molar identities hegemonic society has inscribed onto us.

Being-with characters in *Interview with the Vampire* opens us to becoming-monster, therefore, not because it presents vampirism as a desirable way of being but because it affects us into experiencing the molecularity—the constant changes and passings-between—that Louis and Lestat experience as vampires. Moreover, the queering of creation in the post-human families of both Dracula and Louis and Lestat offers a perspective on the *possibilities* of living our bodies as non-natural. The members of these "families" are not over-coded (based on assumedly natural, biological sex) into binary ways of being that would stop their flows or dry up their potentials—and when they are subjected to those over-codings, the results are disastrous. For monstrous bodies are by necessity *volatile*, always engaged in becoming different-from-themselves, as we witness in Dracula's transformation from young to old, or Lestat's morphing from dark prince to skeletal husk. What produces these volatile bodies cannot be the hegemonic nuclear family. Instead, monstrous bodies are produced by desire, in which nothing is repressed or expelled—in which the desire to go on becoming different-from-oneself is, in fact, the very key to survival.

The Spiral of Time

The importance of time to schizosophy was discussed in Chapter 3, and it should be noted here that *Interview with the Vampire*, like *Mary Shelley's Frankenstein*, is conveyed as an extended flashback, narrated by Louis, whereas flashbacks regularly interrupt the linear narrative flow of *Dracula* (such as when Mina "remembers" Elisabeta's suicide). However, time, or, more accurately, duration, in both *Interview* and *Dracula* is perhaps more affectingly conveyed via montage than flashback.

In *Interview*, although montage, as an aspect of pure movement, also helps to create that "rhythm and energy" of being-with characters, it just as importantly acts as an aspect of what Deleuze calls *composition*, connecting even fixed shots "imperceptibly" and thereby becoming "the assemblage (*agencement*) of movement-images as constituting an indirect image of time" that makes time contemplatable (Deleuze 1986: 30).[3] Consider, for instance, how the film's close-up shots are interspersed with wide shots, or how the editing together of many types of shots breaks down binaries between small/large, interior/exterior because the shots, though distinct, must also "enter into a relationship" that forms the film as a dividual whole (Deleuze 1986: 30). Through *Interview*'s montages, viewers may experience "on the one hand, time as whole, as great circle or spiral . . . ; on the other, time as interval, . . . the smallest unit of movement or action. . . . Time as whole . . . is the bird which hovers, continually increasing its circle. . . . But [time as interval] is the beating of a wing" (Deleuze 1986: 32). Why does *time* matter to becoming-monster? *Interview* makes clear that to survive, vampires must go on becoming. "The world changes," Armand tells Louis; "we do not," which, he claims, leads many vampires to choose death over (eternal) life. That is, as we will see more of in Jim Jarmusch's *Only Lovers Left Alive*, eternity for vampires is only worth living if one continues to grow and change *with* the world, rather than removing oneself from it, as in *Twilight*.

Complementing *Interview*'s emphasis on duration—the ceaseless change that characterizes living things constantly becoming different-from-themselves—is the fluidity of Dracula in Coppola's film. Dracula can *become* anything, be it wolf, shadow, storm, bat, fog, or even a swarm of rats; he can even reverse the aging process and become young again, as there is no *natural order* to Coppola's world: blood can flow from a wounded cross; peacock feathers can fade into a train tunnel; Mina's tears can crystallize into diamonds. Even shadows obey no laws of lighting, moving against instead of with characters. Perfume can drip up, toward the ceiling; wolves can slip through the bars of their cages; the bubbles in a glass of absinthe can become blood cells. These fluid becomings, emphasized via molecular expressions such as morphing and camera consciousness, are furthered by play on/with subjectivity as the intersecting stories of Mina, Jonathan, Lucy, Renfield, Dracula, and Van Helsing fragment and disrupt any totalizing narrative perspective. The film often feels deliberately unmoored from chronological time as scene flows into scene, carrying viewers along with it.

But if Dracula can become anything, then at the opposite end of the spectrum, change, as an essential component of a vampire's molecularity (and duration), is denied most tragically to *Interview*'s Claudia. Although Claudia, Turned by Louis and Lestat while still a child, grows and changes internally, unlike *Twilight*'s vampires, outwardly she remains forever frozen in the body of a child, whose "eyes alone told the story of her age, staring out from under her doll-like curls." The horror of eternity in a fixed-and-frozen, over-coded biological body is revealed to Claudia first when she glimpses a naked young woman through a bedroom window, declaring that she wants to "be" her, and secondly, after the young woman's corpse is discovered rotting in her bed, when she furiously hacks away those "doll-like curls" only to have them instantly grow back. "But it means something else, too, doesn't it," Claudia declares, despondently, after Louis points out that she will "never grow old, and . . . never die." Like the darkest aspect of Peter Pan, "I shall never ever grow up," Claudia says.

The horror of Claudia's realization breathes terrible life into Deleuze and Guattari's observation that "the girl's becoming is stolen first." Claudia's becoming is stolen from her as she is prevented in either a biological or a molecular sense from becoming-woman. It is telling, therefore, that Claudia does not choose to become a vampire, despite Lestat's insistence that he will give Louis, and later Louis's interviewer, "the choice [he] never had." Lestat makes Claudia's destiny Louis's choice, selfishly playing on Louis's desire for a child although Claudia will be the one to live, and die, with the consequences of their choice to "birth" her to darkness. Even Mina is given the agency to choose her new vampire-life; when Dracula hesitates to give her his blood, Mina insists, "I want to see what you see, love what you love," as she persuades her immortal lover to let her "join [him] in eternal life."

But how would an eternal creature experience time? That appears to be the notion upon which *Only Lovers Left Alive* meditates. In *Lovers*, the "crisis of legitimacy" Alice Jardine has pointed to at the foundation of Western narratives—the need, as she puts it, to know "who is the father"—plays no part; in Jarmusch's vampire masterpiece, there is no question of makers or sires, only a post-human family in which the connections between individuals, and between individuals and places or individuals and objects or individuals and ideas, become molecular assemblages capable of tracing a line of flight from molar identities.

Since Jarmusch's film is the least horror-centric of the films in this book and part of my thesis, like Powell's, is that films that center on bodies (in horror, bodies onscreen under threat as well as viewers' affected bodies) may be more likely than other films to destabilize viewers' molar subjectivities, here the question should be addressed of how, or whether, films not centered viscerally on *the body* can still affect viewers. One answer lies again in Rizzo's application of the work of Daniel Stern, who takes a broad definition of *affect*. According to Stern, even films that do not repulse, terrify, or disgust viewers may still exert what he calls "categorical affects"—those which, through viewers' perceptions, create feelings or emotions—as well as "vitality affects," which exceed any particular sense (like revulsion) as they are "dispersed across and throughout the body . . . experienced as . . . 'a rush of anger or joy, . . . an unmeasurable wave of feeling evoked by music'" (Rizzo 2012: 144). Thus, Rizzo argues that even films which do not foreground monstrous transformations or bloody deaths may through their "style" affect the viewer's body in such a way that we assemble with the film's "poetic sensibilities" (2012: 134). Hence, horror may not be the only means of affecting viewers into the cinematic assemblage; the poetic sensibilities of categorically and vitally affective films like *Only Lovers Left Alive* are still capable of producing a perception-image, or what Deleuze calls "an image of thought" created by, and through, assemblages. In such rhizomatic, poetic films, we experience "a logic of thought that is always moving, always dynamic and therefore open to the new" (Rizzo 2012: 159).

Jarmusch's poetic style certainly sets viewers up to experience thought itself as always changing as *Lover*'s vampires form assemblages with different people, places, ideas, and objects. Yet the film, instead of *representing* time from a vampire's point of view, affects viewers into experiencing time as these eternal creatures do—as a duration of nomadic becomings. Perhaps the best example of this is Adam, who connects to himself-across-time through the music he plays and listens to *and* through musical objects like guitars, fiddles, and amplifiers. For Jarmusch's vampires, who often bring the past into the present via memory (Eve, for instance, reminds Adam that he "loves telling [her] these things" as she asks him to relate stories of playing chess with Lord Byron and Percy Shelley), there is indeed as Deleuze asserted an affect that belongs to things, serving in this instance to make the vampires aware of themselves-across-time. Eve's anonymous flat in Tangier, like Adam's ramshackle house in Detroit, is packed with *things*; these things all form a part of the vampires' history. Eve has her books, the pages of which she traces lovingly. Adam spends vast sums of money acquiring guitars and other instruments, for their history as much as for their utility. Marlowe expresses great attachment to an antique waistcoat given to him centuries ago by a lover. Eve even has the psychometric ability to know an object's history by touching it. The tactility of being in the world, connected to the history of people, places, and ideas contained within the objects one touches or possesses, extends even into the vampires' ritual drinking of blood, before which they always rub some personal talisman—a bead or a bracelet, for instance. Blood offers these vampires both an effect and an affect, that is, a simultaneously sensual *and* memorial experience, which the film affects viewers into sharing as the camera leads us to fall backward in slow motion with Eve, Marlowe, and Adam after they drink, while classical guitar music invites us to join in the headily timeless experience, heavy with opioid implications, of "zoning out."

It is tiny, languorous moments like these *Lovers* chooses to extend, to an almost hypnotic degree, as Jarmusch takes deliberate pacing to an entirely new level. (Allegedly, when asked to incorporate more *action*, he responded by cutting what little there already was.[4]) For the majority of the film, viewers ostensibly hang out with Adam and Eve while they talk, dance, read, play chess, listen to music, or simply sleep, until one begins to feel that time *is* the action here, time as Deleuze's endless spiral, open at both ends, a true rhizome with no ending and no beginning, expressed both through those tiny, wing-beat intervals (drinking, dancing, sleeping) and through the whole of time extending endlessly into the vampires' pasts—and futures.

The avian imagery Deleuze uses to describe time (tiny intervals like the beating of wings, a hovering bird "continually increasing its circle") is apropos for *Lovers*, which often takes a bird's-eye view of its characters that complements the spiral of time as its diagrammatic component. The film's opening credits play over a slowly spinning image of the night sky; gradually, the stars elongate into a record spinning on Adam's turntable; from a high angle, the camera circles down over first Eve and then Adam, each sprawled motionless in their respective homes, surrounded by their *things*. The spinning record is superimposed over the separated couple until, in reference to their deep emotional connection, at the same moment their eyes open. This same spiralized effect is repeated throughout the film, as Eve's solitary dance is superimposed over Adam's spinning turntables; as she walks alone, slowly and gracefully, through the twisting alleyways of Tangier; and, most importantly perhaps, as the camera, from its bird-like vantage point, watches Adam and Eve dance, images of the spinning record again superimposed on the lovers as Adam finally lets go of his suicidal ideation—choosing, like Eve, changing, growing, and *becoming* over the self-destruction he had been contemplating.

For there is a fundamental difference in the way Adam and Eve experience time that, as much as their love for one another, forms the film's plot (such as it is). Both Adam and Eve have continued to learn and change throughout their long immortal lives: Adam invents and creates, cobbling together steampunk-style contraptions in his fusty fortress; Eve reads, observes, and acquires. Yet, whereas Adam is existential and brooding, Eve is buoyant, equally and visibly delighted in her solitary watchfulness by the mortals she observes in a Tangier café, the skunk she encounters on Adam's sidewalk, or the mushrooms she discovers blooming out-of-season in the yard. The distinction between these vampires, it seems, lies in the perspective each chooses to take on eternity. Eve's perspective is as expansive as the universe she and Adam often discuss, seeing nothing but opportunities to keep experiencing, learning, and feeling, while she accuses Adam of "self-obsession"—the myopic neuroses of being a monster in hegemonic culture, always separate and outside, Other, unable to either fully escape or fundamentally undo oppressive ideas and institutions. Eve has freed herself from such neuroses because, like the schizo, she seems not to waste energy trying to figure out, or even opt out of, the hegemonic forces humankind subjects itself to. She counsels Adam to spend his eternity "appreciating nature, nurturing kindness, friendship, *dancing*," rather than obsessing over "the zombies," as Adam calls humans: "It's the zombies and the way they treat the world. It just feels like all the sand is at the bottom of the hourglass," he opines, to which Eve brightly replies, "Time to turn it over, then." Where the suicidal Adam feels time to be running out, Eve, the elder vampire, has embraced time as Deleuze's endless spiral—which may be why, while Adam sneers at modernity's innovations, Eve embraces them, video-chatting with him on her smartphone, packing a copy of *Infinite Jest* in her carry-on alongside ancient tomes.

That Adam refers to humans as "zombies" speaks also to duration, since zombies, as Powell has said, have no duration—for a zombie, the only possible change is *decay*. Eve, on the other hand, (fore)sees a future Adam cannot, at least until after their dance seems to open him to a new way of thinking about being in the world. On one of their long, meandering drives, Eve shows Adam how full of possibilities life can be once one empties time of what appears to the limited mortal mind as an inevitable vectorization from birth to death, from rise to fall. Passing shuttered factories and abandoned houses, Eve declares that post-recession Detroit will "rise again" because "there is water here," she says; "when the cities in the south are burning, this place will *bloom*."

Eve, we therefore see, chooses a line of flight from hegemonic culture that allows her to spend eternity as "a disindividuated becoming, a force of impetuous attraction, the torrent of an over-full life . . . bursting beyond the preservation necessity of the individual belonging to a species" (de Miranda 2013: 108). The basis of this line of flight for Eve, who assembles so fluidly with the music, art, technology and literature of different times and cultures, may be her nomadic subjectivity, a subjectivity Adam comes to share, reflected, as Eve's perspective on Detroit's re-creation suggests, in the ways Jarmusch's vampires assemble with *place*.

Like objects, places have an affect all their own in *Lovers*, prompting the vampires to assemble with, without being territorialized by, wherever they currently reside, even as they remain as decidedly aloof as only those who have repeatedly watched cities and empires rise and fall could be. This is not to say that the film fails to evoke a sense of place, since Jarmusch succeeds in capturing both the wild decay of Detroit and the urban antiquity of Tangier: Around the house Adam appears to be squatting in, coyotes howl, and the places he and Eve visit—a hospital, a movie theater turned car park—all have a ruinous atmosphere; in Tangier, electric lights glow in the shadow of ancient minarets. Camera consciousness, montage, and the film's dividual sound-image likewise affect us into experiencing these places alongside Adam and Eve, as the camera pursues Eve through Tangier's alleyways or rides in the car with her and Adam through Detroit. There is no sense of these characters "belonging" to where they live, however—no sense that they are rooted to their "homes," as Louis is to New Orleans or Dracula to his castle. Rather, in the schizosophic sense of the word, Eve, Adam, Marlowe, and Eve's sister Ava appear to be *nomads*.

"The life of the nomad is the intermezzo," Deleuze and Guattari write (1987: 380). Unlike the migrant, the nomad is not on a "trajectory" to resettle (reterritorialize) anywhere; the nomad, therefore, succeeds where the migrant cannot in causing "the earth [to] deterritorialize itself, in a way that provides the nomad with a territory. The land ceases to be land, tending to become simply ground (*sol*) or support" (Deleuze and Guattari 1987: 381). A nomadic subjectivity, similarly, does not reterritorialize itself—does not seek a line of flight from one molar identity in service of arriving at another. Eve's—and later, Adam's—nomadic subjectivity has import for the film's politics of reproduction because, as beings consciously engaged in becoming different-from-themselves, never seeking in their molecular assemblages a fixed-and-frozen identity, Jarmusch's vampires make contemplatable the "coexistence and communication of different durations . . . always becoming and changing with each other through processes of exchange. . . . For example, if the feminine is no longer understood in opposition to the masculine, then . . . [b]oth feminine and masculine must be imagined in new ways" (Rizzo 2012: 69). Or, as Rosi Braidotti puts it,

> sexual difference as stating the principle of "not-one" at the heart of subjectivity . . . is not a quantitative plurality within a one-dimensional and mono-directional system, but a qualitative multiplicity in an open-ended series of complexities. It is not an essentialist instinct or drive, but a vitalist tendency without an aim or an end, a non-self-enforcing and non-capitalizing entity. It is my conviction that this non-unitary, nomadic subjectivity is the prerequisite for an ethics of complex but sustainable subjectivity in the age of the posthuman. (2002: 265)

Reverberating through Braidotti's nomadic subjectivity is Elizabeth Grosz's call for an affirmation of sexual difference. The "not-one" to which Braidotti refers is schizosophy's *thousand tiny sexes*, in which "the two sexes imply a multiplicity of molecular combinations bringing into play not only the man in the woman and the woman in the man, but the relation of each to the animal, the plant, etc.: a thousand tiny sexes" (Deleuze and Guattari 1987: 213). It is important not to confuse schizosophy's thousand tiny sexes for androgyny or even hermaphrodism. Deleuze and Guattari are not arguing for a flattening of difference *between* the sexes but are, rather, observing that if each individual is constantly engaged in becoming-different-from-itself (as we assemble with people, places, ideas, etc., throughout our lives), then one could never be a Man or a Woman, nor could any *body*, constantly engaged in microprocesses of becoming different from *itself*, ever be binarily sexed as Male or Female; such molar categories are incessantly ruptured by molecular assemblages that deterritorialize molar identities. Although *Lovers* may suggest the *imperceptibility* of schizosophy's "sex to the *nth* degree" in the androgynous beauty of its two main leads, more important than the vampires' appearance is how they relate to themselves and to one another as multiplicitous, as sexually different creatures uncaptured by dualisms. Hence, while Adam and Eve may be husband and wife, never do they seem confined by, or even concerned with, gender norms.

This multiplicitous perspective on gender *and* sex extends unto the vampires' reproduction. Although Eve is older than Adam or Marlowe and, it is implied, may have Turned them, she expresses no interest in laying claim to her creations. She takes Adam for her lover, Marlowe for her friend, and Ava, whom it is clear she Turned, for her sister. Thus, we could say that Eve has created her own family, but this family does not exist to (re)press its members into the binary male-masculine/female-feminine roles patriarchal society wants its members scripted into—or into any molar category, for that matter. If indeed Eve's nomadic subjectivity has allowed her to trace a line of flight from Deleuze's "partialities"—if she can speak with such hope of Detroit's resurrection because, like the schizo, she has assumed a durational perspective on time as a great open-ended spiral in which the only constant will be change, allowing her to deterritorialize her interests, relationships, and desires as she enters into molecular assemblages with all she meets, experiences, and touches—then it would seem that Eve might at last offer a post-human model of motherhood in which to give life is to allow others the opportunity to experience era upon era as she has, not for any goal of continuing her species, and certainly not for the purposes of re-production, but to maximize the potential of each individual's *élan vital* by offering mortals like Ava and Adam, and the lovers she and Adam feed from in the film's finale, time to become.

Family as Survivor Assemblage

Of course, for Eve's gift of life to be viewed as a gift, one must conceive of the world as full of possibilities and of the future as promising renewal. Despite their often heavy emphasis on families, this would at first glance appear not to be the view taken by most zombie apocalypse narratives—in fact, zombie films might seem more aligned with the views of anti-natalism, whose adherents believe that bringing children into an already overpopulated world threatened by nuclear war, climate change, economic collapse, pandemics, and a host of other disasters is at best irresponsible, at worst wantonly cruel. Yet in zombie narratives such as the long-running television series *The Walking Dead* or the film adaptation of Max Brooks's *World War Z*, what we find is the almost opposite view, in which survival of the patriarchal nuclear family portends the reestablishment of (phallocentric) civilization itself.

28 Days Later takes yet another view of families, what I am calling a posthuman view, that may at last offer an alternative to the postpatriarchal vacuum Kimberly Jackson identified. In pointing to a brighter future that begins with evacuating society of its current molar organization, making of society itself a BwO, *28 Days Later* reassembles "the family" from *survivors* whose unique individuations, not adherence to molar identities prescribed by (and for the benefit of) hegemonic society, make them indispensable to those they assemble with.

To reiterate, by *postpatriarchal* Jackson refers to the social order as it has been destabilized by evolving gender roles in the late twentieth and early twenty-first centuries. Jackson posits that although we may no longer wish to live under the sway of patriarchal institutions, including the institution of the white, heteronormative, cisgender nuclear family, because an alternative order has yet to be established (in part, I argue, because we have not yet managed to undo the binary thinking at the heart of patriarchal society), in many contemporary horror films we find mothers and children forced to step into roles previously inhabited by fathers who turn out to be weak, insane, possessed, or outright evil. Whether such families can survive, and at what cost to their members, remains an open question, even if from a gynocentric (or as Jackson puts it, "postfeminist") view it might appear empowering to women to destroy The Father.

28 Days Later begins, as most zombie narratives do, with the annihilation of patriarchal institutions. In a curious parallel to *Only Lovers Left Alive*, in which the two-way flow of blood now threatens vampires with contamination by human diseases such as HIV/AIDS (as well as humans with "contamination" by vampirism), humankind's experimentation with a "rage virus" results in the zombie apocalypse after an exposed chimpanzee bites a human. When Jim wakes up in hospital "twenty-eight days later," London, as soaring helicopter shots emphasize, is virtually abandoned, all vestiges of patriarchal society—Government, Law, Media, Capitalism—apparently in ruins. Even Religion seems to have failed, for when Jim seeks refuge in a church, he finds it filled with zombies and is attacked by an infected priest before being rescued by Mark and Selena.

That rage rather than an "alien virus" or some other traditional zombie plot device is what infects humanity matters, because in *28 Days Later*'s survivor assemblage those who do not fill the postpatriarchal void with senseless violence or a new "will to power" offer the ultimate hope for humanity's future. Compare, for example, the motivations of Frank and Hannah, advertising the safety of their flat to other survivors who might be able to escape London with them, to those of Major West, who falsely promises an "answer to infection" as a means of luring women to his estate. It seems, therefore, that only those who successfully extend their sympathies beyond *partiality*, risking their lives to save strangers because they recognize that cooperation with others will be necessary for survival, are likely to withstand humankind's devastation. Yet because questions have been raised about how Selena, as a woman of color, fits into this postapocalyptic landscape, let us turn here to the complexity of race in the cinematic assemblage.

Theories of cinematic spectatorship based in representation and identification (like cinepsychoanalysis) have struggled to respond to the complexities of race, for how can we theorize what it "means" for a person of color to be "represented" in film by, and often for, the white imagination; how can we theorize the ways people of color are meant to "identify" with characters imagined through the lens of racial hegemony? Drawing from the theories of bell hooks, Kinitra Brooks responds with nuance and eloquence to those very questions in the context of zombie narratives specifically, positing the application of hooks's "oppositional gaze as a site of raced and gendered resistance that allows black women to 'critically assess the cinema's construction of white womanhood as object of phallocentric gaze and choose not to identify with the victim or the perpetrator'" (Brooks 2014: 461), that is, with neither the white women nor the men who "construct" them. Insisting on the indivisibility of race and gender as "interlocking oppressions" in the lives of women of color, Brooks forward the oppositional gaze as a way to resist "simplistic explorations of whiteness and masculinity by developing an alternative means of inducing participatory identification in the audience" (Brooks 2014: 461)—an audience that must include people of color, not only the white hegemonic viewer.

Just as LeiLani Nishime was right to insist upon the inclusion of a minoritarian viewpoint on Ava's "liberation" in *Ex Machina*, Brooks is absolutely right to insist upon a viewing position from which women of color can respond to portrayals of raced and gendered "difference." I want to be clear that I am not arguing against the need for such minoritarian inclusiveness. Quite the opposite. What I want to point out instead is that participatory identification already seems to lead us beyond the confines of cinema as cultural apparatus, beyond disembodied spectators "reading" symbolic fictions at a distance, for what lens could those symbols be read through if not the binary lens of a hegemonic majority that imagines difference as monstrous? In arguing for an oppositional gaze that provides minoritarian viewers the agency of an active, participatory role in responding to intersecting race and gender in film, Brooks therefore already seems to be seeking a way to close the gap between viewer and film as Deleuze's *direct event*.

Unfortunately, decrying theories of spectatorship that do not account for non-majoritarian viewpoints does not quite break us free from the tyranny of binary thinking in which *self* is opposed to *other*—in which difference, including racial difference, is defined negatively as lack. Although Brooks does not invoke Deleuze or schizoanalysis, her work does highlight the struggle to, in the first place, create space for an oppositional gaze within a theoretical paradigm that always and inevitably constructs monolithic categories of spectatorship that flatten differences between viewers and, in the second, to engage in *participatory* identification within a paradigm that privileges symbolic representation over corporeal affect. She argues that "the marginalized position of black women [that] influences their negotiated reading of a text that either ignores them or deems them freakish monstrousities" makes them "critical spectators from a location that is disrupted. It is from this interstice outside the mainstream" that Brooks calls for film theory to "move beyond identificatory permeability to a sustained interrogation of the assumed majority status, of male and female, black and white, and the oscillations among those as well as any other intersectional identifications of the viewer" (Brooks 2014: 468).

What Brooks seems to call for is what schizoanalysis may offer: a theory of embodied film viewing capable of *affirming* viewers' intersectional differences. Viewers of color, onto whom are inscribed the meanings of race in a racist society, are likely to be affected differently than white viewers by depictions of difference, racial or otherwise; moreover, how people of color are affected by film needs to be a question asked within an affirmative micropolitics that does not assume all people of color, because they are people of color, will be affected in the same way. The radical potential of Brooks's participatory identification may become realizable only when opposition moves beyond "the gaze"— beyond spectatorship and the eye/I of transcendent subjectivity it privileges. Because it does not weld onto film majoritarian "meanings" of difference that must be embraced or resisted, schizoanalysis may move us closer to an inclusive theoretical position from which to theorize difference, particularly in films like *28 Days Later* that open us up to experiencing difference outside the self/other binary, as difference-in-itself.

Thus, the subversion of molar subjectivities made possible by molecular films may further minoritarian goals in the first place by destabilizing the fixed-and-frozen identities, including racial identities, inscribed onto viewers by hegemonic culture. Let us consider how *28 Days Later* uses molecular expressions to bring about this destabilization through dislocation, discordance, and disorientation. In its opening scenes, *28 Days Later* dis-locates viewers, along with Jim, as the shot vacillates between Deleuze's two tendencies: saturation and rarefaction. When Jim wakes from his coma, the eerie emptiness of the hospital, punctuated by silence in which diegetic sounds like the opening of a soda can seem to echo, makes us question where we are—in reality or some nightmare. This feeling of not being able to *find* oneself increases as wide overhead shots track Jim through London's normally bustling streets, now impossibly emptied of (human) life. Abandoned cars and handmade Missing Persons posters litter the background, never quite coming into focus, so that it is not until Jim stumbles upon the zombies in the church that we begin to realize he has indeed woken to a nightmare.

In contrast to these wide, rarefied shots of streets, buildings, and monuments, the initial zombie attack saturates the screen with close-ups of red eyes, slavering jaws, and decayed flesh, rapidly edited over handheld shots of Jim fleeing, Mark and Selena setting the zombies alight, and a gas station exploding—at which point the set is rarefied again as the camera zooms out to a helicopter shot of the darkened city with a fireball shooting up from the center. This pattern of alternating rarefaction and saturation continues throughout the film, destabilizing our sense of being safely *outside*, separate from, the film event; for in every long, quiet, peaceful shot is contained the dread of when, or whether, the scene will explode into terrifying action. Moreover, these alterations, combined with the film's preference for camera consciousness over shot/reaction shot, prevent us from assuming any monolithic perspective on characters or events, as subjective and objective perspectives do not so much fluctuate as rupture in this film, preventing us from settling comfortably into the worldview of any character.

Music enhances this unsettling of molar perspective, much more so than we might expect from the much-vaunted theme song, in which a simple chord progression and primal drumbeats eventually crescendo into a distorted chorus of guitars. In *28 Days Later*, music oftentimes becomes that "foreign body" Deleuze wrote of in film, although here, even more so than in *Mary Shelley's Frankenstein*, the score discords with the action. Music in film often prompts viewers to know how we should respond to the action—a molar technique viewers will recognize from even primarily molecular films. Yet as the camera accompanies Jim, Mark, and Selena through the empty city to Jim's house, the gentle acapella rendition of "Abide with Me" that plays over the scene in no way accords with the horror of Jim discovering his parents' rotted corpses next to their suicide note. This same discordant combination is applied as the survivors drive into a tunnel filled with abandoned cars and sure to be a hunting ground for zombies, to the melodic accompaniment of Gabriel Fauré's *Requiem: In Paradisum*.

The disconnect between music and action here resonates in us, heightening our sense of dread as we assume the camera's superhuman perspective on these vulnerable characters. Music, in other words, helps to affect us into becoming-camera; this itself destabilizes the molar subjectivity and self/other boundaries hegemonic society would reinforce. Once the zombies attack, our egoistic boundaries are further destabilized through the film's highly visceral effects—spurting blood, animalistic growls, tearing flesh—including the zombies' *speed*. While such effects may appear passé now, zombies that moved with terrifying swiftness were revolutionary to the genre when Danny Boyle first introduced them, overturning what viewers had come to expect from lumbering masses of the undead. The rapid-fire editing that conveys their speed further disorients viewers, serving to dissolve any sense of our subjective borders as we assemble with the film.

Nevertheless, although *28 Days Later* does complicate the binary between *human* and *monstrous* in ways perhaps foreshadowed by the complex origins of the rage virus, the film does make its zombies monstrous, in the most interstitial and abject sense of the word—no longer the heroes but once more that which must be destroyed if our heroes are to survive. Given the seeming molarity of this, it is important to take a closer look at the film's heroes, considering first Selena as a Final Girl before turning to the survivor assemblage.

Harkening back to Teresa Rizzo's schizosophizing of cinepsychoanalyst Carol Clover's Final Girl—the sole female survivor of horror film whose heroism, Clover argues, depends upon her devaluation of the feminine and assumption of the masculine—Selena survives not by becoming female-masculine but rather by adopting that "affective intuitive perception" Rizzo maintains does not fall into the binary trap of masculinity or femininity. There is, for example, Selena's vigilance. She is the first to hear the infected breaking into the tower block stairwell, giving her and Jim time to flee; she doubts Major West's "answer to infection" from the moment Frank plays the recording; and after she and Hannah are trapped by the soldiers, she seizes the moment their captors are distracted to escape. Complementing this ability to respond quickly and effectively to her surroundings is Selena's awareness of herself as a durational being. Like *Scream*'s Sidney Prescott, the Final Girl Rizzo schizoanalyzes, Selena is able to *learn* from her past. When Mark is bitten, she kills him instantly, having learned that the infected cannot be saved or reasoned with; yet the more time Selena spends with Frank, Jim, and Hannah, the more she also learns that she will need others if she wants to do more than avoid infection—if she wants to truly *live*—and so, in the climactic scene, she does hesitate to kill Jim, who turns out not to be infected. Selena is therefore able to assume a perspective on herself that allows her to change *with* others, to her benefit, as well as theirs.

To apply the representational formula of Clover's Final Girl to Selena would assume, moreover, that femininity and masculinity can be applied to black female bodies exactly as they are to white female bodies. This is not the case. Brooks maintains that Clover's Final Girl "relies on the normativity of whiteness" since "the black woman's displays of strength are read pejoratively even as the [white] final girl is read as . . . an expression of independent initiative and not a series of acts threatening castration" (Brooks 2014: 464). Although the problems inherent in any Final Girl needing to become "masculine" to be read as heroic have already been laid out by this book and by Rizzo, the complexities of intersected race and gender, in which a black Final Girl cannot be synonymized with a white Final Girl, drive home an even greater need to consider *how* Final Girls survive from an ethological rather than representational perspective— from a perspective that looks at what Final Girls *do*, without binarily coding their actions masculine or feminine. This is not to say that race can or should be ignored in Selena's character, or in any character; to become-imperceptible is again not to claim that difference does not matter, nor is it to erase difference by assuming, in the case of race for instance, that "underneath" all people are actually *white*, wherein whiteness is taken to be the universal, normal, or natural *human* experience. Rather, once we accept that race cannot be disembodied (assuming Clover's [white] Final Girl to be universal, in other words), through a schizosophic perspective on the intersections of race and gender we are able to examine where and how Selena affects and is affected by the people, places, ideas, and events she assembles with.

One of those assemblages is historic and institutionalized racism, and it is important to take note of where and how Selena remains captured (territorialized,

Deleuze and Guattari would say) by hegemonic conceptions of race and gender, such as in what Brooks describes as her "mothering" of Jim in keeping with the stereotype of "the strong black woman" (2014: 471). In molecular films, which, both as we watch and later as we reflect upon the film, are already prompting us to experience and therefore to think difference differently, moments of reterritorialization and deterritorialization may enable viewers

> to think more fully, more richly, more powerfully a series of concepts or problems related to race and decolonization . . . to think identity not as illusory attribution (including racial categorisation), but rather as the repetition of pure difference, to think the singularity of any entity in terms of its own protean powers of transformation . . . of the virtual self. (Nesbitt 2013: 1, 3)

By "illusory attribution," Nick Nesbitt here refers to the artificial social construction of race as justification for injustice, the *naturalization* of oppression and discrimination accomplished by inscribing hegemonic norms, assumptions, and prejudices onto the body-that-is-raced. Schizoanalysis, because it recognizes the artificiality of race (without negating its very real consequences) and because it is ethological rather than representational in approach, enables us to recognize and to reflect on the moments when Selena does deterritorialize the racial identity inscribed onto her, passing-between or "slipping right through" molar categorizations of what it means to "be," or what is meant by, a black woman, transforming herself—*becoming*—while we, as viewers, are affected into being-with her, in the schizosophic sense of critically empathizing or allying with her.

One powerful way *28 Days Later* enables Selena to become is by transforming the Final Girl of cinepsychoanalysis—a lone hero reliant on her own resilience—into part of the survivor assemblage. Jim and Hannah, we might say, also become schizosophic Final Girls, particularly in their ability to deterritorialize hegemonic identities and become with their surroundings. Jim hides among corpses to escape the soldiers sent to execute him, releases the infected soldier Maylor into the mansion as a weapon, and even uses secret passageways to move unseen about Major West's fortress. Hannah, once she, unlike her doomed-to-die father, ceases to rely for her salvation on the military-industrial complex, has the presence of mind to hide by hanging from the back of a mirror when the soldiers come looking for her. (She is also finally the one to kill Major West by using a car to imprison him with the infected Maylor.) The collective rescue these characters engage in, in which each person's affective intuitive perception contributes to their ability to survive as a unit, is certainly more feminist in its emphasis on cooperation and collective action than Clover's masculinized, self-reliant hero.

Assembling with Jim and Hannah has profound effect on Selena's character, also. Brooks has observed that even though Selena "displays inordinate mental and physical toughness" she "must employ the strength of the communal bonds she has established with her new 'family' to survive intact. . . . Her working partnership with her newly found family ensures her eventual survival and allows her a safe space in which to grow beyond a willingness to kill Jim 'in a heartbeat'" (2014: 472). That Brooks views Jim, Selena, and Hannah as a *family* is important, and will be addressed momentarily, but it is equally important that Brooks sees this family as affecting Selena positively, prompting her to open herself up to loving and needing others despite the trauma she has experienced. Yet there are those who take a decidedly negative view of Selena's part in this survivor assemblage, seeing her need for others as weakness:

> Selena has hung up her machete in favor of a sewing machine, which she uses to stitch together a massive, fabric "Hello" sign. . . . This ending better resonates with the popular rhetoric that fuels anxieties about breakdown and reconfiguration of the nuclear family and "happily ever after" romantic genres. . . . Thus, another largely unexamined revision *28 Days Later* made to the zombie movie genre . . . is the rebuilding of society through re-creating heteronormative family. (Cady and Oates 2016: 315)

In the first place, Kathryn Cady and Thomas Oates here seem to be assuming that Selena is less heroic for building those "communal bonds" to which Brooks refers, rather than, presumably, relying on her own (masculinized) individuality to survive. Furthermore, they also seem to assume that sewing what amounts to a giant S.O.S. banner that leads to the survivors' rescue is less heroic than slaying zombies, presumably because the masculinity "represented" by Selena's machete reads as more heroic than the sewing machine in phallocentric society. This is binary thinking at its most toxic, the ongoing, unexamined privileging of masculinity over femininity that lies at the heart of postfeminism.

In the second place, and perhaps more importantly for the politics of reproduction, there is Cady and Oates's assumption that Jim, Hannah, and Selena represent a heteronormative nuclear family. I will not argue with their assertion that Jim and Selena appear to be heterosexual. However, the film never shows them treating Hannah as *their* child, surrogate or otherwise; she might be better likened to a little sister in this survivor assemblage, as Jim prods Frank to allow her to try tranquilizers when she has trouble sleeping, and Selena, resigned to being unable to save Hannah from sexual assault at the soldiers' hands, drugs her so she "won't care"—quite a difference from Ripley challenging the alien Queen to mortal combat to safeguard her surrogate daughter Newt. Nor do Jim and Selena inhabit hegemonically male-dominant, female-subservient roles in their new cohabitation. Instead, throughout the film they appear to have established an equal partnership that may include romance and desire, but also includes respect for one another's individuality.

Perhaps what Cady and Oates object to is the filmmakers' decision to offer a hopeful, if not entirely happy, ending, rather than the alternate ending (included in the DVD release) in which Jim dies and Hannah and Selena must continue without him, into an uncertain future. Jackson would call that ending postpatriarchal, since it offers no alternative to the patriarchal nuclear family; just as importantly, it can hardly be *feminist* or *progressive* to destroy men in order to empower women. Undoubtedly, there are zombie films in which annihilation of patriarchal structures could pave the way for a new social order, but instead "the resiliency of the heteronormative nuclear family as the central formation in such stories, from which a new social world is imagined to spring" does seem to suggest "that, despite significant subversive potential, zombie narratives offer private and heteronormative models of social order rather than public and countercultural ones" (Cady and Oates 2016: 309), which, therefore, begs the question: Is the reconstitution of *any* sort of family, heteronormative or otherwise, inherently in service to hegemonic society?

There is certainly a resonance to Cady and Oates's argument that the nuclear family in the twenty-first century has become a function of both democracy and capitalism, as governments have shifted "social welfare" from public to private responsibility (having children who can care for us in our later years, for instance) and have privileged the nuclear family, especially the two-wage-earner family, as social insurance against the devastations of poverty; even queer families, as they have been encouraged to adopt practices such as marriage, cannot escape such sociopolitical functions of the family (Cady and Oates 2016: 312).[5] I must concede that Cady and Oates have a point about *the family* as an arm of neoliberal organization. I am not convinced, however, that every family, including the family Jim, Selena, and Hannah assemble, necessarily serves these repressive social functions nor portends the return of patriarchal society.

As evidence, in one of *28 Days Later*'s most subversive plot twists, Selena and Hannah do not become victims of essential motherhood. Their escape from Major West and his soldiers is telling, since, as was noted in this book's introduction, in devastatingly depopulated worlds like Boyle's, women's reproductive capacities often become their defining features. Nor does Cady and Oates's insistence that the film seems "relentlessly nostalgic for family" (2016: 314) account for the molecular expressions of this "nostalgia" in Boyle's film. As Jim, after discovering his parents' corpses, stands in the kitchen of his childhood home, vividly recalling life in happier, simpler times, the camera, which starts out as Jim's perspective, suddenly becomes a zombie running toward the house; the infected crash through the doors and windows and a bloody, disorienting battle erupts that explodes any comfort or safety we might have felt in dwelling on the past, particularly since Jim's "nostalgia" nearly gets him killed. If there is a longing for the nuclear family in the film, it might be better expressed in the horses the survivors watch galloping in slow motion through a field. "They're like a family," Frank observes, and responds, in answer to Hannah's question of whether they might be infected, that "they're doing just fine." Emphasized by Frank's use of the word *like*, as the camera gently shifts between the horses (who have no interest in patriarchal structures) and the human survivors the implication here is that "family" may have lost its hegemonic meaning, opening a line of flight from repressive patriarchal norms.

Yet the true subversion of *28 Days Later* may be that the film challenges us to rethink the binary logic of hegemonic culture by destabilizing the human/monster binary. The infected may be monstrously abject, but they are also to be pitied; references to them as *the infected* insistently remind us that these "zombies" are not evil—they are victims of a virus created by Science. Major West and his soldiers, on the other hand, emerge as the true villains of the piece, *because* of their adherence to the patriarchal order. "What do nine men do except wait to die themselves?" West asks of Jim. In answer to his own question, he confesses, "I promised them women. Because women mean a future." To West and his men, women's *wombs* are their defining feature. Jim has another perspective; he sees Selena and Hannah as much more than a "nesting place" for life. Each time I watch the film, I find it poetically just that the soldiers' desire to reestablish a patriarchal order leads to their re-production as zombies, creatures for whom there can be no duration, no changing of the *self* over time.

Jim may create these monsters using Maylor, the infected soldier West has kept chained up as an object of study, but Jim, in rescuing Selena and Hannah, also becomes-monster, in the sense of molecular intensity with which Deleuze and Guattari write that all becomings are molecular. In becoming-animal, for instance, although barking does not transform us into a dog as a molar entity, Deleuze and Guattari submit that the intensity of barking may allow us to "emit a molecular dog" in the sense that "[i]t is within us that the animal bares its teeth" (Deleuze and Guattari 1987: 275). As Jim, bloody, shirtless, and rain-spattered, slips through the mansion killing soldiers, the intensity of rage he "emits" has him becoming more and more akin to the infected, so much so that Selena almost mistakes him for a zombie and kills him; yet, simultaneously, Jim, who turns out not to be territorialized by the rage that dries up the zombies' durations, also moves further and further from the hegemonic masculinity of West and his men. Boyle's decision to make these villains soldiers rather than simply another band of civilian survivors matters deeply to the subversive content of the film, especially since the Military is typically one of the first patriarchal institutions to be destroyed in the zombie apocalypse. West and his soldiers survive as products of that institution, and the glee with which they proceed with their plan to sexually enslave Hannah and Selena suggests more is at stake here than continuation of the species. To put it bluntly, these are men who reflect patriarchal attitudes about women's inability to deny men sexual pleasure whenever they want it.

As the final fight against these human villains becomes more and more molecular, we as viewers are affected into becoming-monster along with Jim. Shaky, handheld shots; rapid-fire montages; liquid perception (rain falls throughout the entirety of the last scene); and visceral sonsigns (gunfire, explosions, sirens, thunder, growls, panting, screaming) coalesce into a molecular experience that thoroughly destabilizes our egoistic, inside/outside boundaries. The final scene in which Jim, Hannah, and Selena have escaped the horror to await rescue in a tranquil cottage may reconstitute the "family," but this family, as survivor assemblage, provides an alternative to, not a reinstatement of, the repressive, patriarchal nuclear family. As partiality is done away with—our survivors do not assemble only with those who are "like" them or related to them—there is also the possibility for this post-human family to provide a new, equitable and inclusive model for social systems that will extend generosity beyond partiality and affirm rather than exclude difference. Therefore, rather than a hegemonic return to wholeness, what the intact survivor assemblage at the end of *28 Days Later* offers is an ending that is rhizomatic in its hopefulness for a new kind of family, and a new kind of future.

Molecular Motherhood, or the Monstrous Body (Re)imagined

Humanity's future is the primary concern of *Mad Max: Fury Road*. One might say molecularity is *fundamental* to both the film's content and expression, as director George Miller dissolves generic borders between action, dystopian, science fiction, drama, and horror films, assembling aspects of all into a highly stylized, highly affecting film. In that sense, despite being a big budget studio blockbuster, *Fury Road* can hardly be considered "formulaic," to use Anna Powell's descriptor of many mainstream films; rather, the film is decidedly experimental in ways viewers, primed by the generic conventions of action film, might not be anticipating. In fact, while Powell has noted Deleuze's preference for schizoanalyzing "art-house" or avant-garde cinema, she has also argued that mainstream films can affect viewers through molecular expressions in part because their molecularity catches us unawares (Powell 2005: 203–4). *Fury Road* fits this bill exactly, presenting a "poetic sensibility" of categorical and vital affects that prompt viewers to assemble with the film's "rhythm and energy," although that rhythm and energy is quite different from what we experienced in *Only Lovers Left Alive*. What results from *Fury Road*'s cinematic experimentation is a reimagining of the body that destabilizes the human/monster binary, for in *Fury Road* the "clean, healthy, fit, white, decent, law-abiding, heterosexual and forever young" body (Braidotti 2002: 200) is decentered as the ideal human form. At the same time, sexual difference is reimagined affirmatively as the maternal body presents more than a "nesting place" for life and women finally become more than a function of their wombs—yet nevertheless still mothers—in this postapocalyptic landscape.

Let us approach this final film in three interconnected stages, looking first at the ways the body is reimagined in *Fury Road*; secondly at the ways patriarchal control of "the womb" is destroyed; and finally at how the film, through its molecular expressions, opens viewers to reimagining *our* bodies outside the tyranny of hegemonic culture, as the film overturns society's so-called "higher values" and incorporates us into a cinematic assemblage that imagines bodies differently. It is in this film that we at last find the molecular potential of the maternal body being motivated toward the inclusive end of becoming-imperceptible.

Bodies are unexpectedly important in *Fury Road*, which might seem initially to be more concerned with machines. In direct contravention of the typical

Hollywood film, these are not Braidotti's idealized human bodies. Scars, sores, amputations, and tumors abound—yet lest these dis/abled bodies be taken for grotesquery, an othering of that which differs from the "ideal," in this postapocalyptic society there are also widespread practices of scarification, branding, tattooing, piercing, and even a type of poisonous face painting known as "chroming" that deliberately *imperfect* the body. Immortan Joe, the film's archvillain, may require a breathing apparatus, but his disability, which in other films might mark him as "monstrous" to the majoritarian imagination, is far from unique; the film's hero, Furiosa, is an amputee with a prosthetic arm, and Nux, who becomes one of the heroes, has even named the tumors on his neck that are killing him.

What has happened to these bodies could be seen as an indictment of the blight humankind has visited upon its own environment—a horrifying vision of the future in which we will all be diseased or disfigured, in other words. However, there is an ethological topos to *Fury Road* that shifts attention away from what bodies *are* to what bodies can *do*. Furiosa, for example, uses her prosthetic arm as a weapon; she is never defined by her amputation, nor is she confined by it. (In a telling iteration of this inclusive valuation of different bodies, the film employs an actor with osteogenesis imperfecta to play Corpus Colossus, using no prosthetics or special effects to alter or enhance the actor's performance.) Nux accepts the rapid decay of his youthful body as he fearlessly siphons gasoline from Furiosa's engine with his mouth. Already dying, he embraces the posthuman trajectory both heroes and villains in this film seem to be on, a trajectory echoed by the machines they assemble with and rely on, as Miller cultivates a neo-medieval aesthetic in which skulls, spikes, chains, fire, and crossbows couple with war chariot-style race cars and weaponized big rigs.

In short, the world of *Fury Road* is one in which hegemonic society's higher values seem to have been reversed. Immortan Joe promises his War Boys they will "ride with [him] in Valhalla," encouraging them to value death over life; he likewise exhorts the people under his dominion not to become "addicted to water," for it is *oil* that moves this world. Because we are meant to see Joe's outlook as antithetical and villainous, however, the film also prompts us to question his paradoxical—and hypocritical—privileging of "youth" and "beauty" in the women he chooses for his "Wives" (also known as "Breeders"). In both Joe's objectification of his Wives and his reduction of women to their reproductive capabilities, we therefore find patriarchal attitudes toward the value of women cast glaringly into focus—made contemplatable, in other words. It is these very attitudes the Wives react against in the escape that forms the film's plot, writing on the walls of the prison they leave behind "We Are Not Things" and, importantly, "Our Babies Will Not Be Warlords."

To once again quote Ann Hall, Joe also upholds patriarchal attitudes about reproduction as "reproducing sameness" and "upholding the status quo." Joe uses his Wives to "produce" sons who will serve him as warlords, and he seems to believe—erroneously, as his sons Corpus Colossus and Rictus Erectus reveal—that his Wives' "beauty" will result in able-bodied sons. Although Joe's willingness to go to war to retrieve both the Wives and his unborn children is ridiculed by his contemporaries ("All this for a family squabble? Filthy babies," sneers The Bullet Man), there is nevertheless a degree to which women's bodies remain captured by the male imagination in Immortan Joe's society, in which new mothers are hooked to breast pumps like cows to produce milk and the Wives are forced to wear chastity belts, reserving their wombs for Immortan Joe's "seed" alone. Hence, *Fury Road* on the one hand speaks to what Braidotti has observed of the "cyber-teratological imaginary of advanced cultures" in which

> "Mother" has become assimilated into the techno-industrial system; reproduction, especially the reproduction of white, male babies, is a primary asset in the post-capitalist cash nexus, which also bred its own youngsters. The maternal body therefore is at the heart of the political economy of fear in late postmodernity. She simultaneously reproduces the possibility of the future and must be made to inscribe this futurity within the regime of high-tech commodification which is today's market economy. (Braidotti 2002: 207–8)

On the other hand, rather than reifying the "double bind" of this maternal role (as Braidotti claims cyberpunk films like *The Matrix* do), *Fury Road* challenges such postpatriarchal logic via means that exceed even the Wives' successful escape from Joe's Citadel. Viewers are given our first view of the Wives from Max's perspective as they gather in the desert alongside Furiosa's big rig. Draped in scraps of white linen, the Wives initially appear to play into the eroticization of the pregnant female body Kelly Oliver has noted in romantic comedies— yet this subjective perspective is swiftly disrupted by an intense action scene in which the Wives leap in fearlessly to help Furiosa subdue Max and Nux. Furthering this disruption of a molar viewpoint on/of the Wives, we soon learn they are not the only "mothers" to matter in this universe. Furiosa, in fact, is on a mission to bring the Wives to the Vuvalini, or "Many Mothers," who have for generations safeguarded the Green Place outside Immortan Joe's Wasteland.

Rather than the polar extremes of eroticization or abjection, then, what *Fury Road* comes to celebrate in its mothers is *fertility*—yet the film also deliberately resists reducing women's value to their fecundity. As Toast loads guns, Capable keeps lookout, Fragile tricks Rictus Erectus into believing she wants to return to Joe, and Valkyrie leads a motorbike charge against the War Boys, *Fury Road*'s mothers prove to be in possession of that affective intuitive perception, coded neither masculine nor feminine, that enables them to survive by assembling their individuated talents into a formidable familial unit.

Perhaps because its mothers are not reduced to the functions of their wombs, they are also, finally, allowed to have Patrice Diquinzio's "paradoxical" relationship to their pregnant bodies. The most affecting example of this is Splendid, the most visibly pregnant Wife, who uses her body as a human shield to stop Immortan Joe from shooting Max or Furiosa. Cultural ideals of motherhood would have it that a woman must above all protect the child in her womb; for Splendid to place her body, inseparable from the body of her unborn child, in harm's way should strike us as monstrous. Instead, as the camera pulls back to linger on Splendid as she hangs from Furiosa's vehicle, glaring back at Joe, the feeling invoked in us is one of admiration for her courage—so much so that when Splendid falls to her death, we might actually gasp with a dismay that has nothing to do with the fate of her unborn child.

Splendid, in choosing to protect others at the risk of her life and her child's, thus seems to have escaped the partiality Deleuze wrote so scathingly of. Sadly, her body remains in the hands of Immortan Joe, who sacrifices any chance of saving her in a failed attempt to cut the baby from her womb. This son, described as "perfect in every way," is stillborn, but whereas Joe cares only for the loss of his "property," as he calls the child, the Wives weep for Splendid, whose life they understand to have meant just as much as her unborn babe's. *We Are Not Things* indeed, the film drives home—for the rage the Wives express, reflected in the name of their savior Furiosa and the film itself, is not the rage women are typically allowed to express in film, that is, rage in the service of protecting their offspring, including the unborn or surrogate. (Recall, for instance, Ripley shouting at the alien Queen to "stay away from her, you bitch" when Newt is threatened.) The Wives' fury is truly *self*-righteous, fury at the inscription and violation of their bodies, for it is important to remember that none of Joe's Wives have chosen to become mothers. All are victims of sexual assault.

Hence, although the Wives appear to have claimed their unborn children ("*Our* Babies Will Not Be Warlords," they write), there is still a danger that *Fury*

Road could be reinforcing another cultural ideal, one in which "real women" place no value on "motherhood." The Dag seems to express this view when she speaks with resignation of the "warlord" in her womb. However, just as a phallocentric perspective on the Wives' pregnant bodies is swiftly destabilized, The Dag's patriarchal perspective on reproduction—that her baby will inevitably be the same as its father, Immortan, whom the patriarchy would claim gives the child "form, shape, and contour"—is challenged by the Vuvalini, who point out that the child "might be a girl." The Dag takes this idea in with a look of surprise, as though it had never occurred to her that her baby could have a future in which its becoming has not been stolen, *if* the Wives are willing to fight for a world free of patriarchal control. Does the Vuvalini's invocation of the feminine here, however, indicate that another, false binary is being created between the masculine and the feminine, this time from a gynocentric perspective? The film rides perilously close to this line, despite the molecularity of its expressions (to be turned to hereafter). Nevertheless, the dissolution of the male-masculine/female-feminine gender binary, if it is to place us on a line of flight to a more inclusive society, must in some way account for centuries of devaluation of that which has been coded feminine. Ultimately, *Fury Road* does accomplish this recuperation of *the feminine* as culture has come to code it without claiming for women a totalizing "woman's perspective" on the world, in part through its nuanced use of the tropes of climate fiction.

Cli-fi, as this dystopic genre of polluted worlds has come to be called, places a high premium on fertility that equates to many of the philosophies of ecofeminism, a movement that attributes environmental devastation to phallocentric practices and aligns the fight for women's rights with the fight for environmental protection. Writing of the "systematic suppression of the feminine" as "accompanied down the centuries not only by the devaluation of all that is wild and instinctual in our own natures, but by the purposeful destruction of natural ecosystems" (Blackie 2016: 33), for instance, author and psychologist Sharon Blackie traces an historic line between the anthropocentric human/animal binary forwarded by Descartes, who claimed that "animals have neither mind nor reason" (Blackie 2016: 34), and the phallocentric gender binary, in which rationality and industry, coded masculine, have triumphed almost totally over corporeality and sensitivity, coded feminine. Issuing an ecofeminist call to arms that will necessarily involve all people, irrespective of sex or gender, Blackie quotes lawyer and environmental activist Polly Higgins in describing what comes close to echoing Elizabeth Grosz's call for affirmative sexual difference:

"[T]he critical thing of course is to find the right balance of both masculine and feminine energy in each person, in each situation. We need both perspectives, both energies in balance, to make whole decisions. And the suppression of feminine energy . . . pushes down our ability as a civilisation to feel, and especially our capacity to feel great pain. Women give birth, one of the most painful experiences humans routinely endure. We [women] know how to feel that pain and allow it to pass through us with love. . . . But we need to take that ability to feel outside of us, to put it out there in the wider world. . . . If we were to allow ourselves to properly feel . . . the Earth's pain, we wouldn't be able to make the decisions we do, which lead to tar sands, fracking, deforestation. To Ecocide." (Blackie 2016: 54)

What we must remain wary of in narratives like this, which seek to reclaim repressed femininity for *all* individuals, is the gynesitic tendency to make of women a representation: woman as that which is mysterious, wild, *natural*. Even for the purposes of women's "molar politics," as Deleuze and Guattari call them, the tendency to essentialize the experience of motherhood, assuming that all women form bonds with their offspring that *naturally* translate the "great pain" of childbirth into great love for one's children, can be just as tyrannizing to women as phallocentric somatophobia directed toward the pregnant body and maternal non-differentiation. But what if the core tenet of ecofeminism—an anti-egoistic, de-anthropomorphized valuation of the differences between, relations among, and necessity of all forms of life—could be experienced at the level of a *microfemininity* no longer reliant on the masculine/feminine binary even for purposes of femininity's recuperation? What if sexual difference, without being frozen into molar politics of any kind, could be reembodied so that, without flattening the differences between women's experiences of pregnancy and childbirth or inscribing a "maternal instinct" onto the bodies of all women, the creative energy, nurturing sensitivity, and relational thinking dismissed by phallocentric culture as "weak" because it is coded *feminine* could be activated to inform the ways we all feel the pain of other beings, whether human, plant, animal, or mineral? What if motherhood, in other words, could be made molecular, slipping between or passing right through the dualistic machines that have resulted in the most disastrous excesses of phallocentric and anthropocentric society?

Fury Road's Many Mothers, once guardians of the now-devastated Green Place, carry with them actual seeds for trees, flowers, fruits, and vegetables, and it will ultimately not be through human reproduction that the Wives and Many

Mothers, with the help of Max and Furiosa, save the world, but through the return of life-giving water, itself mythologically associated with the feminine. Restoring life to the Wasteland is how the Wives and Many Mothers ultimately defeat Immortan Joe, who, "because he own[ed] the water," was able to control the people who relied on him. From a purely content standpoint, *Fury Road* could thus easily fall into the binary trap of gynocentrically opposing the masculine to the feminine, were it not for the many molecular expressions that prevent viewers from being forced into any molar perspective of/on the narrative, including a gynocentric one. Rather, by affecting viewers into its molecular assemblage *Fury Road* also allows us to imagine—and therefore to experience—our bodies differently.

Once again, this is not a matter of representation. In directing its attention to the female body, *Fury Road* could easily reinforce the phallocentric perspective it sets out to subvert—for the conventions via which the camera "looks" at women's bodies have become so conventional that when we first see the Wives, for instance, we may automatically "read" them as eroticized. As science fiction and other speculative genres reimagine the female body, those reimaginings can only trace a line of flight from objectification or abjection, respectively, if we are somehow affected into sharing the schizo's perspective on our great social deliriums *as deliriums*. That is, just as monsters themselves cannot liberate us from binary thinking, forming a link in the chain toward becoming-imperceptible by helping us embrace difference-in-itself, unless or until we dissolve the self/other borders that solidify our molar subjectivities even Furiosa's reimagined female body could remain trapped within the molar plane of dualistic opposition. Writing of the perhaps as-of-yet unrealized liberatory potential of the female cyborg, for instance, Kaye Mitchell argues that "the female body is not so easily transcended, persisting as it does . . . as what determines female (as distinct from male) humanity. . . . It is therefore erroneous to claim that the cyborg is, in itself and of necessity, either feminist or antifeminist . . . ; what must be attended to are the overarching context and the mode of its use or (re)presentation" (Mitchell 2006: 114).

What schizosophy objects to here, obviously, is the notion that any "(re)presentation" of the female body could ever result in a line of flight, because representation relies on opposition, molarity, and judgment. In place of representation, what Deleuze and Guattari called for was desiring machines freed, in the first place, from the "received wisdom" that forms the fictive foundation of our great social deliriums and capable, in the second, of helping us imagine ourselves and others beyond identity, opposition, analogy, or resemblance—Deleuze's "four branches of the Caught." For *the body* to be reimagined, therefore, the body can no longer represent anything; the body must be experienced directly. If we point to Furiosa's shorn hair as masculinizing her, we are still imprisoned by dualistic thinking that opposes male-masculine to female-feminine bodies. However, if the molecular expressions of *Fury Road* can affect us into experiencing our bodies directly, then we may be placed on a line of flight toward becoming the BwO, for the "problem for Deleuze and Guattari is not one of how to weave together, or even disentangle, but of how to break apart, of how to release and quicken the flow outward of any element which has already begun to exceed any given system of representation" (Jardine 1985: 157). This "unnameable" and "unrepresentable" element is termed *element x* by Deleuze and Guattari, and the "unconscious yet-to-be-produced"—the unconscious becoming-unconscious, in other words—is the "only space . . . where the unnameable element x might freely circulate in a kind of 'chaosmos.' Often described as a Real-in-flux, it is where No-One reigns. The privileged points of entry into the Real-in-flux are the famous Deleuzian 'escape lines': lines for an escape into life" (Jardine 1985: 157).

A chaosmos where No-One reigns might well describe the postapocalyptic *Mad Max* universe. For instance, the escape Furiosa manages from Immortan Joe along her "fury road" might most aptly be experienced by viewers as a disorienting real-in-flux as the film fluctuates between speed and slowness, with rapid cuts and accelerated montages interspersed with slow motion leaps and close-ups of fiery explosions, such as in the extended chase scene inside the sandstorm—a nightmare world of tornadoes, explosions, lightning strikes, and solar flares. What viewers experience during scenes such as these is a "special form of embodied thought particular to the movement-image. For the unified assemblage of film/viewer, thought *is* light, movement, sound, framing and editing" that cannot be "artificially separate[d]" into "response and idea" (Powell 2005: 110) because *the brain is the screen*; in schizosophy, cinematic technology is what we think in and through.

While the potential for viewers to move and think with film is inherent to all cinema, it is again films like *Fury Road*, which seem to set out to destabilize viewers' egoistic boundaries through their molecular expressions, that have the greatest potential to change viewers by producing in us new ideas, new perceptions. Filmed almost entirely on the move with a mixture of crane shots and dash cams that free the superhuman camera to assume a 360-degree perspective on the action, the intensity of *Fury Road's* action scenes may affect viewers as viscerally as scenes of torture and mutilation in a traditional horror film. Director George Miller often saturates the screen with color (red sand, blue sky, black oil), action (spinning tires, flailing bodies), and sound (revving engines, pounding heartbeats, squealing guitars) that overwhelm our viewing senses, affecting us into that unified film-viewer assemblage as we are caught up inside the film, *feeling* the grittiness of the dirt and sand that often rush at and encompass the camera. As we are brought into the film, our reality is further destabilized—made the Real-in-flux—by Max's sudden hallucinations of Glory the Child's death and other disturbing, non-diegetic memories and images, so that by the time we encounter a surrealist twilight landscape filled with vultures, dead trees, and humanoid shapes on stilts, we are no longer certain what "reality" is.

This hellish twilight world does turn out to be "real" (in the film's already-virtual world, of course). Once the Many Mothers' Green Place, the land has now been poisoned, made part of the Wasteland that "kills all that is alive and vibrant inside us" as we slog through a patriarchal capitalist-industrialist society that

> inflicts on us an excess of both connectivity and complexity, ties us to machines and gadgets, keeps us forever moving, forever doing. There is no time or place to develop community . . . [or] a relationship with the planet that sustains us . . . And when we lose our relationship with the land and the other creatures around us, then in the deepest sense, we lose ourselves. (Blackie 2016: 43)

Sharon Blackie is here writing about the metaphorical Wasteland in which many of us now live, which *Fury Road* imagines concretely (virtually?) in its futuristic mythology. But *Fury Road*, an embodied viewing experience of film as a direct event, also has the potential to bring us back to our bodies without dualistically opposing them to the "minds" phallocentric culture has so long privileged. Rizzo writes of this as (re)experiencing the "temporality" of a body that is always becoming different-from-itself (Rizzo 2012: 47). In the view of schizoanalysis, then, film is doing something quite other than (re)producing identification in its embodied spectators. Film is opening us to assemblage with other bodies, including cinematic bodies, that may result in a line of flight from molar identity and the creation of a BwO.

At the culmination of Furiosa's "escape line," a spectacular car crash gives way to an all-black screen—Deleuze's any-space-whatever. Immortan Joe and his warlords are dead; the surviving Wives and Many Mothers are free at last.

But Furiosa is badly wounded, even dying. Max, a universal donor, at this point steps forward, transfusing her with his blood—creating a flow between human bodies, sexually different yet no longer dualistically opposed, that, like the water the women return to the Wasteland, results in *life*.

For those readers who came to these pages hoping to find positive or progressive models of motherhood, this book has no doubt been a disappointment. Schizosophy does not deal in models, representations, or identifications; it deals in flows, vibrations, and intensities—the *embodied* encounters between people, places, objects, ideas, institutions, and technologies, including the technology of cinema, that have the potential, as we assemble with them, to change us, solidifying or dissolving our molar subjectivities.

I found myself motivated to tackle the concept of *motherhood* in this book because I believe the cultural idea/ideal of Motherhood that remains so problematic for feminism, polarizing people of all genders on the question of abortion and reproductive rights; excluding people of color, people with disabilities, people of different ages, and people in the LGBTQIA+ community from many of the cultural and political activities surrounding motherhood; and failing to address issues of political, social, and economic inequality still faced by many "mothers" and their children, not to mention leaving too many women adrift in a sea of cultural expectations that greatly restrict, complicate, and possibly even obfuscate the "choice" to become a mother, cannot be resolved until sexual difference is affirmatively reembodied. To reembody sexual difference is not to equate women, or men, with our biological or reproductive capacities—it is not, in other words, to say that because the female body may have the capacity for pregnancy, all women should want to give birth, or that even if a woman does give birth, she will have a special bond with the child she delivers. Rather, the founding phantasy that is binary gender begins to dissolve once we come to accept that bodies themselves are not "innately psychical, sexual, or sexed," that is, that sex *itself* is an illusion inscribed onto infinitely varied and varying bodies via the molar plane of Biology that would fix and freeze us into the binary categories Male/Female. Once we recognize that sex and gender are not naturally occurring states but are instead hegemonic fictions, part of the great social delirium the schizo sees right through, we may also cease to oppose the male to the female, the masculine to the feminine, enabling us, as Teresa Rizzo has said, to imagine both differently.

What might motherhood look and feel like if it were no longer imagined in opposition to fatherhood, and vice versa? To whom might the choice of when and whether to *mother* become freely available if motherhood were no longer understood in terms of biology and reproduction? Film can play a pivotal role in this affirmative reimagination of sexual difference, both because, as Rosi Braidotti has said, film imagines bodies differently and because, as viewers assemble with the technology of cinema, we may experience our bodies differently. Cinepsychoanalysis has gifted us powerful tools for understanding the psychic structures that underlie our fictions, helping us to see, for instance, why that which is open, fluid, or interstitial figures in the phallocentric imagination as monstrous or abject. But cinepsychoanalysis cannot go much beyond that, other than to propose oppositional readings or identifications, for so long as we concern ourselves with what film *represents*, we will never trace a true line of flight from binary thinking about gender, nor will we ever truly conceive of film's potential to change us.

Film is perhaps even more crucial to the ways we live in the twenty-first century than it was when Deleuze wrote his Cinema Books. The world we live in now is so inundated with cinematic technology that it has become what schizophist Patricia Pisters calls a "metacinematic universe," in which the technology of cinema has changed our relationship to the past, the present, and the future, making them each seemingly accessible to the viewer at any time, consequently breaking down borders between what is virtual and what is actual. We might even say that our world has become *saturated* by cinema, like the superimposition of images on a screen, in which all images, by existing together at the same time and in the same place, create a sort of any-space-whatever that dis-locates our sense of *inside* or *outside,* so that we may occasionally feel we are actually living *inside* a film.

If cinema has the power to so profoundly alter our experience of the world, to make it, and us, "metacinematic," then the stories we tell and the ways in which we tell them through film also have the power to change us, profoundly. Schizoanalysis offers a means for theorizing how those changes come about. What cannot result from schizoanalysis are universal "readings" of what films "mean." As I hope I have made clear in this book, schizoanalysis is not interested in producing such readings. However, schizoanalysis *can* be used to identify molecular films (those which breakdown borders and binaries and prompt viewers' becomings) from molar films (those which reify hegemonic identities). Yet the *experience* of these films will be different for every viewer, and those differences, inseparable into totalizing categories like the Black Spectator, the Female Spectator, the Transgender Spectator, and so on, are important. If feminist film theory is to become truly inclusive, we must open avenues to considering how the content and expression of film works together to affect different viewers differently. This is not to say there is no way to theorize how film goes about affecting its viewers. It is, rather, to say that the emphasis of our theorizing should be on how the embodied experience of film viewing vibrates in viewers both "during and after the film event," as Anna Powell puts it—on understanding how it is that film changes us, so that, as feminist film scholars, we can go about developing an inclusive theoretical position from which to advocate for those films that open viewers up to affirmative experiences of difference.

To me, schizoanalysis offers an opportunity for a long-overdue unraveling of the tyranny of binary gender, and I would call for film and gender scholars interested in this work to focus on developing a corpus of molecular and molar film techniques that can then be analyzed in tandem with a film's content to understand the embodied impact it has on viewers. What I hope I have demonstrated in these pages is that it is possible to bring schizoanalysis out of the sometimes-esoteric world of philosophical gender studies and into mainstream film analysis, enabling feminist scholars to strip away those layers of cultural meaning that have been written onto bodies we too often imagine to be natural. This stripping away will not be simple. Deleuze and Guattari recognized this; that is why they lay out so many "links" in the chain toward becoming-imperceptible, from becoming-woman to becoming-child to becoming-music to becoming-animal—even becoming-plant. If we succeed in becoming-imperceptible, I believe we can begin to imagine for ourselves, and everyone else, new imaginary bodies not captured by what we, or culture, believe male/female, black/white, straight/queer, dis/abled, young/old bodies should *be*. We can instead open ourselves up, in our affirmation of difference as difference-in-itself, to the dynamic processes of becoming.

Although the family is, and likely always will be, an even more potent force than film in shaping how we think about difference—and ourselves—what would *the family* look like if we were to reimagine it from a nomadic subjectivity, to free it from its hegemonic borders so that we no longer remain mired in our partialities, defining ourselves in opposition to those who are different from us? What would happen to our macropolitics if film could open us to a micropolitics of *becoming with* those around us, learning from them, allying with them, empathizing with them without judgment? What if film, in its most molecular expressions, could extend our idea of *the family* beyond those who are like us or close to us, beyond those who speak our language or practice our religion, beyond even those who are human, or animal? Schizosophy offers us the opportunity to expand or contract our universe, based on how we choose to view *difference*. Primarily molecular, highly affective films, whether horrific or poetic, may be one means through which we open up to this expansion. Such films can prompt us to assemble with a radical vision of alterity in which difference is no longer defined in terms of lack, in which the self is no longer threatened by the Other but needs others for (ex)change, and in which the monster, if the monster is that which differs, is in fact each of us.

Notes

Introduction

1 M. Antonia Biggs, Heather Gould, and Diana Greene Foster report that, of women seeking abortions in the United States in 2013, 40 percent stated financial reasons such as being un- or underemployed, while 29 percent cited the need to care for other children. As the reasons stated for seeking an abortion were not exclusive—that is, women often cited multiple factors behind their decisions—the authors report that 64 percent of women sought an abortion due to a combination of economic, relationship, and lifestyle concerns, including the needs of their existing children (2013).

2 As many postmodern scholars have pointed out, the master-slave dialectic itself is nonbinary. Nevertheless, the dialectic does establish an inescapable cycle of superiority/inferiority—slaves desiring to become masters, who are themselves already enslaved—that cannot free us from the tyranny of binary thinking.

3 Films like *Twilight*, for instance, might be classified as "paranormal romance" and films like *Mad Max: Fury Road* as "action-dystopian."

4 Essential motherhood will be taken up again later, when I schizoanalyze *Twilight*. In that analysis, I will look at how the hegemonic content of these films works in tandem with what Deleuze would call their "molar expressions" to reify motherhood as a woman's biological and cultural destiny. When readers look back on this chapter, I do not want to be seen as casting aside my schizoanalytic lens, drawing a false binary between filmic content and filmic expression; yet since the purpose of this chapter is to lay the theoretical groundwork for an embodied politics of affirmative sexual difference, I want to save my film analysis for a later chapter.

5 Primatologist Frans de Waal, the author of *Bonobo and the Atheist*, delivered a fascinating lecture on the morality of animals on the TED stage in 2011; Peter Wohlleben discusses the latest discoveries in the life of the forest in *The Hidden Life of Trees: What They Feel, How They Communicate* (2015); and James Gallagher reported on the "second genome" for BBC Radio 4 in 2018.

6 Denaturalizing *the body*, maternal or otherwise, is an important step toward becoming the Body without Organs. Deleuze and Guattari maintained that no one experiences the body *naturally*; from the moment of birth, if not before, our physical-biological bodies are over-coded with meanings derived from social signifiers like race, class, gender, and ability. We therefore cannot know what it

would mean to experience our bodies *naturally*. For instance, Ta-Nehisi Coates movingly relates the impossibility of living *naturally* in a raced body in *Between the World and Me*—"I saw that what divided me from the world was not anything intrinsic to us [people of color] but the actual injury done by people intent on naming us, intent on believing that what they have named us matters more than anything we could ever actually do" (2015: 120)—and provides a wrenching description of the embodied experience of living in a raced body in a racist society in which "racism is a visceral experience," one that "dislodges brains, blocks airways, rips muscle, extracts organs, cracks bones, breaks teeth. . . . You must always remember that the sociology, the economics, the graphs, the charts, the regressions all land, with great violence, upon the body" (2015: 10).

Chapter 1

1 A far more comprehensive introduction to the collaborations of Deleuze and Guattari can be found in François Dosse's *Gilles Deleuze and Felix Guattari: Intersecting Lives* (trans. Deborah Glassman, Columbia University Press, 2010).
2 To date, some of the most important works to employ Deleuze's cinematic philosophy have been Anna Powell's *Deleuze and Horror Film*; Patricia Pisters's *The Matrix of Visual Culture: Working with Deleuze in Film Theory*; and Teresa Rizzo's *Deleuze and Film: A Feminist Introduction*, all of which have greatly aided my own project.
3 As psychoanalytic theorist Carol Clover noted, horror and pornography are the two film genres most concerned with the body: characters' bodies onscreen and the viewer's body, which must be *affected* in order for either horror or pornography to be successful (1996).
4 Rizzo provides examples like the legal system and the healthcare establishment.
5 It is important not to see Deleuze as drawing another binary here, in which affirmation is opposed to negation or active forces to reactive forces; Deleuze instead describes affirmation as "essentially multiple and pluralist," in other words always-already subsuming within it negation as "a consequence, a sort of surplus of pleasure, . . . whereas negation is always one, or heavily monist" (2005: 74).
6 Grosz goes on to argue that it is perhaps men's conception of women's bodies as "nesting places" for the "products" of male sperm, rather than as bodies with their own specificity and particularity, that leads some men to object not to the idea of abortion but to the idea of *their* fetus being aborted.
7 An excellent example of this, for instance, is Jamie Lee Curtis's iconic character Laurie Strode across the franchise of *Halloween* films, including 1998's *Halloween H20* and 2018's *Halloween*.

Chapter 2

1. Of course, Laura Mulvey argued that the film audience, by adopting the camera's "gaze" when watching scenes of female torture, terror, and death, assumes either a sadistic (for males) or a masochistic (for females) position with regard to "visual pleasure." Yet this argument does not move beyond representation and identification (the audience is identifying with either the male killer or the female victim). Thus, although cinepsychoanalysts may occasionally discuss camera movements, editing techniques, special effects, and so on, theories of "the gaze" remain firmly rooted in spectatorial responses to content, not embodied experiences of expression.
2. I am indebted to Jardine and Rizzo for my understanding of subject-formation as described by Lacan and Althusser.

Chapter 3

1. Ava's two-faced nature is actually implied here as she is doubled during this shot—we are allowed to observe her reflection in the chrome plate directly behind Caleb, whose face as *he* observes *her* is not shown to us.
2. I want to be clear that I am only discussing the film *Mary Shelley's Frankenstein*, not the novel itself nor any other film adaptation. I have neither the expertise nor the inclination to question how literary critics interpret the novel, while analyzing the many adaptations of Mary Shelley's work would represent a book in itself.
3. As Deleuze observes, a film's score and its soundtrack, that is, the diegetic sounds such as a character closing a door while we hear the door close, stand as "two dimensions of musical time, the one [diegetic sound] being the hastening of the presents which are passing, the other [the score] the raising or falling back of pasts which are preserved" (1989: 93). When these two dimensions "intertwine," "time itself becomes a thing of sound" (94).

Chapter 4

1. Selene will perform this miraculous resurrection again with the vampire David in *Underworld: Awakening*, passing on to her surrogate "son" her own imperviousness to daylight.
2. The books and films prove so concerned with Bella's "purity" that she is even given the power to "shield" her mind from psychic penetration, including Edward's

telepathic abilities. In the final film, Bella lifts this shield only for her husband, yet their telepathic communication does not result in the desired two-way flow; Edward sees Bella's thoughts and memories, but Bella remains closed to any reciprocal flow from Edward.

Chapter 5

1. In one of *Interview*'s only truly molar expressions, the film ends with a cover of the Rolling Stones's "Sympathy for the Devil," lest we doubt that Lestat's return is to be celebrated.
2. There is also an undeniable "othering" of the Count and the East in *Dracula*, noticeable, and troubling, even though becoming-vampire is still rendered as sumptuous, compelling, and desirable, even as the vampires themselves are treated as "alien" (Dracula's long nails and hairy palms; Renfield's insect diet) to European sensibilities.
3. Deleuze explains that the "illusion" of time in film is that we believe we are watching something happen, in the present, but, first of all, in the case of recorded (as opposed to live) film, the "something" we are watching has already happened, in the past, and secondly, that "something" is not happening continuously. Film is *edited* so that what we experience as one continuous moment (like a car chase) is comprised in actuality of past moments filmed hours, days, or perhaps even months apart, before being assembled so that we perceive the scene as both instantaneous and continuous (Rizzo 2012: 58).
4. This assertion, unsourced, can be found in the General Trivia available on Amazon's streaming version of the film.
5. As Cady and Oates also note, this is not an argument against the rights of LGBTQIA+ adults to enjoy the same rights and privileges as their majoritarian counterparts, including marriage. It is, however, an acknowledgment that "the ascendancy of gay marriage as a single-issue focus for LGBTQ equality is friendly to neoliberal organization . . . marking a way of deradicalizing LGBTQ equal-rights discourse overall and shifting focus away from queer familial forms" (Cady and Oates 2016: 312).

References

Benshoff, Harry M. *Monsters in the Closet: Homosexuality and the Horror Film*. Manchester: Manchester University Press, 1997.

Betterton, Rosemary. "Promising Monsters: Pregnant Bodies, Artistic Subjectivity, and Maternal Imagination." *Maternal Bodies*, special issue of *Hypatia*, vol. 21, no. 1, 2006, pp. 80–100.

Biggs, M. Antonia, Heather Gould, and Diana Greene Foster. "Understanding Why Women Seek Abortions in the U.S." *BMC Women's Health*, BioMed Central, July 5, 2013, www.ncbi.nlm.nih.gov/pmc/articles/PMC3729671/.

Blackie, Sharon. *If Women Rose Rooted: The Journey to Authenticity and Belonging*. Tewkesbury, Gloucestershire: September Publishing, 2016.

Braidotti, Rosi. *Metamorphoses: Towards a Materialist Theory of Becoming*. Cambridge: Polity Press, 2002.

Brooks, Kinitra D. "The Importance of Neglected Intersections: Race and Gender in Contemporary Zombie Texts and Theories." *African American Review*, vol. 47, no. 4, 2014, pp. 461–75.

Butler, Judith. *Gender Trouble: Feminism and the Subversion of Identity*. New York: Routledge, 2006.

Cady, Kathryn A. and Thomas Oates. "Family Splatters: Rescuing Heteronormativity from the Zombie Apocalypse." *Women's Studies in Communication*, vol. 39, no. 3, 2016, pp. 308–25.

Carroll, Noël. "Horror and Humor." *The Journal of Aesthetics and Art Criticism*, vol. 57, no. 2, 1999, 145–60.

Chodorow, Nancy. *The Reproduction of Mothering: Psychoanalysis and the Sociology of Gender*. Berkeley: University of California Press, 1978.

Clover, Carol. "Her Body, Himself: Gender in the Slasher Film." *The Dread of Difference: Gender and The Horror Film*, edited by Barry Keith Grant, Austin: University of Texas Press, 1996, pp. 68–115.

Coates, Ta-Nehisi. *Between the World and Me*. New York: Spriegel and Grau, 2015.

Creed, Barbara. *The Monstrous-Feminine: Film, Feminism, Psychoanalysis*. New York: Routledge, 1993.

de Miranda, Luis. "Is a New Life Possible? Deleuze and the Lines." Translated by Marie-Céline Courilleault, *Deleuze Studies*, vol. 7, no. 1, 2013, pp. 106–52.

Deleuze, Gilles. *Cinema 1: The Movement-Image*. Translated by Hugh Tomlinson and Barbara Habberjam. Minneapolis: University of Minnesota Press, 1986.

Deleuze, Gilles. *Cinema 2: The Time Image*. Translated by Hugh Tomlinson and Robert Galeta. Minneapolis: University of Minnesota Press, 1989.

Deleuze, Gilles. *Difference and Repetition*. Translated by Paul Patton. New York: Columbia University Press, 1995.

Deleuze, Gilles. *Pure Immanence: Essays on A Life*. Translated by Anne Boyman. New York: Zone Books, 2005.

Deleuze, Gilles, and Felix Guattari. *Anti-Oedipus*. 6th ed. Translated by Robert Hurley. New York: Penguin Classics, 2009.

Deleuze, Gilles, and Felix Guattari. *A Thousand Plateaus: Capitalism and Schizophrenia*. Translated by Brian Massumi. Minneapolis: University of Minnesota Press, 1987.

Deleuze, Gilles, and Felix Guattari. *What Is Philosophy?* Translated by Hugh Tomlinson and Graham Burchell. New York: Columbia University Press, 1994.

Diamond, Fleur. "Beauty and the Beautiful Beast: Stephenie Meyer's *Twilight* Saga and the Quest for a Transgressive Female Desire." *Australian Feminist Studies*, vol. 26, no. 67, 2011, pp. 41–55.

Diquinzio, Patrice. *The Impossibility of Motherhood: Feminism, Individualism, and the Problem of Mothering*. New York: Routledge, 1999.

Fortin, Jacey. "That Time 'Murphy Brown' and Dan Quayle Topped the Front Page." *The New York Times*, January 26, 2018, www.nytimes.com/2018/01/26/arts/television/murphy-brown-dan-quayle.html.

Frohreich, Kimberly A. "Sullied Blood, Semen, and Skin: Vampires and the Spectre of Miscegenation." *Gothic Studies*, vol. 15, no. 1, 2013, pp. 33–43.

Gatens, Moira. *Imaginary Bodies: Ethics, Power and Corporeality*. New York: Routledge, 1996.

Grosz, Elizabeth. *Volatile Bodies: Toward a Corporeal Feminism*. Bloomington: Indiana University Press, 1994.

Hall, Ann C. "Making Monsters: The Philosophy of Reproduction in Mary Shelley's *Frankenstein* and the Universal Films *Frankenstein* and *The Bride of Frankenstein*." *The Philosophy of Horror*, edited by Thomas Richard Fahy, Lexington: University Press of Kentucky, 2010, pp. 212–28.

Hanich, Julian. "Dis/liking Disgust: The Revulsion Experience at the Movies." *New Review of Film and Television Studies*, vol. 7, no. 3, 2009, pp. 293–309.

Jackson, Kimberly. *Gender and the Nuclear Family in Twenty-First Century Horror*. New York: Palgrave Macmillan, 2016.

Jardine, Alice. *Gynesis: Configurations of Woman and Modernity*. Ithaca: Cornell University Press, 1985.

Jones, Steve. "Torture Born: Representing Pregnancy and Abortion in Contemporary Survival-Horror." *Sexuality and Culture*, vol. 19, 2015, pp. 426–43.

Mackenzie, Jean. "The Mothers Who Regret Having Children." *BBC News*, BBC, April 3, 2018, www.bbc.com/news/education-43555736.

Mitchell, Kaye. "Bodies That Matter: Science Fiction, Technoculture, and the Gendered Body." *Science Fiction Studies*, vol. 33, 2006, pp. 109–28.

Morgan, Jack. *The Biology of Horror: Gothic Literature and Film*. Carbondale: Southern Illinois University Press, 2002.

Mulvey, Laura. "Visual Pleasure and Narrative Cinema." *Screen*, vol. 16, no. 3, 1975, pp. 6–18.

Nail, Thomas. "What Is An Assemblage?" *SubStance*, vol. 46, no. 1, 2017, pp. 21–37.

Nesbitt, Nick. "Pre-face: Escaping Race." *Deleuze and Race*, edited by Arun Saldhana and Jason Michael Adams, Edinburgh: Edinburgh University Press, 2013, pp. 1–5.

Nishime, LeiLani. "Whitewashing Yellow Futures in *Ex Machina, Cloud Atlas,* and *Advantageous:* Gender, Labor, and Technology in Sci-fi Film." *Journal of Asian Studies*, vol. 20, no. 1, 2017, pp. 22–49.

Oliver, Kelly. "Motherhood, Sexuality, and Pregnant Embodiment: Twenty-Five Years of Gestation." *Hypatia*, vol. 25, no. 4, 2010, pp. 760–77.

Pisters, Patricia. *The Matrix of Visual Culture: Working with Deleuze in Film Theory*. Stanford: Stanford University Press, 2003.

Powell, Anna. *Deleuze and Horror Film*. Edinburgh: Edinburgh University Press, 2005.

Rajchman, John, and Gilles Deleuze. "Introduction." *Pure Immanence: Essays on a Life*, translated by Anne Boyman, New York: Zone Books, 2005, pp. 7–23.

Rizzo, Teresa. *Deleuze and Film: A Feminist Introduction*. London: Bloomsbury Publishing, 2012.

Rodowick, D.N. *Gilles Deleuze's Time Machine*. Durham: Duke University Press, 1997.

Tomlinson, Hugh, Robert Galeta, and Gilles Deleuze. "Introduction." *Cinema 2: The Time Image*, translated by Hugh Tomlinson and Robert Galeta, Minneapolis: University of Minnesota Press, 1989, pp. xv–xviii.

Williams, Tony. *Hearths of Darkness: The Family in American Horror Film*. Jackson: University Press of Mississippi, 2014.

Films

28 Days Later. Directed by Danny Boyle, DNA Films, 2002.
A Quiet Place. Directed by John Krasinksi, Paramount Pictures, 2018.
Alien. Directed by Ridley Scott, Brandywine Productions, 1979.
Aliens. Directed by James Cameron, Twentieth Century Fox, 1986.
Alien 3. Directed by David Fincher, Twentieth Century Fox, 1992.
Alien: Covenant. Directed by Ridley Scott, Twentieth Century Fox, 2017.
Alien: Resurrection. Directed by Jean-Pierre Jeunet, Brandywine Productions, 1997.
Bram Stoker's Dracula. Directed by Francis Ford Coppola, Columbia Pictures, 1992.
Ex Machina. Directed by Alex Garland, Universal Pictures, 2014.
Interview with the Vampire: The Vampire Chronicles. Directed by Neil Jordan, Geffen Pictures, 1994.
The Island of Dr. Moreau. Directed by John Frankheimer, New Line Cinema, 1996.
Mad Max: Fury Road. Directed by George Miller, Dolby Digital, 2015.
Mary Shelley's Frankenstein. Directed by Kenneth Branagh, TriStar, 1994.
Only Lovers Left Alive. Directed by Jim Jarmusch, RPC, 2013.
Prometheus. Directed by Ridley Scott, Twentieth Century Fox, 2012.
The Stepford Wives. Directed by Bryan Forbes, Palomar Pictures, 1975.
The Terminator. Directed by James Cameron, Hemdale, 1984.
The Twilight Saga: Breaking Dawn: Part 1. Directed by Bill Condon, Summit Entertainment, 2011.
The Twilight Saga: Breaking Dawn: Part 2. Directed by Bill Condon, Summit Entertainment, 2012.
The Twilight Saga: Eclipse. Directed by David Slade, Summit Entertainment, 2010.
The Twilight Saga: New Moon. Directed by Chris Weitz, Summit Entertainment, 2009.
Twilight. Directed by Catherine Hardwicke, Summit Entertainment, 2008.
Underworld. Directed by Len Wiseman, Lakeshore Entertainment, 2003.
Underworld: Awakening. Directed by Måns Mårlind and Björn Stein, Screen Gems, 2012.
Underworld: Blood Wars. Directed by Anna Foerster, Screen Gems, 2016.
Underworld: Evolution. Directed by Len Wiseman, Screen Gems, 2006.
The Walking Dead. American Movie Classics (AMC), 2010–11.

Index

28 Days Later   158–68

abject   24, 46, 56, 60–1, 68–9, 81, 114
   in *Island of Dr. Moreau*   94–6
   and pregnant body   8, 14, 131
abortion   3–5, 13–14, 71, 125, 131
affective intuitive perception   59, 162, 164, 172, *see also* Final Girl
affirmative difference   21, 68, 81, *see also* difference-in-itself
Alien: Covenant   59, 71–4, 78
Alien quadrilogy   61–8
   Alien   21, 39, 60–1, 69–71
   Alien³   63–6
   Alien: Resurrection   66–8
   Aliens   65–6
any-space-whatever   62–3, 65, 177, 179
archaic mother   60–1
assemblage   33–4, 51, 58–9, *see also* cinematic assemblage; survivor assemblage
   molar and molecular   72–3, 106–9, 136–7
   in *Only Lovers Left Alive*   152, 156–7

becoming-animal   95–6, 127–8
becoming-imperceptible   66, 69, 84, 88, 97, 110, 119, 180
becoming-monster   110, 111–12, 118, 132–3, 135, 149, 168
becoming-woman   81–5, 97
   in *Ex Machina*   88, 90
being-with   147–9
Bergson, Henri   20, 30–1, 35, 70, 88, 104
binary machine   44, 88, 90, 142
Body without Organs   16, 45, 64–5, 110, 121, 136, 142
Bram Stoker's Dracula   144, 146, 150–1
BwO, *see* Body without Organs

camera consciousness   73, 85, 100, 151, 155
castrated/castrating mother   46, 59, 61, 78, 97
cinematic assemblage   34, 57–8, 69, 176–7, *see also* assemblage
cinematic synesthesia   102, 147
cinepsychoanalysis   22–3, 31–2, 38–40, 49, 56–9, 76–7, 159, 179
closed set   88, 100
corporeal feminism   81, 141

deframing   86, 127
desire   28, 32, 146–7, 149
   in *Twilight*   122–4
desiring machine   42, 175
diagrammatic component   63
   in *Alien³*   63–5
   in *Alien: Resurrection*   67–8
   in *Ex Machina*   87
   in *Island of Dr. Moreau*   93
   in *Only Lovers Left Alive*   153–4
   in *Underworld*   113, 117
difference-in-itself   2, 19, 37, 45, 81, 137, 175, *see also* affirmative difference
   as pure difference   37, 51, 164
duration   103–5, 121, 133–4, 150–1, 154–5, 157, 163, *see also* temporality

ecofeminism   173–5
egalitarian feminism   10–11, 18, 41–4, 80
essential motherhood   6–8, 13–14, 80
   in *28 Days Later*   166–7
   in *Twilight*   131–2
Ex Machina   85–91

Final Girl   57, 69–71, *see also* affective intuitive perception
   in *28 Days Later*   162–5

in *Prometheus* and *Alien: Covenant* 71–2
flashback 104–5, 120–1, 147, 150
fluidity 39, 46–7, 113, 115, 150

gynesis 75–6, 81–4

identification
 and becoming 67, 97
 and camera consciousness 100, 107, 147–8
 and gender identity 28, 37–8, 49, 56
 and molar expression 117, 125
 and race 159–60
 and representation 15, 179
 spectatorial 31–2, 58, 70, 76–7, 137, 177
imaginary body 37–8, 65, 141
immanence 32, 35–6, 51, 64, 77, 138, 148, *see also* virtual
Interview with the Vampire 145–51
The Island of Dr. Moreau 91–7

language 18, 77
 and cinematic philosophy 98–9, 102–3
 and gynesis 81
 and social machine 89
lectosign 134
light
 in cinematic assemblage 30, 34, 64, 176
 and plane of immanence 64, 105
line of flight 44, 82, 142, 173, 175–6, 179
liquid perception 71

Mad Max: Fury Road 169–78
Mary Shelley's Frankenstein 97–110
maternal instinct 5, 7, 120, 125, 174
molar plane 35, 72
 and biology 37, 178
 and the body 65
molecular plane 35, 72, 130
monstrous feminine 60, 69, 96–7, 98, 121, 131
montage 99–100, 106, 120, 150, 168, 176
morphing 115–16, 118, 119, 130–1, 151
motherhood

 as cultural ideal 8, 172–3
 in patriarchy 4, 11, 21, 149
music 100–2, 161–2

Nietzsche, Friedrich 41–2, 44, 81, 89
nomadic subjectivity 19, 156–7, 180
nuclear family 4, 11, 28
 in horror film 49–51, 139, 157–8, 165–7

Only Lovers Left Alive 151–7
oppositional gaze 159–60
opsign 62

parthenogenesis 72, 97, 114
participatory identification 159–60
postfeminist 2, 12, 78, 121–2
post-human family 51, 152, 168
pregnancy 12–17, 111, 178
 in *Alien* 60, 66
 in *Mad Max: Fury Road* 171–4
 in *Twilight* 125, 130–1
Prometheus 59, 71–4, 78
psychoanalysis 19, 28–9, 32, 37–9, 42, 60–1, 120, 143
psychomechanics 98–9
 as spiritual automatism 102

queering nature 17, 112, 116, 144, 146–7, 149

rarefaction 102–3
reproduction 3, 6, 15, 21–2, 55, 66, 80, 142, 157
 in patriarchy 22, 78, 94, 171
 politics of 12–13, 21, 23, 52–3, 77
rhizome 32–3, 56, 153
 and horror film 68, 146, 168

saturation 102–3
schizo 27–9, 33, 137
schizoanalysis 22, 29–35, 39–41, 57–9, 68, 97, 137, 148, 160, 164, 177, 179–80
sexual difference
 and egalitarian feminism 43
 and horror film 10, 14, 22, 179
 and reproduction 2–3, 16, 178

schizosophic   18, 47, 52–3, 76–7, 80–1, 136–8, 141–2, 156, 173–4
shot/reaction shot   73, 85
   in *Island of Dr. Moreau*   92–3
   in *Prometheus*   74
   in *Twilight*   126, 129
sonsign   62
survivor assemblage   164–6, 168, *see also* assemblage

tactisign   62
temporality, *see also* duration
   and cinema   31–2, 73
   and difference   16, 36, 38, 177
   and time-image   32, 104, 133
thousand tiny sexes   135–6, 156–7
transmutation   44–5, 67
The Twilight Saga   122–5, 134–5
   Breaking Dawn: Part 1   129–32

Breaking Dawn: Part 2   132–4
Eclipse   128–9
New Moon   127–8
Twilight   125–7
two-way flow   88, 95, 120, 137, 144, 158

Underworld   117–22

vampire   111–12, 114, 122, 126–7, 134, 145, 149
   and duration   150–1, 152–3, 154
   and miscegenation   115
virtual   27, 30, 35–6, *see also* immanence
   in metacinematic universe   179
   and time   104, 133
voiceover   91, 93, 117, 126, 145
volatile body   35–6, 149

zombie   154, 167